BENEDICT ARNOLD

A Traitor in Our Midst

Benedict Arnold

A Traitor in Our Midst

BARRY K. WILSON

McGill-Queen's University Press

Montreal & Kingston · London · Ithaca

© McGill-Queen's University Press 2001
ISBN 0-7735-2150-X

Legal deposit second quarter 2001
Bibliothèque nationale du Québec

Printed in Canada on acid-free paper

McGill-Queen's University Press acknowledges
the financial support of the Government of
Canada through the Book Publishing Industry
Development Program (BPIDP) for its activities.
It also acknowledges the support of the Canada
Council for the Arts for its publishing program.

Canadian Cataloguing in Publication Data

Wilson, Barry, 1948–
Benedict Arnold: a traitor in our midst
Includes bibliographical references and index.
ISBN 0-7735-2150-X
1. Arnold, Benedict, 1741–1801.
2. American loyalists – Biography.
3. Generals – United States – Biography.
4. United States – History – Revolution,
1775–1783 – Biography. 5. Canada – History –
1775–1783. 6. Quebec (Quebec) – History –
Siege, 1775–1776. 7. New Brunswick – Biography.
I. Title.
E278.A7W54 2001   971.02'4'092   C00-901320-2

Typeset in New Baskerville 10.5/13
by Caractéra inc., Quebec City

For my brother Bill, who would understand and appreciate
Benedict Arnold's creative daring on the water.
To the memory of a middle-of-the-night call from Rob Hall,
who reminded me of my love of Canadian history.
As always, to Julianne, who puts up with my passion to write.

Contents

Acknowledgments

This project originated more than ten years ago with a late-night telephone call from Rob Hall, a high school friend. He said that a Stan Rogers tune about the War of 1812 "reminded me of you and your fierce Canadian patriotism of twenty-five years ago." Did I still have that passion?

Yes. And the reminder started me thinking about trying my hand at writing Canadian history. In particular, I remembered some snippets of history about the American traitor Benedict Arnold from my days as a young reporter in Saint John, New Brunswick. He had lived there but was little remembered. Why had I not heard more about him in my years of high school and university?

The idea was briefly set aside but quickly revived in the late 1980s when my wife Julianne and I visited Quebec City and I picked up a copy of Ken Robert's wonderful novel *Arundel*, the story of Arnold's invasion of Quebec in 1775. I was hooked.

That spark led to years of research, with help from many people who kindly gave permission to cite material in their care – the staffs at the National Archives of Canada, New Brunswick Museum, Brunswick Archives, University of New Brunswick library, Saint John Free Public Library, and Ontario Archives in Toronto. Many others gave generously of their time for interviews and help. Thanks.

Along the way, I had research help from Thuy Tran and Jill Mahoney. To both, I extend my thanks.

Claire Gigantes, my editor, deserves special praise for her extraordinary work to make the manuscript better. And to Roger Martin at McGill-Queens University Press, who believed in the project and encouraged me to jump through the hoops even when they seemed too high, I offer special thanks.

Low, Quebec, August 2000

Preface

It was the beginning of the most remarkable moment in my search for the Canadian footprint of Benedict Arnold, the infamous American traitor and a player in early Canadian history.

"I have something to show you … We have his coat, you know."

It was a sunny Sunday morning in July. Anita Winteringham, a long-time resident of Oxbow, Saskatchewan, and Arnold's great-great-great-granddaughter, sat smiling at her kitchen table in a modern bungalow in the centre of town, half an hour into a conversation about family history. At eighty-one, the tiny white-haired holder of family memories peered out through glasses that magnified her lively eyes.

When I telephoned from Ottawa, Anita had agreed to meet me to talk about the family's Saskatchewan history. I flew to Winnipeg on business, rented a car, and drove five hours south-east to Oxbow, near the Saskatchewan-Manitoba-North Dakota border. In a phone call the evening before our meeting she was less enthusiastic about seeing me, but eventually she relented. I could come by Sunday morning but not for long. It was Oxbow's seventy-fifth anniversary weekend and the family would be going out. Sunday morning at 10:00 A.M., I pulled up in front of her house. Anita was courteous and offered a coffee but she was a reluctant storyteller. Details and anecdotes of the early pioneering days were offered sparingly and only after much prodding and questioning.

Anita's daughter, Dorothy Mae Usher, was visiting from Edmonton for the town celebrations. "Tell him some of the stories you told us last night," she finally said to her mother, apparently taking pity on me and signalling that Anita actually had been preparing for my visit.

What followed caught me by surprise. Anita warmed up to the stories. "When we went to school, we wouldn't admit we were related to him," she said with a chuckle when asked about her famous ancestor. "The farm was right beside the US border, you know. We didn't want to stir things up."

Then she sent Dorothy off to fetch something. "We have his coat, you know." At first, this aside had little impact on me. "You have Benedict Arnold's coat?" I asked, still scribbling notes from an earlier answer, trying to keep the flow of conversation going.

"Yes, his British coat."

Dorothy reappeared in the kitchen, carrying a long woollen scarlet British military jacket with a buff lining, deep inside pockets for carrying papers, four brass buttons and intricate gold-thread patterns on the sleeves, cuffs, and back.

I was speechless for a moment, taking in the scene, savouring the moment, almost feeling Benedict Arnold's presence in the room. During the next few moments I touched the coat, tried it on (it was too small), held it, and had Anita model it for me.

The story that then spilled out was amazing. According to Anita, Benedict Arnold's coat had been hauled west when a branch of the Arnold family moved from eastern Ontario early in the twentieth century as part of the wave of homesteaders that populated the Prairies under the settlement policies of Sir Wilfrid Laurier and Sir Clifford Sifton. A century earlier, the Arnolds had moved to eastern Ontario from New Brunswick where, in the bustling Bay of Fundy seaport of Saint John, Benedict Arnold had lived for the better part of six years in the late eighteenth century, sinking Canadian roots along the way. He had fled the United States after first helping to create the American Revolution, then saving it through some crucial military campaigns, and finally, trying to destroy it through an act of treason.

There are no identifying marks on the coat, but the Smithsonian Institution of American History in Washington, D.C., has expressed more than a passing interest. That was why Anita had been suspicious at first. She thought I might be another "official" from the East, trying to get the coat away from the family.

Introduction

When not ignoring him completely, Canada's community of historians have either dismissed Benedict Arnold as an insignificant figure in Canadian history or accepted the American view that he was an unworthy blackguard, despised by all, American and Canadian alike.

Walter Stewart, a Canadian nationalist and journalist who wrote a popular history of Canada's Loyalists, apparently found it less a "curiosity" than an abomination that Arnold had a Canadian connection. Like various other writers of Canadian history, he reflects the American view of Arnold as a "turncoat and opportunist."[1] Most historians and writers dismiss Arnold's New Brunswick years as troubled, isolated, unhappy and ultimately unsuccessful. The 1988 second edition of the *Canadian Encyclopedia* said only that his Canadian years were lived in "controversy, resentment and legal entanglements" while in the US, this "arrogant, ambitious man" carries a name "synonymous in American lore with treason and infamy."[2] Canadian school curricula, when they say anything about Arnold at all, tend to offer an American view. The New Brunswick Department of Education, for example, approved for use in Grade Seven a text that mentioned Arnold as a brave American soldier who invaded Canada, but when it got to his Canadian years, the curriculum outline was brief, brutal and not very factual: "After war, hated by both Americans and Loyalists, settled in Saint John but Loyalists boycotted his business and burned him in effigy. Lived in England til his death."

This view of Arnold has even crept into Canadian media. In the mid-1990s, Ottawa's working-class tabloid, the *Ottawa Sun*, began to refer to Bloc Québecois leader and later Québec premier Lucien Bouchard as

"Benedict Bouchard." Then *Sun* editorial page editor Mark Bonokoski said the paper received few calls and little complaint. "I think most readers, particularly those over 30, understand it immediately as a reference to treason. I suppose it has a lot to do with the americanization of our media and our thought processes. To the Americans, he is a traitor. Canadians understand that label and accept it."[3]

The power of Arnold's name as a metaphor for treachery has even made its way into sports reporting. The scene was New York's fabled Madison Square Garden, home of the New York Rangers, a National Hockey League team, on 13 June 1994. Coach Mike Keenan was on the verge of leading the team to its first Stanley Cup championship in fifty-four years but rumours were circulating that he would also abandon the team and his contract to coach elsewhere. The *New York Post* headline of 13 June screamed: "Benedict Arnold had nothing on Mike Keenan." A frenzied news conference followed and a reporter asked Keenan about the report. "This is going to sound naïve but I don't know who he is." Stephen Brunt, columnist for the Toronto *Globe and Mail*, reported the next exchange. "Benedict Arnold, you know, the traitor, revolutionary war, sold out to the British – a helpful reporter filled in the details. 'See, I'm Canadian so I wouldn't know Canadian history very well.'"[4] The next day, on the 193d anniversary of Arnold's death, the Rangers won game seven and took home the championship. Keenan was an instant Broadway hero. Weeks later, he fled the city for more money in St Louis and became an instant New York villian. Benedict Keenan.

Ironically, Arnold's Canadian image has fared better in American fiction. A 1982 novel called *Thundergate* dealt with a Montreal family of Loyalist Macleods during the American Revolution. When father Matthew and son Tom Macleod hear of Arnold's 1780 defection from the American cause, Tom tells his father: "He plans to come to Canada, He's a real Loyalist hero." Matthew had a more complex reaction. "He'll be welcome here but if the Americans ever catch him, they'll hang him. One nation's hero is another nation's traitor."[5]

It may be why *New York Times* reporter Andrew Malcolm chose in 1985 to use Arnold's Canadian presence sarcastically as a symbol of the difference between the United States and Canada. He saw Canadians as more law abiding and civil than Americans and suggested it was because Canada was first populated by conservative Americans who fled the Revolution. "In Canada, the government gave them free land. And students there today learn from history books about the discontented Americans who fomented revolution against their British sovereign and about some heroes who nonetheless stood firmly loyal to the cause of peace and stability, men of character like Benedict Arnold."[6]

Sydney Wise of Carleton University, one of the deans of contemporary Canadian historians and a specialist in military history, is among those who dismiss the significance of this great soldier. "It's an interesting career. It touched many lives," he reflected. "It has its own momentum but it was not sustained. It was episodic. It's hard to place Arnold in the galaxy of doers in the Canadian scene."[7] Wise said history tends to record, and historians pay attention to, those who were elected or played a role in government or in building institutions. Arnold was a soldier and businessman who did none of that. "Historians have tended to consider it a curiosity that an American traitor had land in Canada."

For the record, Benedict Arnold did far more than own land in Canada. As an American general, he came within a whisker of capturing Canada for the thirteen colonies, almost turning British North America into an American outpost. Later, he was a substantial and adventurous businessman who helped write some of the early history of Canada and whose family still thrives here. He was far more than an opportunist. It is true that he did not settle permanently in Canada, but a disastrous economy and tense relations with his neighbours largely explained his ultimate decision to abandon New Brunswick for London, England. He took pains to make sure that his eldest sons stayed and sank roots in British North America.

Arnold's connection to Canada lasted on and off for almost two decades. In pre-revolutionary days, as a Yankee trader, he plied the waters of the St Lawrence River doing business with the New England traders who had moved north, as well as with the growing French Canadian merchant class.

As revolutionary fervour swept through the thirteen colonies, Arnold led one of the most celebrated invasions of Canada, delivering more than seven hundred men to the plains outside Quebec City after an arduous and heroic two-month trek through the Maine wilderness. Through the winter of 1775–76, he led an assault on Quebec that brought the city very close to surrender. It included a dramatic New Year's Eve attack and a five-month siege that had Quebec's defenders despairing for their future. Arnold's role in this pivotal campaign has been largely overlooked in Canadian history, even though, as University of New Hampshire historian Willard Sterne Randall put it, "If

Arnold had succeeded, he would have made Canada the fourteenth American state."[8] There have been exceptions, however, to this rule of neglect. On 30 December 1972, for example, the mass-circulation newspaper supplement *Weekend Magazine* carried a feature titled "When Benedict Arnold almost Conquered Canada: The New Year's Eve Canada Nearly Disappeared."[9]

Of course, Arnold and the American invaders did not succeed. He went back to New England and became the premier soldier of the Revolution and one of the key military players in its triumphs. He also became the most celebrated and reviled traitor to the Revolution, betraying his leader and friend, George Washington.

After the Revolution, Arnold struggled to regain his commercial touch and former wealth, moving to England and then to what remained of Britain's North American empire. His time in New Brunswick, while tumultuous, was commercially noteworthy and, by most contemporary standards, successful. He was defeated, as we shall see, mainly by the lack of currency in the depressed seaside colony and the poverty of his customers.

Arnold became the most successful businessman and trader in early New Brunswick, a supporter of public works and a significant player in the economy of the growing colony. Politically, though, he was inept. He never figured out how to use to advantage the governing system that worked for others who had far less invested in the colony.

He left after being rebuked in the most sensational trial of New Brunswick's early years, a trial that centred as much on character and acceptance as it did on the facts of the case, all of which were on Arnold's side. It was the colony's first libel trial, launched when Arnold sued a former business partner for comments he made publicly about Arnold's character. The jury sided with the aggrieved businessman but awarded him minimal damages, suggesting that his reputation was not worth much.

More than 170 years after Arnold's departure, it was noted that "threads of the Arnold legend are woven into the tapestry of early New Brunswick."[10] The sons Arnold left behind in 1791 soon became part of the Canadian tapestry in their own right. They raised families, helped to colonize Upper Canada (now Ontario), and, a century later, took part in the opening of the Canadian West.

There remain many traces of Benedict Arnold's exploits in Canada – the Plains of Abraham and the gates of Old Quebec where he came so close to ending British control of Canada; the Hotel Arnold and the Arnold River in Wilburn, Quebec, near the Maine border where the young soldier emerged from the wilderness to begin his final trek to Quebec City; the Auberge Arnold in Nouvelle-Beauce, Quebec, where the young commander bought food for his starving men; the old streets of Saint John, the Lower Cove area where he worked and had a wharf and a warehouse, and the King Street site of his residence; the land south-east of Smiths Falls, Ontario, where Arnold's sons farmed and raised their families; the small towns they helped build in the area and the mossy stones of their graves; the Arnold descendants scattered across the country, who have been judges and farmers, businessmen and nurses, wartime pilots and peacetime teachers.

These all bear echoes of Benedict Arnold's footsteps in Canada. He was a dashing, controversial, larger-than-life eighteenth-century man who played a role in the formative years of the country. Canadian historians have largely failed to examine the legacies and legends left by this American villain who chose to remain a British subject. My book, with its emphasis both on the facts of Arnold's life and on the primitive unruly Canada in which he lived, attempts to fill that gap. It is a small slice of the national story, centred around the adventures of one of North America's most controversial figures, written for a general audience with an interest in Canada's past and those who shaped it.

Arnold lived during a time of revolution and intrigue, upheaval and uncertainty. His contemporaries and acquaintances were the giants of the formative years of American and Canadian history – Washington and Jefferson, Carleton and Simcoe. His times were riotous and momentous as American refugees from the Revolution came to Canada with their dreams and the conservative ideologies that played a pivotal role in forming the Canadian identity. It was a time when slaves were sold in the market squares of Canadian communities, when penniless American boat people struggled to create wealth and stability in a sometimes inhospitable wilderness, when the emerging societies of British North America became battlegrounds for the clash between the ideals of democracy and class structure.

Benedict Arnold, trader, warrior, and merchant, was a citizen of these times, sometimes a central player, sometimes a bystander pushed and pulled by the same powerful forces that had turned eighteenth-century North America's political geography upside down. He was also a father, husband, and businessman who bragged about his children, wrote love letters to his wife, tried to provide creature comforts for his family at a time of economic turmoil, and cultivated a circle of friends in Saint John whose members one day would be hailed as the founders of New Brunswick.

Colonel Arnold (1741–1801), by Johann Lorenz Rugenda. Intaglio etching, circa 1776, celebrating Arnold's successful invasion of Canada in November 1775.
New Brunswick Museum, Saint John, NB.

Le Général ARNOLD

déserté de l'Armée des États-Unis

le 3 Octobre 1780

Le Général Arnold, 1780, by Benoit-Louis Prevost (after Pierre Eugene du Simitiere).
Intaglio etching. Print of a painting of Arnold in 1780 when he was military governor
of Philadelphia. It is thought to be the only surviving likeness, although the style
of the day was to add a heroic element to portraits.
New Brunswick Museum, Saint John, NB.

A chair, housed in the New Brunswick Museum, Saint John, NB. Allegedly one of twelve made by Benedict Arnold and sold in auction when he moved his family back to England in autumn, 1791.

Benedict Arnold's British military coat, now owned by Jayson Arnold at Glen Ewen, Saskatchewan. The coat has been passed to the oldest Arnold male during the past two hundred years.

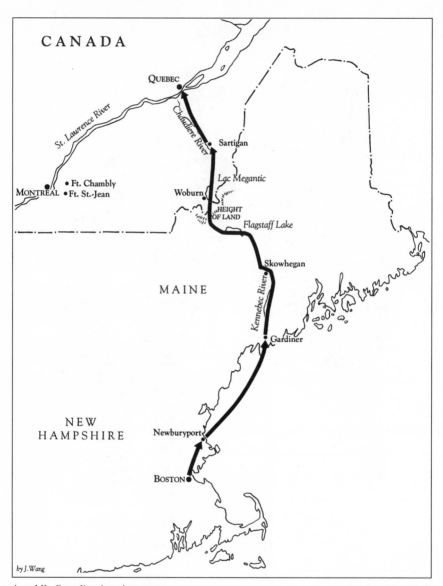

Arnold's Canadian invasion, 1775.   Josephine Wang

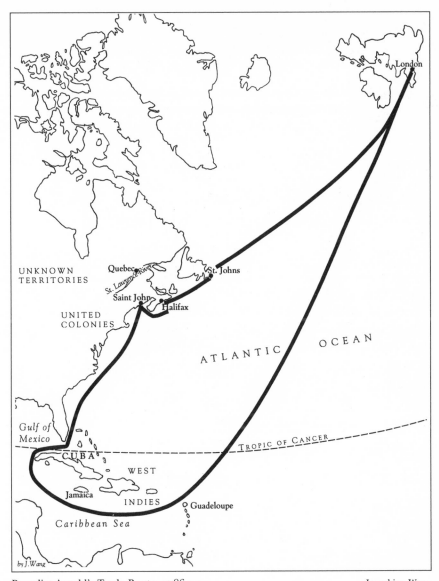

Benedict Arnold's Trade Route, 1786–91.

Josephine Wang

Benedict Arnold

1

Young Trader, Canadian Connections

In a way, Benedict Arnold was born to greatness. In a more profound way, however, he was a self-made man. Arnold was an honoured name in the thirteen colonies. Benedict's great-great grandfather, William, had been a founder of Rhode Island in the seventeenth century after emigrating from England. His great-grandfather, Benedict, had been ten times elected governor of Rhode Island. His grandfather, Benedict II, had spent most of the family fortune. His father, Benedict III, had moved to Norwich, Connecticut, in 1730 as a cooper (barrel maker), married the daughter of one of the town's founders, and become a successful and rich sea captain, trader, and businessman. This was the milieu into which Benedict Arnold IV was born on 14 January 1741, his parents' only surviving son at a time of high infant mortality. It was also a time of constant wars against the French, Indian raids, and yellow fever, which claimed two of his sisters and many neighbours. It was a time of religious upheaval and constant danger. "Benedict Arnold's childhood was full of martial excitement," wrote one biographer.[1]

His mother was a severe and strict Puritan who believed that her only son had been hand-picked by God for greatness. His father was a businessman who plied the high seas and liked a dram or two of liquor. As the son of a wealthy family, Arnold received better schooling than most, studying mathematics, English, Latin, the Bible, history, and logic. In fact, his parent's decision to send him away to a private school in Canterbury, Connecticut, probably saved Benedict's life – he was absent from coastal Norwich in the early 1750s when yellow fever ravished the town, touching his family like most others. Canterbury, located fifteen miles inland, was removed from the disease-carrying mosquitoes that came out of the nearby swamp into Norwich.

It was the first major example of what was to become Arnold's much-noted ability and luck in dodging death. During the eighteenth century, pestilence, war, and disease stalked the population, making arrival at old age something of a miracle. In such a dangerous time, Arnold's ability to beat the odds seemed all the more remarkable.

In battle he was indestructible. Twice wounded, he survived to fight another day. Horses were shot from under him. His coat often was riddled with musket-ball holes at the end of a battle. Several times, he appeared trapped in battle but managed to escape. He took risks that made him an easy target for enemy marksmen. Somehow, though, they always failed to kill him.

In the face of disease, his luck also held as it had in Connecticut of the 1750s. Outside the walls of Quebec City in the dreadful winter of 1775–76, smallpox cut a broad swath through his army, rendering it too weak to make the final decisive assault on the fortress. Arnold survived, in part by being courageous enough to try the new technique of self-inoculation, and in part through luck.

Close calls marked his life, whether he was avoiding a treacherous waterfall and certain death during the Maine march, fleeing from Gen. George Washington's forces after his defection, or escaping from the French after he was captured in the West Indies in 1795 at age fifty-four. Peggy Arnold, his wife of sixteen years and no doubt accustomed to Arnold's luck, still sounded incredulous when she wrote to a friend in Saint John about her husband's late-life escape from the French: "You have no doubt heard of the many wonderful escapes he has had, some of which could only have been effected by his uncommon exertions."[2]

Twenty years before, the American general Horatio Gates marvelled at Arnold's close escapes during the retreat from Canada and his efforts on Lake Champlain in 1776 to stop a British naval invasion. "It has pleased Providence to preserve General Arnold," wrote Gates.[3]

For his part, Arnold was content to praise God for his invincibility. In November 1775, during the invasion of Canada, he sent a letter to his superiors describing how a minor accident helped him avert a potentially fatal disaster. One day, after two hours of rapid and dangerous descent on the Chaudière River, the boats overturned and all provisions were lost. "This disaster, though unfortunate at first view, we must think a very happy circumstance on the whole and a kind interposition of Providence for had we proceeded half a mile farther, we must have gone over a prodigious fall which we were not apprised of and all inevitably perished," he wrote.[4]

Arnold was even more explicit about his presumption of God's protection on 6 January 1776 as he lay in the hospital tent outside Quebec, kept awake by pain in his shattered left leg and trying to organize a siege by his depleted and dispirited army of invasion. Arnold wrote to his sister Hannah in New Haven that he was alive and expected to triumph over the British defenders: "I know you will be anxious for me. That Providence which has carried me through so many dangers is still my protection. I am in the way of my duty and know no fear."[5] It was one of the rare understatements of his remarkable and lucky life.

While he was growing up, it seems that this partnership with Providence was assumed to be true only by his pious mother. His seafaring father figured he would have a better chance of survival if he knew some of the skills that would make him self-reliant in the world of Yankee traders. In the summers, young Benedict travelled with his father on trading voyages to the Caribbean, learning both a love of the sea and the mechanics of sailing.

The accounts of Benedict's childhood, many compiled when he was still seen as an American hero, are exceptional.[6] He is described as an athletic, fearless child who was a strong skater (the climate in those days produced frozen rivers most years in Connecticut), a natural leader, and a daredevil. He watched local militia train and learned the routines. He learned to canoe, snowshoe, and survive in the forests from local Abenaki Indians. Once, he grabbed one of the revolving blades on the water-wheel at the local mill and let it carry him around under the water and up the other side. He impressed local boys by jumping over loaded wagons and by confronting and refusing to back down from local constables. "At thirteen, Benedict Arnold was a leader of boys, and a fighter, but he was not a bully."[7]

That year, 1754, marked the collapse of the world that the spirited, promising boy had known and in which he felt comfortable. His father's trading business had suffered because of the British naval blockades. Debts had built up. His business collapsed and Benedict, Sr, became the town drunk. His wife, Hannah, pulled the young Benedict out of school for lack of money. This was the disgrace that Clare Brandt decided was a character-destroying moment, the time when Arnold changed from being a promising Yankee achiever to being a boy-man with a hole in his soul that could be filled only by money and prestige obtained at any cost, even the loss of his country. At the very least, it gave Arnold a life-long aversion to heavy drinking, particularly by soldiers.[8]

His mother sent Benedict to a wealthy relative, Dr Daniel Lathrop, for an eight-year apprenticeship in the druggist trade. This meant that from age thirteen to twenty-one, Benedict Arnold was supposed to be an indentured employee. In practical terms, those years gave him the best education for life he could have had.

Lathrop took a liking to him and taught him both the druggist business and the trading business. This included an education in trading for fine horses, which Arnold used to his advantage when he became a trader in his own right. Mrs Jerusha Lathrop treated him as a son (her own sons had died) and taught him the finer points of being a gentleman and a gardener.

There were several incidents during his years as an apprentice apothecary that marked Arnold as a young man determined to live in exciting times. In 1758, at age seventeen, he ran away to join the army as it prepared to attack the French-controlled Fort Ticonderoga on Lake Champlain. He was returned after his mother interceded. Early the next year, he ran away again to join the army and was reported as a missing indentured servant, at large without permission. Again he was returned to the Lathrops. By then he had fallen in love with the lure and promise of military life.

By spring 1759, Benedict had persuaded his mother to allow him to enlist and he travelled to Albany, New York, to train for the fight against the French in the planned British assault on their Canadian fortresses. "Benedict impressed his mess-mates with his ability to shoot, to jump over the ammunition wagons, to wrestle, to march long distances without apparent fatigue."[9]

The army was not as impressed when in May Benedict heard that his mother was gravely ill and left camp without permission. His unauthorized leave denied him a chance to serve the British in their successful August/September campaign to capture Canada from the French. It also led the army to put a price on his head. Given Arnold's own invasion of British-controlled Quebec sixteen years later, his participation in the 1759 victory would have been a sweet historical irony. Family loyalties interceded.

An army advertisement offering a reward for his return was placed in the *New York Gazette* in May 1759, but he eluded the army until his mother died, during the summer, and he had handled the details of her death and burial. His father by then was an incompetent alcoholic who died three years later from the effects of the disease.

The Lathrops interceded to get him back into the army without penalty the next spring. By then, however, the battle for Canada was over and there was nothing left but the boring routine of boot camp. It was not for Arnold. By winter 1760, he was back with Lathrop. Again, it was a good career move. His benefactor and mentor made him chief clerk of a flourishing trading business. He sailed to ports in Canada, the Caribbean, and London in search of goods to buy and sell. He learned how to be a shrewd trader and a skilful mariner. There had already been indications that he had leadership qualities.

The combination of these learned and inherited skills proved to be a powerful mixture as the young man set off in 1762, aged twenty-one, to make his fortune. Dr Lathrop gave him an enormous boost with a gift of five hundred pounds sterling (in an age when salaries were usually less than one hundred pounds annually), property, and a letter of introduction.

He moved to the coastal town of New Haven, home to Yale College, to set up his own business as a dispenser of drugs, balms, books, creams, jewellery, prints, maps, and other fine articles imported from abroad. That spring, he hung out his first sign, black wood with white lettering, now on display in the New Haven Colony Historical Society museum:

B. Arnold Druggist
Bookseller & c.
From London
Sibi Totique.

The Latin motto translates: "For himself and for everybody."

Benedict's store was across the New Haven common from Yale and carried an array of goods that would have appealed to the privileged students of the college, which had been founded a century before but named for the Yale family after a generous financial gift in 1716. The store carried the latest books and information from London and other distant, exotic points.

Before long, Arnold began to look to sea again, expanding his fortune by purchasing ships to extend his trading empire, both legal and illegal. Canada would be part of his circuit.

We do not know exactly what Benedict Arnold looked like. It is remarkable that, despite his fame, there are no definitive paintings or drawings of him.

The closest likeness is a profile drawn in 1779 by Swiss artist Pierre du Simitière when Arnold was governor of Philadelphia. It shows a stout man with a strong face and a sharp nose. Yet it is impossible to say this is a true likeness because the style of the time was to inject heroic subjects with heroic qualities. For example, strikingly similar portraits of "Benedict Arnold" were published in Germany, England, and France at the time of his more dazzling exploits. The background was changed to depict Quebec City or Saratoga, New York, but the pose is the same – a plump, rather effeminate-looking young man whom the Europeans saw as a hero of the North American wars. It is almost certain that no artist actually painted him in those locales. It was the practice to rush to print with images of heroes as soon as news arrived of battle victories or feats of survival. The face was interchangeable, the background constructed to resemble what the artist imagined the setting to be like.

There are some recorded hints of his appearance. In an advertisement published by the British army on 21 May 1759 seeking the eighteen-year-old deserter, he was described as having a "dark complexion, light eyes and dark hair."

In those early New Haven days, according to one biographer, Arnold had "a strong physical appearance" with "a distinctive nose, a high forehead suggesting intelligence, a prominent chin and gray piercing eyes."[10] Elsewhere he has been as "short, swarthy and hard-muscled."[11] Almost certainly this was speculation, a writer's license based on earlier scant historical references and an assumption that a warrior who could walk, canoe, or ride miles each day would have to be "hard-muscled." According to the *Encyclopedia of the American Revolution*, he was five foot nine inches tall with "gray eyes set off by black hair and a swarthy complexion." While there are no "authentic portraits," what we have shows "a beak-nosed man with a heavy jutting jaw and a sloping brow."[12] John Joseph Henry, who ran away from home at age sixteen to join Arnold's 1775 march to Canada, described him as "a short, handsome man of a florid complexion, stoutly made."[13] The military jacket that hangs in a Saskatchewan farmhouse would fit a tall, thin man, but over the years it may have shrunk or otherwise altered in shape.

All biographers agree that Arnold displayed both athletic ability, stamina, and remarkable physical presence in his youth. These gifts were taken from him in the Revolution when three times, most notably at Quebec City and Saratoga, he was wounded or injured in the leg. "Arnold refused amputation," writes military historian Robert Spiller, but after October, 1777, "his well-known physical agility was gone for life."[14]

By the time he moved to Canada, repeated wounds had left him with one leg shorter than the other, forcing him to use a cane on many days and to suffer from lingering pain.

Like his physical appearance, his personality remains something of a mystery. The evidence handed down to us is uneven. It portrays a complex, fearless, contradictory personality – impetuous yet calculating, generous yet greedy, well schooled but not scholarly, a doer not a thinker, vain and self-serving yet willing to give credit to others when warranted, warm and loyal to family, friends, and troops yet arrogant and impatient with others.

It is worth remembering that many of the descriptions of Arnold were concocted by people who were prejudiced against him as a traitor. Still, from his recorded actions and the judgments of his contemporaries, unblemished by the weight of historical analysis that has made him an unredeemable villain, it is possible to draw some conclusions about the kind of man Arnold was.

That he was fearless is undeniable, even by his most diligent critics. Years after the 1775 invasion of Canada, long after it became unfashionable and even treasonous to say anything good about Arnold in America, Pennsylvania judge John Henry thought back to his service under Arnold during the heroic march through Maine and gave his former commander much credit. "Arnold was of a remarkable character," Henry wrote in a memoir passed down to his descendent and first published in Albany, New York, in 1877. "He was brave, even to temerity, was beloved by the soldiery, perhaps for that quality only. He possessed great powers of persuasion, was pleasant."[15]

Henry also noted that Arnold was "sordidly" greedy. But that seems to have been an afterthought, influenced perhaps by Arnold's later fall from grace. He surely did not witness Arnold's "greed" in the wilderness of Maine or on the plains of Quebec. In fact, he witnessed the other side of Arnold, his generosity and loyalty to, and popularity with, his men. Henry notes in his memoir that as a young man two days past his seventeenth birthday, he became ill while marching through Quebec. Arnold paid out of his own pocket to have a French couple nurse the young soldier back to health. One of his officers wrote from Quebec that his commander was a man of "invincible courage, of great prudence, ever serene, he defies the greatest danger. You will find him ever the intrepid hero and the unruffled Christian."[16]

Throughout his life, Arnold proved himself a loyal family man, whether by deserting the army in 1759 to be with his dying mother or by making arrangements in his will to ensure that his sons would have a chance to prosper as farmers in Canada.

He was a soldier's soldier, insisting on discipline and effort from his men but admiring them, leading by example, and standing up for them when need necessary. On 13 October 1775 he wrote to Gen.

George Washington from the Maine wilderness to praise his men as they pushed north. "The officers, volunteers and privates have in general acted with the greatest spirit and industry," he wrote.[17]

His compassion and understanding for his men had been evident two weeks earlier when, after a night of drinking and quarrelling, one of his rookie troops, James McCormick, shot and killed another, Reuben Bishop. Arnold did not tolerate drinking among his troops and a court martial was held. He found McCormick guilty and sentenced him to death but then ordered that he be sent back to Washington for a final verdict. Unbeknownst to the condemned man, who had been conscripted to the army rather than volunteering, Arnold sent a letter to Washington recommending mercy. "The criminal appears to be very simple and ignorant and in the company he belonged to, had the character of being a peaceable fellow ... I wish he may be found a proper object of mercy."[18] This letter saved the soldier from what in those days would have been almost certain execution.

In the winter of 1776, a congressional delegation travelled north from Philadelphia to investigate the failure of the invasion of Canada (see chapter 10). Headed by Benjamin Franklin, the four-man committee met Arnold in Montreal in April. Commissioner Charles Carroll was clearly impressed: "If this war continues and Arnold should not be taken off pretty early, he will turn out a great man. He has great vivacity, perseverance, resources and intrepidity and a cool judgment."[19] This praise came before Arnold's heroics of the next two years.

Nor was he always self-confident and assured. As he contemplated the siege of Quebec in early 1776 from a hospital bed, he asked several times to be relieved of his duty. "I find myself unequal to the task," he wrote to Washington in early January.[20] And to his sister Hannah he wrote that command of the army was "a task I find too heavy under my present circumstances."[21] Yet as he healed and the pain subsided, he regained his confidence. Even as he lay on his sick-bed, Arnold never lost his will to fight. He instructed his aides to equip him with weapons in case the British attacked the hospital. He would make them pay a price for his capture or death.

One marked characteristic of Arnold's was his lack of political acumen. He could fight. He could scheme. He could act decisively. He was not, however, an intellectual. Nor was he particularly adept at fighting his way out of the political blind alleys that were so prevalent in the overheated ideological atmosphere of revolutionary America. Alexander Hamilton, an aide to Washington and a master politician during and after the Revolution, was "familiar with Arnold, who had often been at headquarters." It was his impression that "the fighter did not combine

... any intellectual qualities with his physical prowess. Instead of engaging in interesting argument, he shouted and pounded the table."[22]

In fact, Arnold showed contempt for the politicians who sat around in the safety of Philadelphia, engaging in intrigue and setting rules for the army while soldiers put their lives on the line on the battle front. He was "by nature impetuous, aggressive, alert and eager for battle under any circumstances," but he had "never been a good politician. He was tactless, impatient, extremely outspoken and had made numerous enemies unnecessarily."[23]

The last word on Arnold's personality will rest with an American descendant, Isaac N. Arnold, who wrote a defensive 1888 biography of his infamous ancestor. Defensive or not, his assessment has a ring of truth to it. "As a soldier, he exhibited a superb courage that was never surpassed and which made him the idol of his men. He possessed an endurance, a capacity for leadership, an ability for organization, a power over men, a fertility of invention, a coolness in danger and a quickness of perception which marked him as among the best, if not the very best, fighting general of the Revolutionary War."[24]

This view of Arnold was shared by George Washington in the early years of the Revolution. But before he ever ventured into the battlefields of revolutionary America, Arnold had become a successful, astute, and decisive trader who travelled the waterways of North America, developed an extensive list of contacts, and learned a great deal about human nature.

It was key training for his years as a revolutionary fighter.

Malcolm Decker, in his 1932 biography of Arnold, described what he assumed was a typical 1766 scene where the young Connecticut trader Benedict Arnold, then twenty-five years old and beginning to prosper, was working one of his trading networks. "Behold him sitting in the English Coffee House at Montreal, discussing wheat, horses and Rockingham Whigs (a British political movement in favour of making concessions to the American colonies, contrary to the British Tory hard line) with Moses Hazen and Thomas Walker," wrote Decker.

He imagined how difficult it must have been to be a trader in Quebec in those days. "Taken all in all, it was a hard, vicious life, this culling in the North, which challenged the self-motivated bounder and opportunist we see there, pushing through old Kinderhook to Albany and the lakes, through the valley of the Sorel to Montreal, thence up the St Lawrence to Quebec – 'the great circle,' we will call it ..."[25]

In the trading world of the 1760s business was transacted in coffee-houses, Yankee traders dropped in to Quebec to buy goods collected by local traders, often transplanted New Englanders, from the hinterland. The St Lawrence River was the gateway to the rich interior of Quebec, which had recently been acquired by the British. Arnold was in the thick of that trade, making contacts and learning the geography of the colony. It was information that would later be invaluable to the revolutionary invader. It was traditional territory for Yankee traders.

Arnold's trading business began and grew soon after he moved to New Haven and realized that being the proprietor of a shop was not enough to satisfy his energy, ambition, and imagination. After Arnold, Sr, died in 1762, he sold his father's Norwich house for seven hundred pounds, used the money to buy a forty-ton sloop, the *Fortune*, which he used to begin a small trading business. His crews, often with Arnold on board, worked the waters of the Atlantic between the Caribbean and Canada, with stops in Quebec, Nova Scotia, and St John's, Newfoundland. He carried horses, pork, hay, oats, lumber, sugar, and rum on his runs. Often he traded for Spanish gold, for salt or cotton that could be converted to currency in New Haven. He turned out to be a good businessman. "He traded shrewdly and expanded carefully."[26]

By 1766 the twenty-five-year-old Arnold owned three trading ships and his apothecary business was thriving. He used his growing wealth to establish a presence in New Haven. "At home ... he wore fine clothing and white satin stockings, sipped tea and made his way in society."[27] He acquired a family during these years, in 1767 marrying Margaret Mansfield, daughter of the local sheriff and as close to Connecticut aristocracy as he could get. By 1772 they had three sons, Benedict, Richard, and Henry.

Around the time Richard was born, Benedict purchased a two-acre waterfront estate in New Haven and started construction on an elegant house, panelled partly with mahogany from Honduras. Nearby he built stables to house twelve horses and a coach-house for two coaches. He spent £1,800 establishing an orchard with one hundred pear, peach, plum, cherry, nectarine, and apple trees.[28] It was one of the grandest houses in New Haven, but it remained unfinished thanks to restrictive British trade rules and then the Revolution. By 1780 when he tried to sell it, the house still was only half completed inside: politics and war had drained his financial resources in the 1770s and diverted his energies elsewhere.

Arnold's journey to wealth and respectability was not a steady progression. His marriage appears to have been cold and distant, despite his warm and sometimes desperate pleas in letters from ports of call for news from home. Margaret seems to have been largely immune when exposed to the virus of his passion. Through many of these years, he was also hounded by creditors and troubled by debt. It was not until the early 1770s that his wealth began to match his ambitions and pretensions.

This is a shadowy period of Arnold's life, for only part of his commercial and trading business was legal. Like most New England traders of his day, Benedict Arnold had taken to smuggling to get around various strict trading rules imposed by the British government on the colonies in the 1760s. These rules, which are detailed in the next chapter, helped to arouse the powerful commercial class and precipitate the revolution that would defeat the British a decade later.

Thanks to his participation in this underground economy, there are few records of Arnold's commercial life before the Revolution; smugglers are understandably reluctant to leave a paper trail. It was another source of tension in his life in those days, another area of vulnerability. Businessmen with commercial enemies were particularly susceptible. A quiet word to the British authorities and an arrest could follow, a fortune could be seized. This was a particular danger for Arnold, whose strong personality, abrupt manner, and hard-driving, demanding style of leadership made enemies among his competitors and sometimes among his crew.

Arnold learned that lesson one summer day in 1773, almost to his peril. In Quebec City, two of his crewmen went to the authorities to tip them off about their captain the smuggler. Arnold was hauled in to account for himself before the authorities, who threatened to seize his ship. "You cannot imagine how much trouble and fatigue I have gone through," he wrote to his wife. "Two of my people have informed against me, which near cost me my vessel ... had not my friends interposed which, with the addition of ten or fifteen pounds to the villains, settled the matter."[29] Having saved his ship from confiscation, he tried to sell it but could find no buyers. In the end, Arnold purchased a load of horses and set sail for Barbados in search of buyers.

Incidents like that helped to radicalize a generation of energetic colonial traders and merchants, Arnold among them. In fact, a similar incident in New Haven seven years earlier could be considered the beginning of his revolutionary awakening.

In February 1766 Arnold was involved in the public flogging of a former crew member who tried to turn him in for a reward from the British. The man had been given several chances to leave town but stayed in the hope of getting some British coin. Other members of

Arnold's crew, possibly with his collusion, attacked the man who was prepared to take away their livelihood by having the ship seized. Under Arnold's watchful eye the unfortunate man was run out of town on a rail – that is, he was tied to a wooden rail or log and carried through the town for all to see – after enduring forty lashes. Arnold and other members of the mob were charged with disorderly conduct and fined; but instead of feeling chastened, Arnold felt justified. The problem was not the mob's actions, or the self-serving act of treachery by the former crew member, he said in a series of letters to the *Connecticut Gazette* newspaper. The issue was the attempt by Great Britain to impose trade restrictions and taxes on the colonies, eroding rights and liberties that had been guaranteed in British law.[30]

For all his revolutionary bravado, the fear of being closed down by the authorities was a constant worry, a hazard of the job. Yankee traders like Arnold, operating on both sides of the law, were tough, no-nonsense risk-takers willing to do what had to be done to stay in business. Sometimes, that involved meting out rough justice to crew members or competitors with a grudge, staring down inquisitive British naval officers or greasing the palm of some corrupt port official who was willing to be absent from the docks the day that contraband molasses was unloaded.

In the meantime, Arnold was learning and honing the qualities of leadership, toughness, decisiveness, and daring that marked his greatness. His trading connections gave him Quebec contacts and a window into the commercial class and intricate society of this recently conquered land. It was a far more complex society than many in the thirteen colonies or the British Isles were willing to concede.

The story of Samuel Jacobs, one of Arnold's merchant contacts, illustrates the point. He was a German Jew who moved first to Great Britain and then to the thirteen colonies before moving north in 1759 as a supplier to a unit of General James Wolfe's army of invasion.

When the British won, Jacobs decided to stay, settling in the Richelieu Valley town of St Denis, north-east of Montreal near the St Lawrence River. He bought an abandoned distillery, produced rum from molasses purchased in the West Indies, and then used the money he earned from selling the rum to buy local grain and pelts for sale to merchants trading into New England. He prospered, buying local farms, acquiring some small ships to transport goods to Quebec City or Montreal, and establishing widespread commercial links. He was a general merchant, selling clothes, household goods, and farm equipment to peasant farmers in the Quebec countryside. From them, he bought farm produce to sell to the traders whose ships plied the river during the summer months.

The business was based on cheap rum, and it was rum, "imported at low prices from New England and the British West Indies, that quickly became the liquor of mass consumption in the Canadian countryside after the Conquest."[31] Benedict Arnold was one of the traders who supplied Jacobs with rum, or the molasses to make it, as well as other items in demand in peasant homes. In return he wanted the produce from the rich farmland of the Richelieu Valley.

It was a complex commercial life for the local middleman merchant, who had to balance delicate relationships with local farmers and with foreign traders. To that was added the uncertainty and danger of politics, the need to weigh the interests of local French Catholic peasants against the common-law traditions of the British governors. What's more, come 1775 the egalitarian, democratic rhetoric of the invading Americans had to be balanced against the requirements of feudal stability that the middleman's neighbours, suppliers and customers expected. Jacobs and his merchant colleagues in Quebec in the 1760s and 1770s were for the most part well equipped to undertake this delicate balancing act.

The peasant farmers with whom Jacobs dealt had few buyers for their crops. Yet despite their portrayal in nationalist literature and legend, defiled as pawns in the hands of the British conquerors and smooth Yankee traders, they were not totally powerless. They had some bargaining leverage. For one thing, they knew the merchants wanted and needed their wheat, which fetched top dollar from the traders. "Samuel Jacobs and the other merchants showed almost no interest in other products or potential products of this rich farming region," according to one historian. "A few head of cattle were shipped down to Quebec but peas and oats were only purchased reluctantly as a favour to insistent Habitants."[32] While the traders wanted wheat, the farmers grew peas for food and oats for cattlefeed. When there was a surplus, they naturally wanted to sell it as well and used wheat as a bargaining chip.

To get supplies of the coveted crop, merchants offered peasants free grain storage over the winter until the trading ships appeared again on the St Lawrence. Merchants sometimes took possession of the grain as soon as it was threshed, promising that if the market price increased before it was sold to the trader, the benefit of the higher price would be passed back to the farmer. Even with such inducements, the merchants often had to sweeten the deal a bit more. "To secure the wheat of a large producer, Jacobs would often agree to accept some peas as well or to take damaged or sprouted wheat along with the good. At times of heavy demand, he might also offer a cash advance or a few gallons of rum ... on striking a bargain."[33]

Once in possession of the goods, Jacobs and his merchant colleagues still had to cut a deal with a trader who had access to foreign markets for local produce and to the merchandise needed to satisfy the consumer needs of the Lower St Lawrence region. Part of the negotiation invariably centred on the currency of exchange.

In those days, there was no common currency. A common Canadian currency did not appear until 1817, so when Jacobs and Arnold were cutting deals, they would first have to decide on the currency to be used, which would be written into the agreement. They had a number of choices – the Spanish dollar, Portuguese coins, Halifax currency, Montreal currency, and York currency. Each had its own value, depending on demand and availability.

To complicate matters even more, there was a shortage of currency in Quebec in those days and sales were often made using "bills of exchange" rather than currency. It was like a futures contract, promising cash or goods later as compensation. "The money system was in chaos in those days," according to Carleton University Economics professor Robin Neill. "There wasn't much cash around and there were many competing currencies."[34]

It was with that structured yet chaotic commercial system as a background that Benedict Arnold and Samuel Jacobs met in Quebec City on 4 October 1774 to conduct some business. The result shows how diverse a business Jacobs ran. He was not simply selling local farm produce for export. At times, he also imported farm produce, in this case oats that could be sold to local horse owners. The two traders were making plans for the 1775 trading season when they agreed that Arnold would deliver oats to Jacobs at Montreal, to be paid in Halifax currency. The contract specified that if either failed to meet his end of the bargain, there would be a penalty of two hundred pounds Halifax currency.[35]

There is no follow-up document but it is unlikely that Arnold met his end of the bargain. It is equally unlikely that he paid the penalty. By the next year Arnold had exchanged his trader's clothes for military garb. The next time the two men met, Arnold was leading an invasion force and Jacobs was trying to make money from both sides, selling to whomever could pay him for his goods.

In virtually any other era, Benedict Arnold would have continued to prosper at the trading business he had clearly mastered. He would have accumulated a fortune and probably donated enough of it to have public buildings, institutions of higher learning, or possibly even a city named after him.

History, however, intervened. Forces in his life, both past and present, came together in a compelling mix of self-interest and destiny that would drive him onto the public stage of grand events. His training, experience, personality, and inclination revealed him to be a master of the military stage but a bumbler on the more important political boardwalk.

2

The Rustle of Revolutionary Winds

When Arnold and Jacobs sat down together in October 1774 to do some business, the events that changed Arnold from a trader to a revolutionary leader with few peers were already at work. They were a mix of his religious background, his personality and self-interest, and the simmering political unrest that permeated his society, a unique mix of radical action and political thought that defined his era. One key ingredient was the British inability to understand the powerful concoction that was being created in its North American colonies.

At thirty-four, Benedict Arnold was very much a product of the unsettled times in which he lived. His boyhood was coloured by the religious turmoil that divided society in the thirteen colonies and reverberated into the revolutionary years three decades later. At its core was the issue of how the dominant Puritan church should be organized: whether as a liberal, congregation-oriented church or a hierarchical conservative church.

It started in the early 1730s when a Massachusetts preacher named Jonathon Edwards, later president of Princeton University in New Jersey, galvanized congregations with an emotional pitch for their souls. In one of his most noted sermons, delivered in Enfield, Connecticut, six months after Arnold was born, he regaled his frightened and emotionally charged audience with predictions of their demise. "O sinner! Consider the fearful danger you are in. It is a great furnace of wrath, a wide and bottomless pit, full of the fire of wrath, that you are held over."[1] A contemporary witness reported that the audience was moved. "The shrieks and cries were piercing and amazing."[2] In such fearful religious days was young Benedict raised.

In 1739, the preacher George Whitefield had come to New England
from England to warn that the local Puritans were becoming too liberal. He embraced a fundamentalist brand of religion, featuring sub-
servience and loyalty, that appealed to many and repelled others. The
divisions became political as well as religious, a battle between the old
and the new. Defenders of the old faith became known as Old Lights,
while the more radical modernists were the New Lights. The debate
between the two is now seen as a precursor to later revolutionary
debates about local versus central control, democratic versus hierarchical political structures.

The dispute divided the Congregationalist church in Norwich, Connecticut. Arnold's devout mother, Hannah, sided with the Old Lights
while the boisterous young Benedict, as he matured, gravitated to the
opposite view. The dispute centred in Connecticut and neighbouring
Massachusetts but echoed throughout the thirteen colonies. "Suddenly, Connecticut and Massachusetts had become places of conten-
tion," wrote one historian of the revolutionary years. "The revival was
a force that surged through the life of every New Englander."[3] Benedict
Arnold, raised in a divided town by a devout mother, early felt the force
of defiance and political tension.

He also witnessed an early harbinger of revolution. "The Great Awakening was one of the first truly national events in colonial history. Every
district from New England to Georgia, from the seaport towns to the
scattered cabins of the far frontiers, felt its impact," wrote Columbia
University scholar John Garraty. "In a sense, it casts light on the growing interrelationships that would eventually make America a nation.
Thirteen isolated settlements, expanding north and south as well as
westward, were becoming one."[4] By happenstance, Arnold's birth coin-
cided with the early stirring of national feeling that he would help
convert into political reality.

As a young man, Arnold also would have absorbed the politics of
the sea – the creed of self-reliance, daring and the need for team work
and discipline when employed on the water. As a businessman who
invested thousands of pounds in ships and cargo, he would have
become fiercely entrepreneurial and suspicious of anything – whether
government regulation, competitor, or privateer – that would threaten
profit margins and potential prosperity. As a smuggler working in the
underground economy, he would have been very wary of governments,
their laws, and their law-enforcers who could threaten his reputation
and his very livelihood. As one of the leading businessmen in his area
of New England, Arnold, like his trader and business colleagues, was

suspicious of authority, particularly an authority thousands of miles away that imposed rules and charges on a population that did not even have the vote.

The ham-handed British government made the situation worse. It was strapped for cash after the enormously expensive Seven Years' War, which ended with Britain's capture of Canada. That victory itself was costly because there were ongoing expenses involved in administering and protecting the North American properties. Since the economies of the American seaboard colonies were relatively prosperous, it was debated in London whether the colonists should be expected to pay some of these expenses, incurred in their name but not with their approval.

The British government that was elected in 1763 settled the question. Tory prime minister George Grenville decided that the colonies could and should pay some of their own costs, even if they did not have representatives in Parliament to plead their cause.[5] His government's first move was to pass the Sugar Act, aimed at clamping down on the molasses trade that flourished along the coast of North America. It turned many Yankee traders, including Arnold, into smugglers, since the low-grade molasses that came from the sugar cane refining industry was the basis of the rum industry. Then, in 1764, came the Stamp Act, a simple tax bill, designed to raise revenue to pay the bills of the Seven Years' War. It required colonists to buy stamps for most of their commercial transactions. More than the sugar tax, this tax stuck in the colonial craw because it was pervasive. "Any colonist who bought or sold land, became an apprentice, went to church, married, read a newspaper, drank in a tavern, gambled, took public office, shipped goods elsewhere or went to court would feel its effects."[6] It was constantly visible, collected at each transaction. It required payment in British sterling, which, as we have seen, was not always readily available in the colonies.

It was, in other words, brilliantly crafted to alienate everyone and to unite in opposition to the British government groups as disparate as the low-life tavern dwellers, the merchants of Benedict Arnold's class and the traditionally pro-British colonial élite. Eventually, the London government realized its mistake and withdrew the law, but the damage had been done. "The movement that nullified the Stamp Act and forced its repeal was the first great drama of the revolution," wrote historian Edward Countryman. It was seen as a premonition of things to come, "a danger signal indicating that a more general threat (to American liberty) existed."[7]

Across New England, there were protest rallies and riots against the imposition of British taxes. In New Haven and across Connecticut, the uproar took on religious tones as New Lights opposed Old Lights – young merchants and traders with the most to lose against the old establishment that had grown up with British rules and did not want to rock the boat.

Arnold, in debt to some British financiers and finding his ships and his commerce continually under threat from the British, was clearly sympathetic to the New Lights and the dissidents, who began to form into vigilante groups calling themselves the Sons of Liberty. After the incident of February 1766 in which one of his crew members was flogged (see previous chapter), Arnold was identified by the British as a forceful member of the resistance. His letters to the *Connecticut Gazette* painting the incident in the broader context of British oppression exposed him as a potential dissident leader.[8]

Back in coastal towns like New Haven, a boycott of British goods was organized, and unlike modern-day efforts at consumer pressure by persuasion, Arnold and his Sons of Liberty friends enforced the boycott with threats and retaliation against anyone caught buying or in possession of British merchandise.

Anti-British sentiment was further inflamed by evidence that the hierarchy of the Church of England was being strengthened at the expense of local churches, that London increasingly was sending customs agents to oppress the locals, and that local officials were misleading the king about conditions in the colonies.

Arnold was being drawn into the conflict both from commercial self-interest and from a sense of indignant outrage at high-handed British tactics. Still, he was absorbed in his business affairs, watching his family grow, trying to reconcile himself to his standoffish wife, and working hard to make money and to get out of debt. By 1770 his hard work was paying off. Early that year in Boston, the first real blood of the Revolution was spilled. It changed everything for Arnold.

Under provocation, British troops had opened fire on a rampaging mob that had formed at the instigation of the Sons of Liberty to protest British laws and the British presence. A number of citizens were killed, left to bleed in the snow of a Boston winter. When, after several months, there had been no uprising against the British, Arnold wrote to a friend: "Are Americans all asleep and tamely giving up their glorious liberties or are they all turned philosophers that they don't take vengeance on such miscreants. I am afraid the latter and that shall all soon see ourselves as poor and as much oppressed as ever heathen philosopher was."[9]

The Boston Massacre radicalized the colonial population. But it was a series of British parliamentary decrees enacted in 1774 that settled the matter. Among them was the Quebec Act.

Debated in London through the early 1770s, the legislation was the brainchild, the handiwork and achievement of one towering figure in early Canadian history – Guy Carleton. In design and concept, this "act for making more effectual provision for the government of the province of Quebec in North America" was simple and straightforward. It established the right of the Roman Catholic church to exist in Quebec, despite a general British prohibition on Catholicism within the realm. It affirmed the seigneurial system with its church tithing and protections for the power of the land owners. It did not provide for an elected assembly, though English-speaking North Americans, including those in Quebec, were clamouring for democracy. Such British legal institutions as trial by jury and habeus corpus were not to be extended to Quebec, despite the pressure from English merchants. And the boundaries of Quebec were to be extended into the Mississippi Valley, west of the thirteen colonies.[10]

Carleton's motives for this reactionary legislation were largely political, although the feudal rules affirmed by the Quebec Act also appealed to his class sensibility. He was an Ulsterman, born in County Tyrone in 1724, an army man who was befriended by the military up-and-comer James Wolfe, who brought him to Quebec City in 1759 as deputy quarter-master general during the siege of the city. Carleton was wounded, not for the last time, in the assault that took Wolfe's life. Just seven years later, after involvement in army campaigns off the coast of France and in Cuba during which he distinguished himself as a soldier, Carleton was sent back to Quebec as governor.[11]

As part of Wolfe's army, he had run a camp on Île d'Orléans, within sight of the fortress on the rock. He organized food, drink, clothes, tents, arms, and hospital facilities for the British army. According to one biographer, he "also seems to have acted as engineer, supervising the cannon that blasted Quebec."[12]

In the late 1760s, Carleton's instincts as Quebec governor were that the conquered French Canadians could not be assimilated. The best way to keep them loyal, or at least pacified, was to appease their religious leaders and most influential citizens, giving them their religion and exemption from British common law. It was also hoped that this would insulate the French from the democratic tensions that were sweeping the thirteen colonies and, to a lesser extent, Great Britain. Carleton also played up to the Quebec merchants who wanted to see the boundaries of Quebec, and therefore their natural trading area, extended south-west into the Ohio and Mississippi Valley regions.

As early as 1767, Carleton was advising London that Quebec would have to remain French and Catholic if it was to be pacified.[13] On 9 August 1770 he sailed to London to speak directly to the government, imagining a sojourn of several months. Instead, he was there for four years.

The first task was to convince the British government to take Quebec seriously if it wanted to avoid a repeat of the political agitation that was growing in New England. The second step was overseeing the legislative drafting and the parliamentary debate. He had to face down the wrath of opponents such as Edmund Burke, who balked at the idea that Quebec should remain Catholic but that there should be no elected assembly to advise and direct the governor. Carleton also had to defend the absence of the right to a jury trial and other common law institutions that the British had come to take for granted.

Carleton testified several times after the legislation was first introduced on 26 May 1774. On 16 June it was approved by a vote of fifty-six to twenty. The House of Lords passed it and on 22 June King George III gave royal assent as a mob outside the House of Lords, aroused by the rhetoric of Burke and other Whigs, shouted "no popery."[14]

Now fifty years old and with a young bride acquired in London and the two small sons she bore him while he worked the parliamentary corridors promoting the Quebec Act, Carleton returned to Quebec City on 18 September 1774, expecting the gratitude of a colony. But the response he received from the colonists was mixed. The clergy, seigneurs, and other upper-class French Canadians welcomed the Quebec Act. Since they had no official voice, the opinion of the French peasant farmers was not evident. The small English-speaking merchant class, however, was not amused. "From the beginning, they had disliked the arbitrary militaristic government of the province," wrote Carleton's biographer. "Now, they had confirmation that the province was going to continue to be administered for the benefit of French Canadians."[15] As a result, many of these merchants allied themselves with the Americans in the revolutionary war.

But first, they tried unsuccessful petitions to London to have the law withdrawn, and then a shocking bit of political theatre and defiance in an age when disrespect to the monarch was a serious crime. On 1 May 1775, the day the Quebec Act took force, a marble bust of George III in Montreal's Place des Armes was found to have been desecrated, painted black, adorned with a rosary of potatoes and a wooden cross around its neck. A makeshift Roman Catholic bishop's mitre had been placed on its head and underneath was a hand-printed sign: "*Voilà le pape du Canada, le sot Anglais*" ("Behold the pope of Canada, the English fool").

Later that day, the bust of the king was thrown down a well, later to be retrieved by loyalists. Authorities were outraged but the vandalism was never legally pinned on anyone. The bust of George III so roughly treated that day is now on display at the McCord Museum in Montreal.

If the reaction in Quebec to Carleton's political handiwork was mixed and confusing, in the thirteen colonies his accomplishment met with nothing but abuse. It touched the traditional New England fear and dislike of the French, the inherent disdain for Catholicism in colonial America and the New England resentment against anyone who suggested that they could not expand their commercial empires westward. Some leading revolutionaries saw the Quebec Act as one of the final straws, one of the key events on the road to the Declaration of Independence and the Revolution. Among these dissenters was Thomas Jefferson, who wrote, with radical simplicity, "The British Parliament has no right to exercise authority over us."[16]

Similarly, an eighteen-year-old Alexander Hamilton, who became Gen. George Washington's aide-de-camp and, later, a towering political figure in post-revolutionary America, circulated a pamphlet throughout the colonies in which he "protested the resulting denial of English civil liberties, argued that catholicism had been made the established religion of Canada and reasoned that since no Protestants would submit while Catholic immigrants would be drawn in from all over Europe, a papist state was being created to encompass Protestant America 'with innumerous hosts of neighbors disaffected to them both because of religion and government.'" The danger in this was something that "every man of common sense" should judge.[17]

In the New England of 1774 this was a tame reaction. In Massachusetts, Dr Joseph Warren wrote what were called the Suffolk County Resolves. On 17 September, the day before Carleton arrived at Quebec City, Paul Revere, a Boston silversmith and eventually one of the heads of a rebel spy ring, delivered them to the first Continental Congress meeting in Philadelphia. The Congress was a collection of sometimes elected and sometimes self-appointed businessmen, lawyers, and local leaders from all thirteen colonies who convened to discuss their relationship with England, and to consider how to deal with growing popular anger and English obstinance.

Congress endorsed Darren's resolves and had them printed and circulated in America and England. They were inflammatory, anti-French, and anti-Catholic. "The late act of Parliament for establishing the Roman catholic religion and French laws in that extensive country now called Canada is dangerous in an extreme degree to the Protestant religion and to the civil rights and liberties of all America, and therefore, as men and Protestant christians, we are indispensably obliged to take all proper measures to protect our safety."[18]

Congress approved a petition of protest to the British Parliament and in October 1774, John Jay disseminated in Great Britain a letter attacking Catholicism for spreading and promoting "impiety, bigotry, persecution, murder and rebellion through every part of the world."[19] The text of the letter was sent to Quebec and Governor Carleton had it translated into French and posted throughout Quebec in market squares, on church doors and in other public places to show local French leaders and habitants that he was defending them against such south-of-the-border bigotry.

This blunted the effect of a congressional letter, sent to Canada in late 1774, that deplored the slavery of Quebec's inhabitants and invited them to send delegates to the second Continental Congress in 1775. Another letter, this one from John Adams, was carried north that winter by the lawyer John Brown. He met in a Montreal coffee-house 9 April with local English merchants he expected to be allies. They started the evening that way, but an assertion by Thomas Walker, a Boston trader who had moved to Quebec after the British took control in the early 1760s, that there would be no exception to the congressional prohibition against trading with Britain cooled their passion. Most of these businessmen depended for their livelihood on British trade and access to the new lands offered them through the Quebec Act. Suddenly, ideology and their self-interest began to conflict. In the end, the local businessmen decided not to send delegates to Congress. Instead, they created a correspondence committee to keep in touch. It was an early example of a Canadian non-committal, compromise solution.[20]

To the south in the thirteen colonies, meanwhile, the Quebec Act was seen as one of the so-called Intolerable Acts that led to revolution.

One other idea in the colonial revolutionary stew has resonance even today in the violent streets and murderous neighbourhoods of the United States – the political conviction that everyone has the right, the obligation almost, to own a gun.

The issue was inflamed by Britain's insistence that soldiers be a regular feature in the rebellious communities of the colonies and that colonials be forced to billet troops. This was grist for the mill of those who argued against the presence of a permanent standing army. In colonial

America, this translated into a call for the presence of a citizens' army that would be able to resist the presence of armed state enforcers.

The ideologues cited John Locke, the British philosopher who influenced the 1688 English Revolution with his claim that individuals have the right to protect themselves, "a right to defend themselves and recover by force what by unlawful force is taken from them."[21] He argued that "self-defence is a part of the law of nature, nor can it be denied the community, even against the king himself." In 1776, as the American Revolution swelled, Scottish liberal and free market theorist Adam Smith wrote: "Men of republican principles have been jealous of a standing army as dangerous to liberty."[22]

The Boston Massacre of 1770 had raised the stakes and led John Adams and his cousin Sam to dispute the power of the British army. By 1774 George Washington was helping to organize the Fairfax County Militia Association to defend the county against the standing British army.[23] As the British monarch wondered why the colonials were not being disarmed, Americans were arming themselves and justifying doing so on the self-righteous grounds of the need for self-protection.

One decisive moment came when a young Virginian lawyer, Patrick Henry, spoke to Virginia's assembly in favour of an armed citizenry. "They tell us ... that we are weak, unable to cope with so formidable an adversary, but when shall we be stronger? ... Will it be when we are totally disarmed, and when a British guard shall be stationed in every house? ... Three million people armed in the holy cause of liberty ... are invincible by any force which our enemy can send against us."[24]

This kind of rhetoric led to the American Second Amendment – "A well-regulated militia being necessary to the security of a free state, the right of the people to keep and bear arms shall not be infringed" – which because law on 15 December 1791, and the tenacious belief that guns are the oxygen of American freedom. There was a growing American ideology of defiance, grievance, and anger.

The story of the intellectual birth of the American Revolution is a tale of strange mixtures – a declaration of the rights of man made by slave owners; a call for political equality made by a group of men prepared to extend political power only to a small male land-owning élite like themselves; a declaration of freedom of expression made by a group of Protestant zealots hostile to anything that promoted Roman Catholicism or French. In the mix was a feeling of Divine Providence, that those in the thirteen colonies were the Chosen People, a phenomenon that was seen again a century later when the Boers, as they believed, made a "covenant" with God to be His Chosen People in southern Africa. Thus, in the 1760s, John Adams, the Boston lawyer who became the second president of the republic, wrote: "America was designed by Providence for the theatre on which man was to make his true figure, on which science, virtue, liberty, happiness and glory were to exist in peace."[25] Almost fifty years later, in 1815, the old man looked back on the events that had created a new nation and decided that the war against Britain was merely the consequence of the real revolution, which occurred, as he wrote to Thomas Jefferson, "in the minds of the people and this was effected from 1760 to 1775 in the course of 15 years before a drop of blood was shed at Lexington."[26]

At a time when politics was commonly viewed as an exercise in élite control, Adams developed a vision of it as "the science of human happiness." By late January 1776, Adams had articulated a view of politics and the growing revolution that sustained him through eight years as George Washington's vice-president and four years as the second president. It was strangely undemocratic, reflecting a belief in the future of America and "the system" with little regard for the individual caught up in it. "Individuals are but atoms," he wrote to his wife, Abigail. "It is scarcely worthwhile to consider what the consequences will be to us. What will be the effects upon present and future millions, millions of millions, is a question very interesting to benevolence, natural and Christian. God grant they may, and I firmly believe they will, be happy."[27]

In a class by himself among the revolutionary intellectuals was Benjamin Franklin, the Philadelphia renaissance man whose support for the Revolution gave it credibility at home and abroad.[28] When independence was declared in 1776, Franklin was seventy years old. He was internationally recognized for his scientific accomplishments and political thinking. He had been a newspaper owner and journalist, a man born into relative poverty who became wealthy, a widely read colonial whose curiosity and creative mind led him to the experiments that created the Franklin stove, bifocal eyeglasses, and theories on electricity. He helped found hospitals and libraries, charities and political debating societies. In the 1750s, he began to dabble in politics, undertaking a trip to London in 1757 on behalf of the Pennsylvania assembly to argue a financial case for the government of the colony.

The trip turned out to be Franklin's most important contribution to Canadian history. He helped persuade the British government, at the end of the French and Indian War, to keep Canada as a possession, rather than the French sugar islands.[29]

Franklin's most important contribution to history, though, was his decision as an old man to join the revolutionary cause. The irony is that during the decade before the Revolution started, Franklin spent most of his time in London, lobbying British politicians to repeal some of the legislation that was irritating the colonies. He was not on the ground in America as the revolutionary cauldron reached a boil. Still, as he sailed back to the colonies from London in April 1775, he wrote that England had become an "old rotten state."[30] With a reputation throughout the colonies and with experience abroad as a diplomatic colonial representative, he was ready to be the Grand Old Man of the Revolution.

Clearly, then, beneath the increasing sense of defiance, grievance, and anger among American colonials was a headier ideal of freedom from oppression that was strongly influenced by European thinkers such as Jean-Jacques Rousseau. "Man is born free," he wrote at the outset of his *Social Contract* (1762). "And everywhere he is in chains. One thinks himself the master of others and still remains a greater slave than they."[31]

In 1776, the year of the American Declaration of Independence, Great Britain was mesmerized by the first volume, just published, of Edward Gibbon's monumental work *Decline and Fall of the Roman Empire*. For many readers, it seemed to be a warning to the powers that be that the demise of the British Empire could come through overindulgence and insensitivity.

Gibbon, an overweight, heavy-drinking man-about-town in London, was also a member of Parliament, a position purchased for him in 1774 by a wealthy cousin. It was a time when money could buy a seat in Parliament and when the rich or otherwise favoured were able to become MPs without the messy necessity of convincing voters of their merit. There were voterless "rotten boroughs," seats that had long ceased to exist in reality but were kept on paper for the "deserving" who did not want to subject themselves to the humiliation and uncertainty of democratic politics.

Gibbon's reaction to the events in America was typical of a class of British Whigs (liberals) who were the intellectual backbone of the American Revolution. In early 1775, when revolution was stirring, he was "convinced that we have both the right and the power on our side" in the colonial conflict. By late 1777 Gibbon the MP was lamenting: "What a wretched piece of work do we seem to be making of it in America."[32]

It was a sign of the times. American intellectuals and revolutionaries were heavily influenced by the radical British Whig tradition, by British writers such as John Milton and other seventeenth-century intellectuals who objected to the growing power of Parliament and its control by the English upper class. These British radicals used pamphlets, speeches, and any medium available to argue against the power of élites, the Church, and the idea of a standing army paid for by the State. They railed against the power of Prime Minister Robert Walpole and his "robinocracy," against the corruption of Parliament, against the power of the king. In England much of this debate took place on the fringes of the Body Politic. In the thirteen colonies, it was mainstream. "More than any other single group of writers, they shaped the mind of the American revolutionary generation," wrote a chronicler of the ideological forces at play in the Revolution. "Opposition thought in the form it acquired at the turn of the seventeenth century and in the early eighteenth century was devoured by the colonists."[33]

Many of the leading colonial revolutionaries – John Adams, George Washington, and Thomas Jefferson among them – looked to England and her radicals for their inspiration. "The colonists' attitude to the whole world of politics and government was fundamentally shaped by the root assumption that they, as Britishers, shared in the unique inheritance of liberty."[34] Their growing revolutionary fervour was based on a belief that their English rights were being violated by the English overlords, a growing feeling that their concept of the privileges and benefits of English liberty was being betrayed by the English themselves.

Enter Thomas Paine, a hero of the Revolution but not always the heroic figure portrayed by the revolutionary myth makers.

Tom Paine was, wrote John Keane in his 1995 biography, "the most prominent political thinker and writer during the revolutionary struggle against the British."[35] He also called him "the greatest political figure of his generation" – an amazing and exaggerated claim because he belonged to a generation that included George Washington, James Madison, and Thomas Jefferson in the colonies, Edmund Burke and Adam Smith in Great Britain, the creators of the French Revolution, and a host of other luminaries. Others have portrayed him as a brilliant propagandist whose personal financial and emotional life was largely a failure, a man who expected society to conform to perfect rules of democracy that he did not always embrace in his personal life.

Paine was in his mid-thirties when he came to America in 1774, a failed and bankrupt English businessman, leaving behind two failed marriages, several young children, and a mountain of unpaid debt.[36] He has been unkindly described as a degenerate "pock-marked English immigrant with a bulbous nose, a fondness for the bottle and a hot, restless eye who had abandoned a wife and several small children to cast his lot with the cause of liberty in America."[37]

When he arrived in America with a letter of introduction from colonial icon Benjamin Franklin, whom he had met in London, Paine had shown little interest in politics or the theories he would soon popularize. He was vain, unemotional, and arrogant, a man who actually came to believe that if he returned to England after the American Revolution, his writings alone would be enough to inspire a revolution that would overthrow the king. He was single-minded in believing that his revolutionary ideas were the Truth. At one time, he wrote that the American Loyalists who refused to join the Revolution were traitors who "must forfeit their heads."[38] This uncompromising view of the correctness of his views served him well as he inspired the intellectuals and the mobs of both the American and French revolutions to overthrow their establishment figures. They served him less well when the mobs turned against him and his populist theology, infused as it was by a conservative view of the need for order. He was, at times, despised in post-Revolution America and jailed in revolutionary France, narrowly escaping the guillotine. He spent his final years in lonely poverty in New York City, suffering from palsy, drinking heavily, and raging against those who used their position in the new nation to undermine the egalitarian, republican principles he had espoused. He died on 8 June 1809.

Despite his flaws, Paine stands as one of the pivotal figures in American revolutionary lore. For Paine turned out to be a brilliant propagandist, capable of stating popular beliefs in a way that made them sound revolutionary and commonsensical. He wrote eloquently about the need for a citizen militia to oppose the British army. More decisive was his January 1776 pamphlet *Common Sense,* which captured the mood of the moment and moved it further. Until then, the intellectual base of the American insurrection had been to search for a better deal from Britain, a recognition of American rights. But Paine called for independence, rather than reconciliation, and he did so in clear, inflammatory language that could be understood by all. "The success of Paine's *Common Sense* was not then due to any originality of his ideas but to the fact that Paine, by a happy inspiration, spoke out strongly and uncompromisingly for independence at precisely the moment when American public opinion was ripe for the suggestion."[39]

Common Sense was followed in April 1776 by the essay "To the People," which called for decisive action. "It is not a time to trifle," he wrote. "Reconciliation will not go down, even if it were offered." America would only be happy with self-government. The country "hath a blank sheet to write upon, Put it not off too long."[40]

He also urged freedom for black slaves. American revolutionaries, awash in the desire for equality and liberty, heeded his call to arms against the British but not his call to consider their own position as oppressive slave owners. That would take another revolution, fought by their grandchildren and great-grandchildren.

Benedict Arnold had already cast his lot with the Revolution. While Paine, Adams, and Jefferson were filling the Philadelphia and Boston nights with earnest rhetoric about the rights of man and the evils of the British army, Arnold was on the front lines fighting for those ideas.

3

Arnold the Revolutionary

By the time the first Continental Congress was convened in Philadelphia in 1774, the thirty-three-year-old Arnold had become a prosperous trader, merchant, and businessman with a fine New Haven home, three young sons, and a passionless, if functional, marriage. He had position, wealth and respectability. He was well on his way to redeeming the family name, which had been tarnished by his alcoholic father.

What led Arnold to risk all this for the uncertainty, turmoil, and danger of war? As a trader, of course, he had little choice but to take a side, in the event of war, and both sides had their risks. As one of his biographers put it, Arnold's decision to become a revolutionary was typical of his time and of the young men of commerce attracted to the cause. "An arbitrary self-interest was the basis of their careers. Courage and the restless demand for action and power led them on."[1]

Arnold already identified with the agitators. As early as 1764 when Britain imposed the Sugar and Stamp acts, Arnold became active in the opposition underground. He was heavily in debt to various London lenders. In New Haven, there were rallies to oppose the prospect of new taxes and Arnold attended. Soon, he either joined or helped organize (depending on the historical account) the Connecticut branch of the thuggish Sons of Liberty, who took the law into their own hands to destroy stamped paper and to intimidate stamp commissioners into resigning. On 10 September 1765, riots against the Stamp Act spread to New Haven and "there is little question that Benedict Arnold was at least somewhere on the edge of the crowd."[2]

By February 1766, as noted earlier, he had come out of the dissident closet by condoning the public flogging of the crewman who tried to tell the British about Arnold's smuggling. Then he wrote public articles justifying the violence as a protest against British attacks on citizens' liberties and rights. "At 25," wrote one biographer, "Benedict Arnold emerged from the Stamp Act crisis a vocal and popular hero in New Haven and a conspicuous political figure."[3]

Through the first half of the 1770s, revolutionary politics in New Haven became increasingly violent and defiant. On 10 August 1774, John Adams, the Boston lawyer who became the second president of the republic, passed through New Haven on his way to Philadelphia for the first informal Continental Congress. Adams had joined the Sons of Liberty in Boston, and his home was a gathering place for anti-British fighters and refugees. He was one of the revolutionary stars, and as his entourage wended its way, it attracted attention and support, nowhere more than in Connecticut. "Seven miles outside New Haven, carriages and horsemen were waiting, the sheriff of the county, the constable of the town, the justices of the peace among them," reported a chronicler of the journey. "As the party approached the city, all the bells were set to ringing and the doors and windows were crowded with people watching the procession as if it were a coronation. At nine o'clock, some dozen cannon were fired on the Common and such a stream of visitors came to pay their respects that Adams could not keep track of their names."[4]

Arnold was clearly interested in the impending Congress. In one of his few purely political gestures, he left home late in August to travel to Philadelphia with the Connecticut delegation. He used his time in Carpenter's Hall, where the delegates met, and in Biddle's Tavern, where he stayed, intriguing with other Sons of Liberty radicals about appropriate ways to show physical defiance.[5]

The first Continental Congress pledged allegiance to the Crown but called for an end to British trade sanctions against the colonies. A boycott of British goods was threatened. Arnold apparently sensed that political resolve would have to be backed up with military preparedness. He returned to New Haven from Philadelphia and joined sixty-four others in learning military drills and manoeuvres from an army veteran. A military company of volunteers was formed, the Governor's Second Company of Foot Guards, for which each man bought his own uniform. Arnold was elected captain.[6]

In early April 1775, the militia had its first taste of war. News of an outbreak of violence in the Boston area reached New Haven, whose conservative local establishment decided to remain neutral. Arnold, as militia captain, felt otherwise and proposed that his unit march north to reinforce the Massachusetts militia. Most of the men were persuaded by Arnold but the local military establishment, led by war veteran and local Masonic Lodge founder David Wooster, disagreed: these were still the days of British rule, and the idea of armed insurrection was not yet widespread. He withheld the keys to the local armoury and on Sunday, 22 April, Arnold and his men confronted Wooster, got the keys, armed themselves, and headed north. Wooster would confound Arnold again a year later during the Quebec campaign, on the same military team but barely speaking.[7]

Arnold's men reached Cambridge, a model of military prepared-ness. The colonial forces under siege at Boston suffered from a woeful lack of arms, particularly cannon. Arnold, who had travelled the Upper New York area as a trader, knew that the British had let Fort Ticonderoga on Lake Champlain fall into disrepair. If it were captured, its guns could be used to help lift the siege of Boston.

Arnold persuaded Massachusetts revolutionary leaders Dr Joseph Warren and beer maker Samuel Adams that the scheme was viable. They liked the idea and took it to the colonial assembly, which approved the campaign on 3 May. Arnold was given some funds and a colonel's commission. It was his first military appointment.[8]

May 10, 1775: Mr Allen, finding he had a strong party and being impatient of control and taking umbrage at my forbidding the people to plunder, he assumed the intire command and I was not consulted or advised with for four days, which time I spent in the garrison as a private person, often insulted by him and his officers, often threatened with my life and twice shot at by his men.[9]

Benedict Arnold's diary entries from the summer campaign of 1775 against the British fort at Ticonderoga show many sides of him. He was a soldier who expected discipline among soldiers. He was a commander who expected the obedience of his underlings. He was prepared to take risks to make gains. He was a decisive, impulsive commander whose preference, in a crisis, was to take direct military action rather than go the political route. He was a strong-headed, egotistical man who easily made enemies among those who should have been friends. His rela-tionship with Ethan Allen, as we shall see, is a case in point.

The facts of the Ticonderoga campaign are relatively simple and unchallenged. The fort had been built at a strategic site on the south-ern tip of Lake Champlain by the French in 1755. It was midway in a fortified line between Quebec City and New York. It was well designed and proved itself functional in 1758 when a small French garrison staved off an attack by a much larger British army. Commemorative plaques to that epic battle dot the treed countryside around the National Historic Park.

But the French lost the overall battle for North America on the Plains of Abraham in 1759 and as the army retreated, it blew up the fort. The victorious British rebuilt it but put no further resources into the fortifications. By 1775 the foundations were cracking and just forty British soldiers maintained it.[10]

Arnold and a small group that volunteered to go with him travelled north from Cambridge to the Massachusetts-Vermont border, a slow 110 miles over bad roads. It was at the border, in early May, that he first learned about Ethan Allen, who held a conflicting commission from Connecticut and had his own plan to capture Ticonderoga. Arnold rode through the night and found Allen and his self-styled Green Mountain Boys at a tavern in Bennington, Vermont, which they were using as a headquarters.

What followed was a test of wills between Arnold and Allen, with their colliding commissions and styles. Allen had the advantage. He had the troops and they refused to serve under anyone but him. Arnold and Allen agreed reluctantly to cooperate in leading the attack on Ticonderoga. At dawn on 10 May with fewer than a hundred soldiers, they captured the unsuspecting fort and roused its sleeping commander.[11] The first revolutionary battle had been won, but it was more important for its symbolism than for its strategic worth.

For Arnold, the trouble began that dawn. He and Allen had a frosty relationship, a circumstance that some hostile biographers blame entirely on Arnold's arrogance. Thus: "Another man might have bowed to superior organization and experience and offered his services in the spirit of co-operation but Arnold's spirit did not encompass co-operation," wrote Clare Brandt, describing the pre-attack tussle over who would be in charge.[12]

Once inside the fort that misty May morning at the dawn of America, Allen's men proved to be undisciplined and rowdy. They wanted to enjoy the first spoils of war and began looting and drinking from the fort's liquor stores. When Arnold ordered them to act like soldiers, Allen stripped him, at gunpoint, of his joint command. Arnold wrote in his regimental log about the threats made against his life. Meanwhile, since one of the main purposes of the campaign had been to capture guns for use in the relief of Boston, Arnold used his time to inspect and to take an inventory of guns in the fort.

Even Brandt gives Arnold credit for his Ticonderoga performance. "Arnold was justifiably furious at the feckless behavior of Allen and his men. Although vastly less experienced than they, he sensed instinctively the shape and urgency of the strategic situation and was enormously frustrated at his inability to act on his insight."[13]

By most measures, Arnold's first foray into revolutionary fighting had been a success. However, thanks to the unflattering accounts of his actions at the fort that were reported to his political superiors by his military rivals, the easy victory at Ticonderoga turned out to be Arnold's baptism by fire into the vicious politics of revolutionary forces. On the word of Allen and his allies, the politicians decided to question and dispute the campaign expense accounts Arnold submitted.

Clearly, he underestimated the political wiles of the northern frontier revolutionary Ethan Allen and his allies. For the relatively sophisticated and educated Yankee businessman, that was probably not hard to do. Allen was a study in contradictions.

Ethan Allen and his Green Mountain Boys are usually portrayed as American originals, rough-hewn hillbillies who, at a crucial time in the early days of the uprising, came to the aid of their country with a decisive intervention against the British. It is one of the quirks of history, and a symptom of the historical American hatred of Arnold, that Allen has won so much of the glory for the capture of Ticonderoga.

In reality, Allen was hardly a hero. He was a rural bully, an outlaw who liked to throw his weight around, particularly when he was backed up by the fists, knives, guns, and boots of his ruffian hillbilly buddies. But he was no coward; in fact he was courageous to the point of recklessness. He was a glory seeker with enough force of personality and charisma to entice others to sign on to his dreams. In many ways, however, he was an incompetent soldier who brought as much trouble to the revolutionary cause as glory. He spent many of the crucial years of the Revolution in a British jail after a botched invasion of Canada. It is a delicious irony that the man who is embedded in the American historical psyche as a heroic counterpoint to the traitor Arnold later tried to turn his back on his new country by striking a deal with the British to deliver what is now the state of Vermont to the Redcoats. Despite his best efforts, he was less successful as a traitor to America than Arnold was.

Allen was born on 10 January 1738 at Litchfield, Connecticut, the son of a well-established family of colonial farmers who had moved from place to place over the previous century, searching for wilderness land to settle. Allen wrote a self-aggrandizing autobiography in which he describes his early life on the Connecticut frontier as a time when he worked hard to learn the finer points of reading and grammar: "In my youth, I was much disposed to contemplation and at my commencement in manhood, I committed to manuscript such sentiments or arguments as appeared most consonant to reason."[14]

He became a Connecticut businessman and married a stern illiterate woman six years his senior. Eventually, he moved north to the New Hampshire grants, land opened for settlement by the 1763 Treaty of Paris, which made a British colony of most of North America.

The New Hampshire lands became a battleground between two colonies. The governor of New Hampshire began assigning land to new owners but in 1764 the king accepted a claim by the governor of New York that it was New York land. Settlers with a deed from New York began to appear in the territory to claim land already occupied by settlers with deeds from New Hampshire.

In the turmoil, a vigilante group was formed, the Green Mountain Boys, led by Ethan Allen. Their aim was to defend New Hampshire owners against New York usurpers. Biographer John Pell argued that Allen became colonel commandant of the Green Mountain Boys much as he had run his private businesses – with his mouth: "In every case, he talked the others into letting him run the show. There was something about his enthusiasm, volubility, self-confidence or smile which fascinated these people."[15]

Through the late 1760s and early 1770s, the Green Mountain Boys became the *de facto* law in the wild hills of the verdant territory east of Lake Champlain, modern-day Vermont. They threatened New York surveyors and settlers, beat them, and sometimes subjected them to what they called "chastisement with the twigs of the wilderness" – being stripped, tied to a post, and whipped with branches. To other Green Mountain settlers, Allen and his ruffians were heroes. To New Yorkers, they were outlaws who soon had a price on their heads.

By 1775 Allen had become well known for his direct and unsophisticated writings in defence of the rights of the New Hampshire grants settlers. He was taking on the appearance of a leader. Still, an incident in January 1775 illustrated his continued preference for terror over the quill as a way to spread his message of colonial rights. Benjamin Hough, a Church minister who had complained to New York authorities about the activities of the Green Mountain Boys and then accepted a New York commission as a justice of the peace in New Hampshire, was arrested and put on trial for what the Green Mountain Boys considered collaboration with those who would steal land from the settlers. Allen was called upon to be one of the judges. On hearing Hough's confession of his "crime," Allen had him tied to a tree, stripped, lashed two hundred times, and then released to walk the 250 miles to New York.[16] Even by the standards of those days, it was rough justice.

In early 1775 as Allen was travelling the countryside to sell a book outlining the Green Mountain side of the argument, he made a connection that would catapult him into revolutionary fame. He met the Massachusetts lawyer John Brown, who worked for the Boston Committee of Correspondence. Brown wanted to get to Canada to find out how the Canadians viewed the revolutionary stirrings in the thirteen colonies. Brown also thought Fort Ticonderoga should be captured in the name of the Revolution. Allen gave Brown an escort of Green Mountain Boy, through the mountains into Canada. In return, Brown recommended to the Massachusetts politicians that Allen be commissioned to capture Ticonderoga. "The people on New Hampshire Grants have ingaged (*sic*) to do this business and in my opinion, they are the most proper persons for this jobb, (*sic*)" he wrote.[17]

Allen accepted the challenge and later wrapped the decision in the shroud of revolutionary foresight and historical knowledge: "Ever since I arrived at the state of manhood and acquainted myself with the general history of mankind, I have felt a sincere passion for liberty,"[18] he wrote later.

There followed the head-butting with Arnold over command, the capture of the fort, and Arnold's shunning. Allen supporters crowed that he had been "shunned, derided and even shot at by the Americans. He probably spent the time hobnobbing with the British officers while Ethan ruled the garrison after his own ideas of military conduct."[19]

Barnabas Deane, a soldier at the fort and a brother of Congressman Silas Deane, a friend of Arnold's, had a different view of the scene. From Ticonderoga, he wrote his Connecticut politician brother:

Col Arnold has been greatly abused and misrepresented by designing persons, some of whom were from Connecticut. Had it not been for him, everything here would have been in the utmost confusion and disorder. People would have been plundered of their private property and no man's person would have been safe that was not of the Green Mountain party. Col Arnold has been twice fired at by them and has had a musket presented at his breast by one of that party who threatened to fire him through if he refused to comply with their orders, which he very resolutely refused doing as inconsistent with his duty and directly contrary to the opinion of the colonies."[20]

By 15 May Arnold had found a small schooner fitted with guns and he convinced a crew to go north with him to the end of Lake Champlain where Fort St John, as the Americans called it, lay on the Richelieu River (it came to be called St Jean-sur-Richelieu, St Jean to the habitants). He crossed the watery boundary into Canada on 17 May. Two days later he attacked Fort St John, captured a British sloop, and destroyed other boats that could be used in a counter-attack down Lake Champlain. Then, realizing he did not have the troops or resources to hold the fort, and recognizing that success had been possible only because of the element of surprise, he quickly decided that there was no percentage in an occupation. He withdrew and headed south down Lake Champlain.

It was a brilliant and blood-free foray into foreign territory, an early sign of Arnold's bold, decisive style and clear strategic thinking. It also was an historic moment for the fledgling American nation. The attack on Fort St John was "the first American invasion of a foreign country and an act which committed the Continental Congress to extend the revolution to Canada, an enormously ambitious step."[21]

As Arnold sailed north, Allen was incensed; he wanted to be the first to gain military glory in Canada. He ordered his men to row north up Lake Champlain, in the hope of beating Arnold to the fort. Arnold's forces won the race handily. When he met the triumphant Arnold's southbound ships, Allen was all the more determined to outdo his rival by capturing and holding St John. It was a foolhardy plan, as Arnold no doubt told him. His military diary notes the meeting between his own ship sailing south, buoyed by victory, and Allen's bateau rowing north, fuelled by envy: "At noon, met Col Allen and his party of 100 mad fellows going to take possession of St Johns and not being able to dissuade him from so rash a purpose, supplied him with provisions."[22] Allen's forces were defeated by a now-alert British force at the fort and had to retreat. On Sunday, 21 May, Arnold recorded: "Received advice of Col Allen's defeat at St. Johns and return with loss of three men, which did not in the least surprise me as it happened as I expected. Returned to the fort and made preparations to proceed to Crown Point."[23]

The Americans, reunited, moved on to the fort at Crown Point, south of Ticonderoga, and captured it. At that point, Allen and his allies, including Maj. Samuel Elmore, demanded that Allen be given command, since the Green Mountain Boys would not serve under Arnold. The proud New Haven merchant, with his first military command and two victories under his belt, refused and Allen backed down.

Still, Arnold did not trust him. In his dealings with the insolent Colonel Easton, an Allen ally, Arnold showed his growing disdain and lack of tolerance for the challengers. On 11 June he wrote in his diary:

Went on shore early and gave orders to have the guards doubled to prevent any mutiny or disorder. Col Allen, Major Elmore, Easton and others attempted passing the sloop without showing their pass and were brought to by Capt. (illegible) and came on shore when in private discourse with Elmore, Easton intruded and insulted me, when I took the liberty of breaking his head and on his refusal to draw like a gentleman, he having a hanger by his side and cases of loaded pistols in his pocket, I kicked him very heartily and ordered him from the point.[24]

On the political battlefield, Arnold would pay dearly for his cocky behaviour. Allen and his allies John Brown, who was married to a cousin of Arnold's, and James Easton, a tavern owner, sent reports back to politicians in Boston and Philadelphia indicating that Allen had been the main reason for the victories and complaining about Arnold. Meanwhile, Arnold had spent more than one thousand pounds sterling of his own money on the troops under his command, as well as on his personal expenses. He billed the Massachusetts assembly, only to have many of his expenses challenged while a committee of politicians travelled to Ticonderoga to investigate. Arnold resigned his commission in disgust and disbanded his regiment on 23 June 1775 when the committee from the Massachusetts arrived. Many of the soldiers, lacking alternatives, enlisted in a regiment raised by Easton, who was responsible for some of the influential anti-Arnold reports sent back to the congress.[25]

On 24 June Arnold made a final entry in his regimental log book. The men who had followed him into battle and whom he had fed and clothed with his own money had turned on him in frustration:

Applied to the committee from Mass. Bay for cash to pay the regiment, which they refused. I am reduced to great extremity, not being able to pay the people who are in great need of necessary and much in debt. This gives me much trouble to pacify them and prevent disturbances. At noon, went on board to dine. When at dinner, I was confined in the Great Cabin by the people who man and sent a boat after the committee from the congress who had left this place for Ticonderoga about three hours before. I complained much of the insult offered me and received for answer that they bore me no personal ill but were determined to stop the committee and oblige them to pay of the regiment or at least such part as would inable them to go home to their families with honor.[26]

It must have been heart-breaking and infuriating for Arnold to see his soldiers go hungry because of political bickering. Soon he was released when pork and flour were brought to Crown Point from Ticonderoga. He left the fort and the army to return to Boston, where he managed eventually to clear his name against charges that he was fiddling with the expense accounts.

On his way home to New Haven he received the sad news that his wife had died. Arnold arrived home a widower with three small children. His sister Hannah became their surrogate mother and the operator of his business.

Arnold was alone. His shipping business was being ruined by the British blockade and by his absences. His political enemies had debased the value of his recent military heroics on Lake Champlain. The malaria he had picked up in the West Indies recurred. Yet he also had the military and revolutionary bug. He had tasted victory. He had felt the glory without any of the real hardship of war. He had heard reports of the Battle of Bunker Hill in Boston, which many consider the real beginning of the Revolution. On 24 June Arnold noted in his military log book, "Had a rumor of an engagement at Cambridge between the regulars and the provincials, in which it is said there is many thousands killed on both sides."[27] Exaggerated as the report had been, it clearly made an impression on the thirty-four-year-old military man. Benedict Arnold was itching to go to war.

4

Preparing to Invade Canada

Arnold left no written record of why he chose, in mid-life, to abandon his young, motherless family to go to war. His critics have attributed it to Arnold's insatiable need for glory and fame. But given his personality and experience, the logical conclusion to draw is that his undoubtedly painful decision was based on a complex stew of calculations, emotions and inclinations.

As long as the war was underway and the British blockade was in effect, his business was going nowhere. The soldier in him could not imagine sitting at home as a businessman while his country was at war. And he had long believed that one way to end the war quickly was to invade and capture Canada, cutting the British off from their northern supplies and potential invasion route and expanding the political authority and trading area of the new United States. It was to pursue this Canadian option that Arnold rode to Cambridge in late August to meet General Washington, recently appointed commander-in-chief of the rebel forces, along with his military and political advisors.

It is likely that the Philadelphia congress of 1774 marked the first meeting between Arnold and George Washington, an aristocratic Virginian plantation and slave owner who, like Arnold, had been heavily indebted to London merchants at one point in his career. Washington had won some renown as a British soldier in the earlier Indian War and he was a local leader, but he had yet to acquire the larger-than-life image that was his after the Revolution. He was an imposing, handsome, towering man who, despite some historical speculation that he might have been impotent, lived in a comfortable marriage with a rich widow, Martha Custis, and her two children – though he coveted his neighbour's wife: Washington's letters reveal his emotional passion and unfulfilled longing for Sally Fairfax, the wife of a powerful Tory who lived nearby.[1]

He was a reluctant revolutionary, a farmer who made his own wine, a gardener who developed new plant varieties, and a talented tinkerer who invented a plough. From his home in Mount Vernon, Virginia, Washington chaffed under the burden of British commercial laws but did not engage in literary or rhetorical rabble-rousing. Like Arnold, Washington was not an intellectual consumed by ideas. He was a soldier, businessman, and practical citizen.

The close and productive relationship that developed between Arnold and Washington early in the revolutionary war can be explained in part by the similarities between them. They "had much in common. Classically educated, both men had made a thorough study of modern European warfare. They had observed the British army at close range and understood its weaknesses in fighting a war thousands of transatlantic miles from supply bases." They were both aristocratic in attitude. "Most of all, they were daring soldiers by inclination and they sensed and admired this trait in others."[2] In Cambridge, the two men spent several days conferring. They got along well. Each respected the other for their past military exploits and their strategic analysis. Washington appreciated Arnold's planning and proposals. He trusted Arnold's military and leadership instincts. He recognized that Arnold had already led the first successful American military foray into Canada and had displayed the essential military wisdom of knowing when to attack and when to retreat. His battlefield judgments were based on calculation and strategy, rather than enthusiasm, optimism, and hopeful assumption. Like Washington, Arnold was a soldier.

As important, though, was the fact that Arnold's proposal for an invasion through the wilderness of Maine dovetailed perfectly with Washington's evolving plans for the capture of Canada.

The revolutionary commanders who had been in or near Canada during the summer of 1775 were optimistic about an invasion of Canada. After the capture of Ticonderoga and Crown Point, Ethan Allen had written to Congress to suggest such a move: "It is my humble opinion that the more vigorous the colonies push the war against the King's troops in Canada, the more friends we shall find in that country ... should the colonies forthwith send an army of two or three thousand men and attack Montreal, we should have little to fear from the Canadians or the Indians and would easily make a conquest of that place ..."[3]

Benedict Arnold also argued that a few thousand men could capture Canada for the Revolution. Arnold sent Congress a bold proposal, detailed below, suggesting that he lead a force to capture St John (now St Jean-sur-Richelieu), leaving soldiers behind to hold Lake Champlain. Friends inside Montreal would open the gates of the city. A force of two thousand well-armed and disciplined American troops could take Canada, he said, as long as his force included "no Green Mountain Boys."[4]

Part of their optimism was the result of intelligence the Americans were receiving from the network of Yankee traders who had moved to Quebec and were convinced that the colony was ready to join North America in revolt against British laws and restrictions. Although they had declined to send delegates to Congress in early 1775 for fear they would lose access to British markets, these American informants remained confident that given a choice, most Canadians would join the Revolution.

Among the group was Quebec City trader John McCord, a leader in the demands for a democratically elected Quebec assembly who left the fort in late 1775 with twenty-eight other merchants rather than join the British defence force. McCord's fellow American sympathizers included James Livingstone, a Montreal merchant who met visiting American propagandists and supplied them with information; William Holton, a Quebec City hat maker who came under suspicion and was jailed for supplying arms and information to the invaders; Jason Livingston, a former New York lawyer who became a wheat merchant in Sorel and an early collaborator in the American cause; and John Halstead, a New Jersey native and longtime Yankee trader in Montreal who thought he saw the writing on the wall in 1775 and became one of the first locals to join the invading American forces. He was appointed commissary to the American army, in charge of the books. His records now lie in the National Archives of Canada. For the cause, he gave up most of the property he had accumulated in Canada and retreated with the Americans when the invasion ended.[5]

The most important local "friend of the Americans" was the trader Thomas Walker. He was a contact for Ethan Allen and a contact and spy for Arnold. He had never been a fan of the British army and a decade before his cousins in the thirteen colonies were taking their punishment, Walker was standing up to the colonial authorities in Montreal. In 1764 he refused an order to billet British soldiers. "In consequence of their resentment, he suffered a cruel and unparalleled attack on his person in his own house, the 6th of December, 1764, by a party of soldiers led by their officers who, after giving him more than 50 wounds and contusions, many of them of a very dangerous nature, and cutting off part of his right ear, left him for dead," he said in a statement filed years later with the Continental Congress.[6]

Walker complained to the government in London about the attack. The mayor of Montreal was charged with assault and acquitted. Walker was then counter-sued by the Montreal authorities and the case dragged on as a form of official harassment. Still, Walker stood by his beliefs. In 1767 he was agitating for an elected assembly, despite the opposition of the authorities who feared it would be a way for the English-speaking merchant minority to dominate the French-speaking majority.[7] When the American colonists began to make noises and to send pleas to the Canadians, Walker made sure they were distributed. He was under British surveillance and the Americans assumed that his mail was being read. They used that assumption to send some destabilizing misinformation, allegedly for Walker but really intended for British eyes.

In May 1775 Arnold wrote to Walker from Crown Point, asking about the state of British defences and warning that any Canadian mobilization in defence of the British would bring retaliation from rebellious American colonials. This normally careful and precise soldier greatly exaggerated the number of American soldiers at the ready. It was probably a deliberate lie, rather than the result of self-delusion. In fact, it was intercepted by Quebec British governor Guy Carleton and taken as an early sign of American strength by nervous British defenders.

"I wrote you a line the other day from St John's but omitted being particular as expected it would fall into the hands of the enemy," Arnold wrote on 24 May.

I have now to beg the favor of you to advise me, from time to time, of the number of troops with you, their movements and designs if possible and if joined by any Canadians or Indians ... If any number of the former, you can assure them they will soon see an army of men in the heart of their country. I have here in Ticonderoga about 1,000 men and expect to be joined in a few days by 2,000 more. We are making new carriages for the guns and expect tools and artificers every minute to repair, tie and put it in a formidable condition. We yesterday received advice that your hundred regulars were making preparations at St John's to come this way but to our great mortification, the news has been contradicted.[8]

Given the underwhelming state of American arms on Lake Champlain, this was evidently intended as propaganda or bravado. The Americans were hardly ready for a fight just yet.

The letter indeed was intercepted by the British and included in a packet that Carleton sent back to London. Still, despite the clear evidence that Walker was a contact for the Americans, Carleton left him in his home. Perhaps he considered Walker too good a source of information about what the Americans were doing.

When word of the Battle of Bunker Hill and the British siege of Boston reached Montreal, Walker openly led a campaign to raise money to help the city. He was under constant watch by the British and was suspected of being involved in the defacement of the statue of George III the night the Quebec Act was proclaimed into law. Yet despite his legal troubles, mutilation at the hands of the British army, and general intimidation, Walker, now chairman of a Montreal committee urging the Quebec colony to join with the thirteen to the south, remained a ready informant for the Americans.

There were reports through the summer of 1775 that the entire colony of Quebec, stretching along both sides of the St Lawrence from Montreal to the Quebec fortress and south to Lake Champlain, was guarded by just six hundred British soldiers. There were reports that politics in the northern colony were volatile, that the French peasants would welcome the Americans as liberators, that the British and Brigadier General Guy Carleton were isolated from the population, its merchants and peasants. It was said that Carleton was supported only by the the church hierarchy, which was the true winner in the Quebec Act. And of course, Arnold and Allen had shown at Fort Ticonderoga, and Arnold had shown at the St. John fort, how vulnerable the British defenders were to a disciplined attack.

A diary, author unknown but purchased from Carleton's descendants in the 1930s and possibly written by him or a colleague, offers an inside look at the political developments in Quebec's countryside during the summer of 1775, tales of which would have filtered south to buoy American expansionist dreams. "The country people, the Habitants, as they are called in Canada, began to show an inclination to disobey the orders of their superiors," said the diarist. "They refused to take arms as militiamen."9

In London that summer, there was concern. On 2 August Lord Dartmouth, the British cabinet secretary of state for the northern district (Quebec), wrote to Carleton: "The backwardness of the Canadians is a discouraging circumstance for the present. I trust the resolution here to act with vigor and the knowledge of measures intended for exerting ourselves on the side of Canada ... will have a good effect and inspire more confidence."[10]

Adding to the intrigues of the summer was a batch of letters – fifteen hundred in French and fifty in English – sent north in May and June by the provisional congress of New York, insisting that the capture of Ticonderoga and Crown Point were acts of "self-defence" and appealing to Canadians across the border to join them in the struggle for liberty.[11]

All this and more was known to the politicians gathered that summer in Philadelphia. Politics and guns were running ahead of the politicians. Yet all through the summer, Congress dithered. It wasted valuable time debating the proposition of a Canadian invasion, fearing it would lead to a final break with Great Britain that many did not want. On 5 July Congress adopted the "Olive Branch" petition to the king, offering to remain a part of the British Empire if the controls were loosened and Americans were given more economic freedom and some say in London. The politicians did not want to be seen invading British territory at the same time as they proposed an end to tensions and hostility.

As the congressional debate opened in early June, John Adams emerged as an advocate of invasion, as long as Canadians wanted it. "Whether we should march into Canada with an army sufficient to break the power of Governor Carleton, to overawe the Indians and to protect the French has been a great question," he wrote. "It seems to be the general conclusion that it is best to go, if we can be assured that the Canadians will be pleased with it, and join us."[12]

June was also the month that Congress appointed Washington as commander-in-chief and authorized the issuance of two million dollars in continental credit to finance the army. On 6 July it adopted "the Declaration of the Causes and Necessities of Taking up Arms," written in part by Thomas Jefferson, which rejected outright independence while laying out grievances and vowing that Americans would rather die than live as slaves.

At the end of the month, Congress rejected an offer of reconciliation from the British government. In turn, King George rejected the Olive Branch petition on 23 August and declared the colonies to be "in open rebellion." The news did not reach Philadelphia until 9 November, by which time the two sides were careening towards open war.[13]

The political dithering delayed decisive military action. Arnold biographer Willard Randall has joined with several military historians to argue that, "if Congress had moved at once and authorized Arnold to strike before Quebec's governor Carleton could be reinforced, Arnold's plan to conquer all of Canada with a few thousand men very likely would have succeeded."[14] Instead, Congress delayed for several months before finally deciding to set up a Northern Department under General Philip Schuyler, a wealthy landowner from Albany, New York. Finally, in August Congress sent what one American historian called a "simple but splendid message" to Schuyler – that he should invade Canada "if (he) finds it practicable and it will not be disagreeable to the Canadians."[15]

Schuyler took along as his second-in-command New York estate owner and former British officer Richard Montgomery, thirty-eight years old and a veteran of the British campaign against Quebec sixteen years before. With reports of a British push to build a fleet for an attack south through Lake Champlain, the Americans cobbled together a small fleet and launched it from Ticonderoga on 28 August 1775. As the invasion began under harsh conditions and inclement weather, Schuyler's health broke down and Montgomery took charge.

The invasion of Canada by the traditional water route was underway.

Meanwhile, Arnold had won approval for an audacious invasion plan that involved a daring route: north along the Kennebec River of Maine, across a largely unknown wilderness called the Height of Land, down the Chaudière River into Quebec, across the plains to the St Lawrence River, a river crossing and then an appearance on the Plains of Abraham outside the walls of Quebec. It would set up a potentially decisive battle on the field that just sixteen years before, in September 1759, had witnessed the epic battle between Wolfe and Montcalm that decided the fate of a continent.

The unlikely nature of the invasion route was a large part of its attraction. The British would never expect to be confronted suddenly by an army appearing out of the wilderness. The route that nervous British leaders expected the Americans to use was the easier trek north up Lake Champlain to the Richelieu River and then to the St Lawrence. This was the route the British would be guarding.

It was not a new idea to use the Kennebec River through Maine as a route to and from Quebec. In 1759 the British had sent a messenger from the Lower Colonies to General Wolfe at Quebec via the Kennebec River. In 1763 the engineer John Montresor was dispatched with a party of Indians to travel the route down the Chaudière River across the Height of Land and down the Kennebec to the Atlantic Ocean.

He did so, wrote a journal, and drew a crude map. It was this journal and map that Arnold was relying on as he argued that an invasion force could be led up the river.[16]

Arnold would find out that it was one thing for a small mobile party to travel this route but quite another for an invading army, with all the baggage of war. Moreover, the map in many ways was flawed and in the end, the invaders had to grope their way north using the intelligence provided by scouting parties travelling ahead. On the ground, it was a much more brutal and formidable route than it appeared on paper. It involved a journey up the meandering Kennebec, portages around several daunting waterfalls, then a difficult portage over the Height of Land and a series of lakes and dead-end rivers to the mouth of the Chaudière River. From there, the invaders would have to travel down the often-wild Chaudière (boiling water) – so named by Samuel de Champlain because of the rough water, rapids, and falls that marked its descent from the mountains of northern Maine into the plains of Quebec.

The American invasion planners, who had never travelled the route and had little knowledge of the unpredictable autumn weather of the Maine mountains, had little idea of the difficult terrain, faulty directions, dangerous waters, and hardships that lay ahead. If they had known, it is unlikely the invasion would have been launched so late in the year, with such hurried preparations and planning.

Before he would authorize the invasion, Washington insisted that Arnold clear his name before a committee of the Massachusetts Congress, some of whom had accused him of financial improprieties during the Ticonderoga campaign. Arnold faced the committee and won a settlement that satisfied both sides. Then on 2 September a representative arrived from Schuyler's camp to endorse the scheme of a second invasion force. Washington promoted Arnold to the rank of colonel in the colonial army and gave him authorization to choose one thousand men from the army besieging the British garrison in Boston.[17]

On 12 September the first of Arnold's troops started the march northeast from Cambridge to Newburyport about twenty miles northeast of Boston on the Atlantic coast. That same day in Philadelphia, Congress reconvened and with a delegation from Georgia in attendance for the first time, the thirteen colonies were united in their stand against Britain.[18]

In the pocket of his military long coat as he left Cambridge on 15 September, Benedict Arnold carried a paper of instruction from Washington on behalf of Congress, announcing to the Canadian population that the invasion force was arriving as friends and liberators. This address to the Inhabitants of Canada explained that the tensions between colonies and Mother Country had become so heated that only arms could settle it. The army of Britain, so gloriously deployed around the world, "are now tarnished with disgrace and disappointment."[19]

Washington boasted that the colonists were doing better against the British army than expected, and then he tried to flatter the French Canadians into joining the cause:

Above all, we rejoice that our enemies have been deceived with regard to you. They have persuaded themselves, they have even dared to say, that the Canadians were not capable [of] distinguishing between the blessings of liberty and the wretchedness of slavery; that gratifying the vanity of a little circle of nobility would blind the eyes of the people of Canada. By such artifices they hoped to bend you to their views but they have been deceived. Instead of finding in you that poverty of spirit they see, with a chagrin equal to our joy, that you are enlightened, generous and virtuous; that you will not renounce your own rights, or serve as instruments to deprive your fellow subjects of theirs.[20]

Washington called on Canadians to unite with the invaders, who had arrived "not to plunder but to protect you, to animate and bring forth into action those sentiments of freedom you have discussed and which the tools of despotism would extinguish through creation." To help the cause along, Washington had "detached Colonel Arnold into your country." He was there to act as an ally and "best friend." Washington asked them to provide Arnold's army with the supplies they needed and they would be compensated.[21]

Washington made the same point to Arnold in a private memorandum detailing how the Canadian population was to be treated. He wanted his young brigadier general to make sure his troops respected the locals and their traditions. "Upon your conduct and courage and that of the officers and soldiers detached on this expedition, not only the success of the present enterprise, and your own honor, but the safety and welfare of the whole continent may depend."[22]

Despite the anti-Catholic tone of the congressional petition to the British Parliament (which the American revolutionaries seemed to assume would not make its way to Quebec), Washington insisted that Arnold and his troops "avoid all disrespect or contempt of the religion of the country." American Protestant Christians should "look with compassion upon their errors, without insulting them." Only God can decide who is right or wrong. Washington gave Arnold fourteen specific instructions, including a plea that he avoid plunder, try to win Canadians to his side, pay full value for all goods purchased or acquired, compensate volunteers who join the cause and avoid at all cost the humiliation or ridicule of priests or Catholic ceremonies.[23]

Given that Arnold was advanced little money for his invasion, that it was to last much longer than expected, and that these Protestant revolutionary advance troops had been raised and radicalized on anti-Catholic rhetoric and invective, this was a tall order indeed.

5

The March through Maine I

Newburyport is a quiet, industrial town hugging the Atlantic coast of Massachusetts, more than twenty miles northeast of Boston. It is filled with commemorations of its storied past. The first wharf was built in 1665 to accommodate a trading post. The town itself was established in 1764 along a picturesque natural harbour. Running along the harbour was a common, the typical communal green space of seventeenth- and eighteenth-century towns. It became a base for American privateer ships during the Revolution and claims credit as the founding site for the American coast guard. On 23 July 1791 the USS *Massachusetts* was launched as the first vessel employed in the service of the new federal state, assigned to snuff out the smuggling trade.

Strangely, there is little in modern-day Newburyport to celebrate the fact that, at the very dawn of the American Revolution, it was the staging point for one of the most remarkable campaigns of that war.

On 16 September 1775, the little town was swollen with more than a thousand young colonials recruited (sometimes conscripted) to take part in America's first sustained foreign invasion. The men had spent the past several days marching east from Cambridge to await passage to their grand adventure – Arnold's audacious scheme to march north to capture Canada. Many of them were without military experience but were willing to enlist for the excitement and the honour of serving under one of the Revolution's early luminaries: Arnold, the hero of Ticonderoga and author of the humiliation of the British at St John. On that sunny Saturday, the men sprawled about in tents set up along the common, waiting for him to appear.

Soldier Joseph Ware of Needham, Massachusetts, had arrived on Friday evening after a brisk march from General Washington's base camp outside Boston. Arnold arrived the next day, having "dined at Salem, where I procured two hundred pounds of ginger and engaged a teamster to transport that and 270 blankets, received from the Committee of Safety ..."[1] On the Sabbath, he ordered his would-be army out for an inspection. The young revolutionaries tore themselves away from the Newburyport girls to stand at attention. "This day, had a general review and our men appeared well and in good spirits and made a grand appearance and we had the praise of hundreds of spectators who were sorry to see so many brave fellows going to be sacrificed for their country," the self-important young Ware wrote in his diary.[2]

On the town common, the Reverend Samuel Spring, chaplain for the expedition, preached a sermon invoking God's protection for the troops. The next day, the men were ordered to board eleven transports heading east. Already, some were having second thoughts. Guards had to be called out to herd some of the eleven hundred revolutionary vanguard soldiers on board. The destination, three hundred miles to the north through wilderness and the unpredictable weather of a New England autumn, was the fortress of Quebec City and the colony of Quebec.

A few days earlier, as the troops left Cambridge for Newburyport, an enthusiastic Cambridge patriot had written to a friend about the departure of the troops for a far-off land and, as he imagined, inevitable glory. "If the season is not too far advanced and the Canadians and Indians not unfavorable to the scheme, we flatter ourselves that in a few weeks, we shall hear of his [Arnold's] being in possession of Quebec. There is only a company of 25 men there at present," he continued, "and the American cause is highly favored by French and English. All our accounts from that province are very promising and afford the pleasing hope that e'er long, that province will accede to the American league."[3] Another witness of the triumphant march out of Cambridge wrote with the same air of optimistic certainty: "The drums beat and away they go as far as Newburyport by land, from there they go in sloops to Kennebec River, up it in bateaux ... scale the walls and spend the winter in joy and festivity among the sweet nuns."[4]

Arnold left no diary note about what he was thinking that Sunday in Newburyport as he strode before his troops. As a military man who had tasted war already and who was a strong believer in troop discipline, he must have been apprehensive as he looked at this field of rookies. They gave the appearance of a group anxious to get the trip over with so they could share in the inevitable glory and the spoils of victory. Most had never been to battle, although a few were veterans of the Battle of Bunker Hill, which had been fought earlier that summer. Many were raw recruits.

At Washington's headquarters, Arnold had called for volunteers and received more applicants than he could handle; Washington had agreed to send just eleven hundred men north. As he chose his army, Arnold applied certain standards. The men were to be younger than thirty, taller than average, and familiar with boats and survival in the woods. In the end, he chose 747 from the Cambridge volunteers and just over three hundred riflemen led by Virginia marksman Daniel Morgan. The riflemen had marched more than six hundred miles from their base in Lancaster, Pennsylvania, to join the campaign. One historian has reported that Washington was glad to see these rambunctious, unmanageable hillbilly rebels join Arnold's crusade. They were a problem, with their unauthorized sniping at the British and their undirected harassment of Americans whom they considered to be British sympathizers. Now, they would be Arnold's problem.[5]

As Arnold questioned the applicants in an attempt to screen out inappropriate candidates for his revolutionary army, many lied about their familiarity with water, boats, and the woods, as well as about their age. Nonetheless, they were a remarkable group of men (and a few women), and some of them were destined for fame. On 11 September, as Arnold conducted his last review of the chosen group on the campgrounds of Cambridge, he looked into the faces of many who went on to write the history of the young nation they were trying to create.

Arnold assembled his invasion force into four divisions. The officer core consisted of Capt. Morgan; Lt Col Christopher Greene, a leader of the Rhode Island recruits who made up the second battalion; Maj. Return Meigs; and Lt Col Roger Enos. Morgan, a renowned Virginian marksman who led his men by example, had once submitted to five hundred lashes for punching a British officer. He became a guerrilla leader, harassing British soldiers on the north-south road that ran through Virginia, and a battle leader who, after the Revolution, retired to the life of a rich plantation owner on 250,000 acres of Virginia farmland. His troops would be Arnold's vanguard. He was captured at Quebec City. Meigs was a revolutionary who shared with Arnold a Connecticut background. His odd name came from the fact that his father had unexpectedly returned home to sire him. Enos had already developed a reputation as an expert in supplying an army in the field.

He was picked to lead the rear division whose job it was to keep Arnold's army in provisions.

Among the troops, there were interesting characters as well.

Dearborn, Michigan, was named after Henry Dearborn, who in 1775 was a twenty-four-year-old physician from New Hampshire and a veteran of the Battle of Bunker Hill. On the trek, he took along his pet Newfoundland dog. In later years, Dearborn fought in some of the decisive battles of the Revolution. After the war he became a Massachusetts politician, serving eight years as secretary of war in Thomas Jefferson's cabinet in the early nineteenth century.

Dearborn also fought against Canada during the War of 1812 when he served as a general, operating out of Michigan. By then, however, he had become a caricature of the daring young revolutionary who had marched with Arnold thirty-eight years before. Canadian historian Pierre Berton imagined him as an indecisive military leader in 1812, well past his prime; "a ponderous, flabby figure, weighing 250 pounds with a face to match, Dearborn does not look like a general, nor does he act like one. He is a tired sixty-one. His soldiers call him Granny."[6]

The youngest member of the troop was John Joseph Henry, a sixteen-year-old Pennsylvanian who ran away from his home and apprenticeship in order to join a Lancaster regiment being raised to invade Canada. He barely survived the trek, suffering from hunger and fatigue. At Quebec City, he was taken prisoner and developed scurvy in prison. After the war, Henry became a judge in Pennsylvania, dying in 1811 as a relatively young man, still suffering from afflictions that had begun during the march with Arnold and his imprisonment. He entered Canada on his seventeenth birthday.[7] Years after his death, his account of the trek to Canada was published. Because it was written after the fact, some historians question its accuracy. Still, real or exaggerated, Henry's account offers a glimpse of life as a teenager caught in the swirl of an historic march.

Other than Arnold himself, no member of the expeditionary force acquired more fame and notoriety than Aaron Burr, at nineteen already a scholar, ladies' man and charismatic character. He was a product of the New Jersey upper class, the son of the president of Princeton College. Although his father died when Aaron was young and he was raised by an autocratic uncle, Burr inherited his father's academic bent. Aaron first attended Princeton at age thirteen. He was just five and a half feet tall, but energetic and talented. Burr showed up for the march with his Indian mistress in tow, an Abenaki girl called Jacatacqua whom others on the trek dubbed "Golden Thighs."[8]

At first, Burr had been one of Washington's favourites; the general described him as "a gifted young officer." But the two had a falling out when Burr was caught reading some of Washington's confidential mail.[9] Burr compiled a credible revolutionary record and later became a successful politician, lawyer and senator, and one of Thomas Jefferson's friends. He came within a hair of being the third president of the United States. And he too became a traitor.[10]

Many of the troops arrayed before Arnold on that September day in 1775 were dressed in the style of the time and equipped with a rifle, a small axe, and a long knife. They wore coarse hunting shirts, animal-hide leggings over their woollen trousers, short coats and moccasins, and they carried a blanket. John Henry later described it as a bush style of dress influenced by the Indians of the area. "It was the silly fashion of those times for riflemen to ape the manners of savages."[11] Two of the Pennsylvania riflemen, Joseph Grier and James Warner, brought their wives along for the march.[12]

At first, the American commanders imagined the trip from Newburyport to the mouth of the Kennebec River in Maine would be the most most dangerous part of the adventure. Eleven ships, financed and prepared for Arnold's army by Newburyport patriot and wealthy businessman Nathaniel Tracy, left the harbour on Tuesday, 19 September, and made their way along the coast of Maine, praying that the British warships enforcing an embargo against the colonies would not see them.

On Saturday, Arnold noted in his diary that his entire force had arrived and he had sent three boats along the shore to the Kennebec "to look out for men of war and cruisers, with orders to give us the earliest intelligence if they discovered any on the coast."

On Sunday, Arnold reported "head winds and thick weather" as he made preparations to leave. The next day, he got the men onto their boats and he received word back that the coast was clear of the British.

Arnold's diary tells the tale of the next few days:

Tuesday, Sept. 19: Weighed anchor at seven o'clock a.m. and at noon, all the transports, being eleven in number, got safe out of the harbor, except the Schooner *Swallow*, which run on the rocks and could not be got off this tide. Took all the men from on board her, except twelve, including Captain Scott, whom I ordered to follow us as fast as possible. As soon as our fleet passed the bar, ordered the captain of each vessel to be furnished with a copy of the signals ... This being done, bore away for Kennebeck, wind (west southwest). About four o'clock, brought to and spoke with two fishing schooners, who could give us no intelligence. The weather came on thick and foggy. Continued a (north northeast) course till twelve o'clock at night.[13]

They settled down at 2:00 A.M. on Wednesday, 20 September, and left early the next morning. "Weather still continues very thick and foggy, attended with rain," wrote Arnold. By 9:00 A.M., they had arrived at the mouth of the river "without the least molestation from the enemy." After a six-hour ride at anchor to let the seasick sailors recuperate, the ships went up the Kennebec as far as Georgetown.

At 5:00 A.M. on Thursday, they lifted anchor to head north but after a few miles, discovered the river was too shallow. "Left the transports in the river, wind and tide unfavorable, and proceeded as far as Gardinerstown."[14]

Arnold had hoped to get much further up the river with his transports but they had to be abandoned for smaller boats. The problems were starting.

The first unexpected setback surfaced almost immediately. The invasion army arrived at Gardinerstown on 22 September only to find a disaster in the making at Reuben Colburn's shipyard.

When Arnold had ordered two hundred bateaux in advance from the shipyard, he had been assured they would be light, mobile, stable, and flexible enough to handle the currents, rapids, and portages of the river. When he arrived, they turned out to be ill-made misfits. Instead of light dry wood, the boats were made of green pine and oak frames. Each boat weighed four hundred pounds or more and often the seams were poorly caulked. "The result was a meadow full of ill-suited, badly-made, undersized, overweight boats to carry Arnold's army through 400 miles of rough water and portages to Quebec."[15] The Colburn creations have been described as an attempt to marry the traditional Maine logging boat with a lighter craft designed for speed and portability. "About 20 feet long, the bateaux constructed by Reuben Colburn had bottoms solid enough to withstand the sharp glacial material of the Kennebec bottom and flared sides to carry them over the waves in white water."[16]

An angry Arnold complained about the construction, demanded better caulking, and ordered twenty more because some of the two hundred were smaller than he expected. The "fleet" of bateaux that awaited him was not up to the task of moving 1,100 men and forty-five days' worth of provisions through a wilderness river. For the first of several times on the invasion route, the trek north had to be halted unexpectedly. It was the first hint that Arnold's estimate that the invasion would take twenty days was far too optimistic.

During the sojourn in Gardinerstown, some of Arnold's troops became unruly, vandalizing houses whose owners were suspected of being Tories and fighting among themselves. The commander resorted to traditional military brutality to keep his troops in line. Early in the adventure, he wanted to teach them the lessons of discipline and restraint that he expected of soldiers and that George Washington demanded of his invasion force.

Meanwhile, hundreds of miles north in Canada, events were unfolding that would have an effect on his venture.

On 21 September as Arnold's small fleet struggled north to reach Gardinerstown, the lieutenant-governor of Quebec sent a message to London with the first news of the American invasion. It was a report of the arrival of Montgomery's troops before the fort at St Jean on 7 September. Hector Cramahé, second-in-command to Guy Carleton and the commander of Quebec City since Carleton had travelled to Montreal to direct its defence, reported the first evidence that the French Canadian habitants might side with the invaders. It was based on the fact that Montgomery had captured the fort at St Jean easily and was on the way to Montreal. "Had they remained firm in our interests, probably the province would have been saved for this year," Cramahé reported. "But finding the Canadians, in general, adverse to taking up arms in defence of their country, they withdrew and made their peace."[17]

The British, of course, had some allies. "Justice must be done to the gentry, clergy and most of the bourgeoisie that they have shown the greatest zeal and fidelity to the king's service," wrote Cramahé in his report to London. But many of the English merchants and some of the peasants, were on the side of the invaders. "Some Canadians, I understand, are with the Bostannais upon every road."[18]

What he could not have imagined is that the most ham-handed military operation of the entire venture was about to take place, courtesy of Ethan Allen. Schuyler had sent Allen ahead of the main invading army, imagining him to be a persuasive revolutionary capable of winning French peasants and Indians to the American side.

General Montgomery, once he took command of the invaders from the ailing Schuyler, apparently agreed. On Sunday 17 September, as

Arnold reviewed his troops in Newburyport, Allen left St Jean with a small group to check out the defences of Montreal, where Governor Carleton and some troops lay waiting. Within three days, Allen wrote to Montgomery, he had collected 250 French peasant supporters and purchased supplies from farmers and rum for the troops.[19] He reached Longueil across the river from Montreal and waited there several days as he made contact with local New England revolutionaries who thought they had troops to contribute.

They decided to attack Montreal, despite Montgomery's private misgivings. One of the co-conspirators was the New England lawyer John Brown, who convinced Allen that if he crossed the river from Longueil with his small force of 110 American and local fighters, Brown would join him with more troops from further down the St Lawrence River. Allen crossed, Brown did not, and Carleton mustered enough of his tiny defence force to capture Allen and put him in chains, alerting the British to the extent of the invasion.[20] Allen spent the next months in a British jail while the early days of the revolutionary drama were being plotted and played out.

For the record (since the plaques at Ticonderoga credit Allen with the capture of fort, and since modern-day Fort Edward, further down Lake Champlain, has an Ethan Allen Street), it is interesting to note that Allen played no further role in the Revolution and in fact, tried to become a traitor. He bungled that too. His main interest was in making the Vermont Green Mountain territory a state separate from New York or New Hampshire. When it appeared that certain of the thirteen colonies would not accept Vermont as a separate jurisdiction, Allen turned to the British. In 1781 he established contact with British General Frederick Haldimand, offering to make Vermont a British jurisdiction if it was accepted as a separate entity. "I shall do everything in my power to render this state a British Province," he wrote the British general.[21] The scheme did not materialize, Allen did not become the leader of a new British colony, and instead of being tried for treason, the new united states let him live out his life in obscurity. He is an odd figure to be revered as a revolutionary hero.

Allen's enthusiasm and lack of caution during his amateurish attack on Montreal had some dire consequences. It cost the American invaders the element of surprise in their attempt to capture Canada. It jeopardized the safety of some of his Canadian collaborators. On 5 October, acting on evidence that Thomas Walker had helped the invaders by passing on information and distributing their propaganda, Governor Carleton sent troops to Walker's house with a warrant for his arrest.

When Walker resisted, the troops fired on his house and set it ablaze. His wife had to be rescued from a second-storey window by ladder. Walker himself stumbled out of the smoky building and into the arms of the waiting British soldiers. He was not one to hold his tongue and in the confusion that followed, a British soldier aimed his rifle, threatening to shoot him. An officer intervened to protect Walker and then took him before Carleton, who ordered him onto a ship bound for England where he would be tried for treason. Walker was taken aboard and chained while the ship awaited the rest of its cargo and passengers. For days it sat in the Montreal harbour while Walker no doubt contemplated his likely execution at the hands of British justice.

Meanwhile, his Montreal house was all but destroyed and he accused British troops or their civilian supporters of pilfering supplies. He later estimated the value of the loss at £2,500, a sizable sum in those days.[22]

News of the American defeat, the capture of a well-known revolutionary leader, and Carleton's tough new crackdown on American collaborators had the effect of convincing some of the habitants that if they wanted to back the winning side, the British might be their best best. "For the first time, many French Canadians dared to side openly with the British," wrote historian Robert Hatch. "Habitants poured into Montreal from all parts of the district."[23] He estimated that within days, as many as one thousand appeared to check out the prospects of siding with the government.

In a dispatch to his political masters in London, Carleton offered his own view of Walker's arrest and its impact on Canadians who were watching the developing struggle between two societies of British subjects. After Ethan Allen was defeated, there was renewed interest in the British side from local peasants, Carleton reported.

Our information [was] that Mr Walker still continued to preach up disobedience and rebellion. A party of troops were sent to apprehend and bring him prisoner. He had prepared his house for defence and fired several shots at those who surrounded it. Ensign Macdonald was wounded in the arm and a soldier received a bad wound in the thigh, occasioned by their humanity. The house was then set on fire and Mr Walker, his wife and servants surrendered. This occasioned our numbers to increase and, willing to profit by these favorable events, several officers were employed to make another effort to bring up some militia.[24]

Meanwhile, Arnold and his invading army were preparing to make their way north. In the American camp at Fort Western, now Augusta, on the southern Kennebec River, Arnold was beginning to realize he knew little of the expanse of territory that separated his army from the Plains of Abraham and the fort at Quebec. The maps that he had were old and Arnold suspected that they were inaccurate. While he worked out the logistics of moving one thousand men, 220 boats, and provisions for forty-five days upriver, he began to dispatch scouting parties and advance troops.

On Sunday, 24 September, after a church service, Arnold sent seven men forward in two birchbark canoes. The orders, recorded in Arnold's diary, were to make it to Chaudière Pond "to reconnoitre and get all the information he possibly can from the Indians, who I am informed are hunting there."[25] He sent a second ten-man group, with a surveyor, to measure exact distances ahead. The following day, he sent Capt. Daniel Morgan forward with three companies of riflemen to act as an advance party and to cut a road through the bush to help with the army's portage across "the Great Carrying Place" between the Kennebec River and the Dead River, which would take them to the Chaudière River and into Canada.

Even in his naïvety, the prospect of moving a fully equipped army north through the wilderness must have seemed formidable to Arnold. In the South, as it flows through Augusta where Arnold was camped, the river is slow-moving, confined between steep banks crowned with thick forest. But the peacefulness of the river through this stretch is deceiving. Not too far north, a series of rapids begin and the river's meandering path becomes more pronounced, adding miles to the journey as it weaves and backtracks. At Norridgewock a powerful and wild waterfall, now tamed by a dam, forced a hard portage over steep terrain. Further north still, the Kennebec would have to be abandoned as the trail turned north-west, through miles of untracked wilderness and mountainous territory, swamps, bogs, muskeg, and the occasional lake. In the northern distance loomed the Height of Land with the towering peaks leading to it – Poplar Mount, Sugarloaf Mountain, and what now is known as Mount Bigelow, named after one of Arnold's soldiers. The army would have to struggle through this mountain range before beginning the descent into Canada via Lake Mégantic and the Chaudière River, which led to the St Lawrence River and Quebec.

It was a stretch of more than three hundred miles punctuated by long and difficult portages through thick bush, swampland, and over steep, rocky terrain. Clearly the American planners underestimated what lay ahead. It would have been a treacherous trip in ideal conditions; as it turned out, conditions were far from ideal, and the army endured a six-week nightmare.

6

The March through Maine II: America's Hannibal

Before Arnold could leave the makeshift camp on the banks of the river at Fort Western, he had some bureaucratic matters to deal with.

The first item of business concerned one James McCormick, a young and uneducated lad who had been drafted into the army. McCormick got drunk on rum one evening, was drawn into a fight, and killed fellow soldier Reuben Bishop. He was convicted by a jury of his army peers and condemned to death. Arnold put on a stern public face for the sake of discipline, but privately he felt sorry for the young soldier, who had been caught in a web of circumstances largely beyond his control. On Wednesday, 27 September, Arnold sent him back down the river with a private letter to Washington asking that his life be spared.

At noon on the same day, he sent four companies of men north, one led by Dearborn and his Newfoundland dog. Meanwhile, Colonel Enos and his company of logistical and provisions specialists remained downstream near the mouth of the river, controlling most of the supplies. A few carpenters had remained with Arnold to repair the leaky bateaux. Arnold sent word back that all the flour was to be sent forward for the trip.

On Thursday, he sent a letter to Nathaniel Tracy, the Newburyport merchant who had been his host the week before and who had been responsible for arranging the eleven transports to carry Arnold's army to the mouth of the Kennebec. At the time, and for the next few years, Tracy prospered as a merchant who sold goods to the congressional army and whose privateering ships captured goods on the High Seas. Later in the Revolution, however, his fortunes turned. Congress could not repay loans they had taken from the businessman, private debtors took their cue and also refused to pay, and many of Tracy's ships were captured by the British. "His losses were immense."[1] For the moment, though, he was a revolutionary sympathizer living in a grand style with purebred horses, coaches, and country homes. Arnold wrote to thank him for the fleet and his hospitality. The voyage, wrote Arnold, "has been very troublesome indeed."[2]

Two days later he sent a note to Enos ordering him to move his men – close to one-third of the force – forward to join the invasion. Enos should continue to bring up the rear, sending the sick back to Boston but ordering all the stragglers forward. And the carpenters were needed up front to try to patch up the faulty boats built at Gardinerstown. "Leave two or three men with the commissary to assist him and hurry on as fast as possible without fatiguing the men too much. Bring on with you all the carpenters ... and as much provision as the batteaux [sic] will carry. When the Indians arrive, hurry them on as fast as possible."[3] He sent a second command to another officer in the rear, ordering that some supplies be left behind "until the event of this expedition is known."[4] However, all the newly constructed boats, poles, oars, pitch, nails, and other repair supplies should be sent forward immediately.

The invasion force was about to depart. Arnold had been sending smaller groups forward. At 10:00 A.M. he left Fort Western to head north, propelled in a birchbark canoe by Indian guides. After eight miles, the canoe was leaking so badly he exchanged it for a bateau. This slowed him down and he ended the day four miles short of his destination of Fort Halifax, where some of the troops that had been dispatched earlier were camped above a waterfall.

The next day Arnold crossed the river and portaged around the falls, then hired a local man with a team of horses to haul baggage up a five-mile portage to avoid rough water. By late afternoon, the supplies had arrived and he left to travel a mile and a half north where he camped with Maj. Return Meigs and his troops.

On Sunday Arnold travelled twelve miles upriver, dined at 4:00 P.M., then carried on eight more miles north, including a tour around the waterfall at Skowhagen, Maine[5] before arriving five miles above the falls at the home of a widow who put him up for the night. He said the river along the way was a "great part of the way small falls and quick water."[6] This was an ill omen for the hundreds of soldiers, several hundred boats, and tons of supplies that were to follow.

Arnold was out of the widow Warren's house early on Monday morning and heading north toward Norridgewock Falls, six and a half miles away through tangled bush, along a raging river that must have made his heart sink. "At 10:00 A.M., arrived at Norridgewock Falls ... great part of the way swift water and rapids. The land from Fort Western to this place appears in general very good and fertile and is thickly inhabited. Here we leave the English settlements, no inhabitants being above the falls, which by the best estimation are 50 miles from Fort Western."[7] In three days he had covered the fifty miles from Fort Western. Norridgewock was to prove a turning point, the beginning of the expedition's very bad luck.

The most forbidding challenge was the portage itself – close to a mile of steep, forested hillside over which hundreds of men would have to pull tons of supplies and more than two hundred boats weighing four hundred pounds each. "We were half leg deep in mud, stumbling over fallen logs, one leg sinking deeper in the mire," wrote one soldier. "Then the other, then down goes the boat and the carriers with it. A healthy laugh prevails."[8] At least their sense of humour was still there. Soon it too would disappear.

Norridgewock became a place to stop after the difficult portage, take stock, and try to fix the leaky boats. The first troops to arrive took an inventory of their food and found that spray from the rough water had spoiled much of the bread. Some of the beef, dried fish, and peas had also been spoiled. Arnold's diary is remarkably restrained about this first major setback. "Examining bread, great part of which is damaged by the boats leaking and the difficulty of passing the rapids, where it is impossible for people unacquainted to get up the boats without shipping water." The next day, he wrote: "Carpenters employed in repairing batteaux [sic] and several companies in carrying over their provisions, some of which proves unfit for use."[9]

The army was delayed almost a week at Norridgewock, drying out their supplies, throwing out bad food, and getting around the treacherous portage. By Sunday, 8 October, the last of the troops and supplies had made it up the hill, but they could go no further that day. "We have not been able to get all our baggage over the portage until this morning, tho' we have constantly had two sleds going with oxen, owing to the height of the hill and the bad road. A storm of rain prevents our proceeding this day."[10]

These were remarkable diary entries for a man with a reputation for arrogance, short temper, and wilfulness. The boats for which he had paid full price were inadequate. The soldiers he had chosen because they said they were experienced boatmen could not keep their supplies dry. And the week-long delay at Norridgewock meant that the expedition that he had expected would take twenty days had already eaten up more than two weeks and they had not yet left the settled area of Maine. More than one hundred miles of wilderness lay ahead before the troops emerged into Canada, still scores of miles from Quebec. But if Arnold was feeling panicky or bitter about his unravelling schedule, his diary did not show it.

On 9 October the army broke away from its camp and began to move up river, through rapid water and tough terrain. The next day, there was a five-mile journey against a strong current in "very rapid and shallow water." The army began to encounter the soaring mountains that soon became their enemy. "We encamped late at night much fatigued," wrote Arnold on 10 October.[11]

The next day, the troops reached the point in the Kennebec where they had to veer off the river and across the "Great Carrying Place" to get to the Dead River. In the distance was Sugarloaf Mountain. It was a twelve-mile portage through thick forest, over rough land, across swamps and mountains. The men, already tired, had to carry their supplies and their four-hundred-pound boats.

The first portage was more than three miles, "rising ground, bad road but capable of being made good,"[12] wrote Arnold. The first lake, more than a mile long, was filled with trout, which the soldiers caught and cooked. Then came a tough half-mile portage, a lake more than two miles long, a third portage of one-quarter of a mile through almost impassable terrain, and a third, three-mile pond. At last, unexpectedly, came the final hellish portage, almost three miles long with the last mile through a "savanna," as Arnold called it, that looked lush and stable but really was a mire, almost a foot deep, that the men had to wade through, carrying hundreds of pounds of supplies.

In his 1903 history of the march through Maine, historian Justin Smith tried to capture the agony that this portage created for the men, already tired from more than two weeks of tough slogging, diminishing food and hard work. He said that going into the five-day ordeal, the men were in good spirits: "It was this last division of the portage that nearly broke the hearts of the toiling soldiers. At a distance, the savanna seemed like a beautiful plot of firm ground, covered by an elegant green moss, divided by a large grove of spruces and cedars with grey moss and half-withered bushes here and there and in places, almost impenetrable thickets but at every step, the men sank eight or ten inches through the treacherous moss into mud and found at the bottom the sharp snags of dead trees. In a word ... the first part of this carrying place was very bad and the rest of it a hundred times worse."[13]

On Thursday, 12 October, Arnold matter-of-factly recorded in his diary that Lieutenant Steele had returned with some information about the terrain ahead and no reports of Indians. In fact, according to John Henry's account of the trip, the men on Steele's excursion suffered incredible hardships, ran out of food, and barely made it back from their twenty-six-day exploration.[14] Without mentioning their hardships or condition in his diary, Arnold noted that he had assigned the men to duty as guides for the main force. He conceded, however, that some of his men were suffering. That day, he authorized construction of "a small logg house" to be used for the sick. It became known as "Arnold Hospital."

In his diary, Arnold was optimistic: "Our men are much fatigued in carrying over their battoes, provisions etc., the roads being extremely bad. However, their spirit and industry seems to overcome every obstacle and they appear very cheerful. We have had remarkable fine weather since we left Cambridge and only one death has happened and very few accidents by water, which is the more remarkable as there seldom passes a season without some people being drowned in the Kennebec, which is very difficult and dangerous to ascend."[15] Justin Smith, basing his judgment on the diaries of some of Arnold's men, provides a grimmer description of the army that bedded down that night during the long, hard portage over the Great Carrying Place: "Exposure and fatigue began to tell upon them and indeed, a small number were already ill."[16]

While Arnold's troops slogged their way through the Maine wilderness, the politics of the Revolution continued apace, back in the safety of Philadelphia where the politicians met and watched carefully for any evidence of failure or weakness among the commanders at the front. In the history of the emerging nation 13 October was an important day: congressional delegates voted to authorize creation of an American navy. This had been in the works for more than a month. In September Washington had asked Col. John Glover of Massachusetts to convert colonial fishing vessels into fighting ships. A congressional committee was created to prepare a plan for intercepting two British ships. Friday the thirteenth, the congressional committee authorized the installation of ten guns on each of two fishing boats. Over the next months, the number of authorized armed ships was increased, rules of engagement were written, and the decision was taken to fight back against British ships raiding American coastal towns.[17]

While congressional politicians were creating a navy, the soldier who had created and led America's first tiny fighting fleet on Lake Champlain sat in his tent in the Maine wilderness, writing letters.

To Schuyler in Quebec Arnold wrote that his army had made progress "after a very fatiguing and hazardous march over a rough country up the Kennebec River against a very rapid stream through an uninhabited country and meeting with many other difficulties which we have happily surmounted." Having done all that, he hoped "in a fortnight of having the pleasure of meeting you in Quebec."[18]

A second letter was written to Lieutenant Steele, who was to act as a scout and advance party. Arnold wrote that he had sent letters to Quebec and he hoped that the French-speaking John Hall would be able to get to the first settlement, Sartigan, where could get information about French support and British defence; he might also get information from the fort at Quebec. To grease the spy wheels, Arnold sent twenty dollars. He wanted to know whether the American boats were designed properly to make it down the Chaudière River into Quebec.

Arnold also wrote his first letter to Washington in two weeks. He noted the fatiguing journey; he said that the bateaux had to be hauled halfway up the river but that after the first portage, the men were in high spirits and expecting to reach the Chaudière River within eight or ten days, "the greatest difficulty being, I hope, already past."

He estimated that he had twenty-five days' worth of provisions for 950 men. He had ordered that one hundred barrels of provisions be left behind in case a retreat was necessary. He had not yet heard from American commanders in Quebec and did not know how they were doing. He hoped for the best as he moved forward.

Then, in case there were political complaints about the delays in the invasion, Arnold offered his commander-in-chief an explanation in a postscript:

Your excellency may possibly think we have been tardy in our march, as we have gained so little. But when you consider the badness and weight of the batteaux and the large quantity of provisions, etc. we have been obliged to force up against a very rapid stream, where you would have taken the men for amphibious animals, as they were great part of the time under water; add to this the great fatigue in portage – you will think I have pushed the men as fast as could possibly have been. The officers, volunteers and privates have in general acted with the greatest spirit and industry.[19]

The next day, 14 October, Arnold wrote to Colonel Farnsworth, a commander in the rear, under the charge of Enos, that they should send forward the provisions they had been storing in case of a retreat. In the afternoon, Arnold left the camp at the first pond to move forward. He quickly found out how hard the going would be. "We soon arrived at the second pond, which makes as desolate an appearance as the first does bountiful, the lake being very irregular, long and narrow, the trees all dead and full of moss, the water very thick and muddy." They got through the lake, portaged along a trail overgrown with roots, and reached the third lake. "There, the prospect is very beautiful and noble, a high chain of mountains encircling the pond, which is deep, clear and fine water."[20] In the distance was a beautiful snow-capped mountain. The group camped on the shore of the lake for the night. The next morning, Arnold sent letter directly to Enos in the rear, ordering him to send the oxen forward to the Dead River "as I intend killing them there for the whole detachment." He said he would be holding a council of war with his officers once they arrived at Dead River. By then, he hoped they would have better intelligence about conditions and prospects in Canada.[21]

On that same day, 15 October, the troops crossed the three miles of lake in three hours. Then they portaged through a mile-long trail up the mountain and down to the edge of a savannah, where they camped. Arnold received a letter written by Enos on 14 October and he sent back instructions that provisions be forwarded, that a boat be kept at each lake to handle sick soldiers being sent back, and that the remaining troops and provisions push ahead. Arnold still thought his troops had enough food for twenty-five days.

On 16 October, Arnold's small group left camp, wading through mud almost to their knees for close to three miles. "Here," he told his diary, "the men had a most fatiguing time in getting over their batteaux, baggage, etc." By early afternoon they had arrived at a brook that could accommodate their boats and they rowed a mile to the Dead River. Arnold left a crew behind to try to cut a better road for those who would follow and continued down the Dead River as it meandered aimlessly. They passed several divisions of troops that had been sent ahead and were labouring to get their boats and provisions up the river. Arnold's group stopped to camp late in the day, "much fatigued."[22]

In camp the next day there arose the beginning of a crisis. Colonel Green's troops were almost out of food. Spoiled provisions meant they were reduced to just four barrels of flour and a bit of pork, a "great part of their bread being damaged." They fished and caught some trout in the river. Getting supplies from the rear became more urgent. Why were they taking so long? What was Enos doing? Rations for his men were cut in half, from three-quarters of a pound each per day of flour and salt pork.[23]

Arnold sent Major Bigelow and close to one hundred soldiers south to help bring supplies forward and to lighten the load of the troops bringing up the rear. "If you find your men much fatigued and this party can bring on more of your provision than their share, let them have it," he wrote to Enos.[24] During the wait for their return, Arnold kept his troops occupied by having them make rifle cartridges. During the day, Morgan's division of riflemen arrived and passed north through the camp, on their way to Chaudière Pond.

On Wednesday, two companies of soldiers arrived at camp, led by Captains Goodrich and Dearborn. At the end of the day, Maj. Return Meigs arrived with the last of the divisions, save for the third of the army that remained behind with Enos. On Thursday morning, it started to rain. When it let up in the afternoon, Arnold ordered his men forward seven miles up river to the next portage. They stopped there and caught some fish for supper. "Night coming on and the rain increasing, we encamped on the portage," Arnold wrote in his diary.[25] The rain continued through Friday.

On Saturday morning, Arnold awoke early, determined to press on. He recorded in his diary that the rains of the past two days had swollen the Dead River by three feet. He saw this as a good thing, since the once-shallow river could now better accommodate the boats. The troops broke camp and headed north, covering nine miles before hitting the first of a series of waterfalls that had to be skirted. As the men struggled through the bush in heavy rain, they came upon the miserable camp where Morgan had stopped with his advance party of riflemen. Morgan's troops were soaked and their camp poorly located on low ground. Arnold ordered them to join his troops and the entire army struggled on one more mile through the rainy darkness, "very wet and much fatigued." They made camp, built what fires they could to dry clothes and cook food, and then settled in near midnight to sleep.

There has been some speculation about what happened next; suggestions that the events of the following twelve hours occurred because the edge of a Caribbean hurricane passed over the Maine wilderness. To the men in the midst of it, the night of terror must have seemed like a biblical warning. As they lay in their tents, exhausted from the day and shivering from the wet chill, a high wind blew up, making the surrounding forest roar. There was the swoosh of the forest, punctuated by the crash of shattering trees, some of which were uprooted. All the while, the rains continued and the Dead River, which is fed by ponds littered through the hills and mountains of the area, received more overflow than it could handle. High in the mountains of the Great Divide, it began to overflow its banks and pour southward, picking up water, speed, and force as it rushed towards the sleeping soldiers.

At 4:00 A.M., the camp awoke to the sudden sound of cascading water, "which came rushing on us like a torrent, having rose eight feet perpendicular in nine hours," Arnold wrote.[26] The flood hit too quickly to save most of the tents, baggage or food. The army straggled, wet and forlorn, to a nearby hilltop to wait out the night.

Daylight broke over a dismal scene, recorded by Arnold: "This morning presented us a very disagreeable prospect, the country round entirely overflowed, so that the course of the river, being crooked, could not be discovered, which with the rapidity of the current renders it almost impossible for the batteaux to ascend the river, or the men to find their way by land ... add to this our provisions almost exhausted and the incessant rains for three days has prevented our gaining anything considerable, so that we have but a melancholy prospect before us, but in general in high spirits."[27]

The men spent most of the day trying to get their baggage dry. On Monday morning the troops moved on, pushing three miles upriver to a fork. Morgan and his land party had taken the wrong turn, and after rowing two miles up the river, Arnold concluded this was a dead end. The march was halted for two hours while Arnold sent scouts ahead to bring Morgan back. Meanwhile, on the main river, the army struggled three miles upstream against a strong current until it arrived at another waterfall, which required a portage. Here, disaster struck again. During the carry up the steep hill, seven of the boats were upset when their carriers fell. All the provisions in the seven boats were lost in the river and an already tight food supply suddenly became tighter. And still there was no information from Canada, nor from the army in the rear.

Faced with a deepening crisis, growing doubts, and plummeting morale, Arnold ordered a halt to the day's travel, set up camp, gathered his commanders together, and put the future of the invasion on the line. Enos, the commander at the rear, did not attend. That council of war – convened at the low point of the campaign when the weather was bad, provisions short, and the men wet and discouraged about their prospects of making it over the mountains – was a turning point. The officers talked and argued into the night, considering whether to turn back, pick up the supplies that had been left behind, and admit defeat, or to press ahead. Arnold, by his determination, optimism, and calmness, won the debate: they would press on. Even Arnold's critics see that night in the sodden tent in the Maine wilderness as one of the finer moments of the Revolution and early American military history. Historian Clare Brandt, normally contemptuous of Arnold, gave the general his due: "With his army on the verge of disintegration, Arnold summoned all his powers of mind, spirit and instinct in order to preserve the one thing that was keeping his men going – their courage. In the process, he demonstrated for all time that he was a leader of men."[28]

The council of war took two decisions to support the primary conclusion that the invasion would continue. First, twenty-six sick men from the main army at the front were sent back to Enos with instructions that he give them provisions for the remainder of the trip back to Massachusetts. To preserve the provisions that remained, Enos was also ordered to send back the sick and weak from his contingent, pick the hundred or so most fit men, outfit them with fifteen days' worth of provisions, and lead them forward with the flour, meat, and ammunition that could be distributed to the rest of the army. Arnold made it clear in a letter of 24 October sent back to Enos that the future of the expedition and hundreds of lives were at stake. "I make no doubt you will join with me in this matter as it may be the means of preserving the whole detachment and of executing our plan without running any great hazard, as fifteen days will doubtless bring us to Canada. I make no doubt you will make all possible expedition."[29] He sent a separate letter to Colonel Greene, urging him to move quickly. "Pray hurry on as fast as possible."[30] The second decision was that Arnold would lead a small party to the Chaudière and into Quebec so that he could send provisions back from the French *habitants.*

Having written his orders that morning and sent fifty men forward into Quebec in search of provisions, he left at noon and travelled seven miles until progress on the water was halted by the foaming spectre of yet another waterfall. It was the tenth portage on the Dead River and as the men struggled over the hill, it began to rain again. After a mile of travel above the falls, the group decided to camp, tired and once again wet to the skin. That night, the temperature plunged, rain turned to snow, a cold wind started to blow, and by morning, two inches of snow lay on the ground. Frozen clothes added to the misery of the troops.

The next day, Wednesday, 25 October, Arnold's party rowed, paddled, and portaged more than ten gruelling miles through the snow.

They were often forced to spend valuable time in the back-breaking work of cutting and clearing logs that clogged the river, possibly fallen during the high winds that had blown through the area several days earlier. Arnold's diary entry was a stark description of a hellish journey: "Snowed and blowed very hard all this day. In the last lake, the sea ran so high we were obliged to go on shore several times to bail our batteaux, which was with much difficulty kept above water ... Night coming on and we being much fatigued and chilled with the cold, we were obliged to encamp without being satisfied whether we were right or not as our guides gone forward had made no marks or we had missed them."[31] It was not until 11:00 P.M. that the exhausted men were able to get to bed.

Early the next morning, Arnold sent a scouting party forward to look for a portage while the rest of the men had breakfast and packed up. Conditions were bitter. The scouts returned without having found an easy route so the group struck out blind. With more than six inches of snow on the ground they made ten miles that day, almost half of it in portage. They stopped in mid-portage, finally pitching their tents close to midnight.

The next day, as Arnold and his party struggled north, news reached him from the south about a shocking betrayal that had taken place behind the lines.

Roger Enos, Arnold's second-in-command and an experienced soldier with a reputation as a logistics and supply expert, had been receiving Arnold's letters urging him to move troops and supplies forward to save the army from disaster. At noon on 25 October, as Arnold and his party struggled through the brutal wintry conditions at the head of the invasion, Enos and his officers arrived at Greene's headquarters near the rear. Greene's troops were increasingly hungry, lacking in supplies, despairing. Enos, suggesting that the invasion was a lost cause, wanted to retreat in defiance both of Arnold's direct orders and the decision made several days earlier at the council of war. Greene and his officers, including Dr Isaac Senter, voted to continue. Enos and the majority voted otherwise. Whether through cowardice or arrogance, they sent Greene and his men forward with just two barrels of flour and two barrels of pork, while retreating with more than three hundred men, close to half the supplies, and all the medicine. It could have been a death sentence for the seven hundred increasingly hungry and illness-prone men at the front.

Word of the defection spread northward among the soldiers straggling through the Maine wilderness, some of them a hundred miles from Quebec settlements and hundreds of miles from American towns. It caused anguish, fear, and anger. On 27 October Capt. Henry Dearborn wrote in his diary: "Our men made a general prayer: that Colonel Enos and all his men might die by the way, or meet with some disaster equal to the cowardly, dastardly and unfriendly spirit they discovered in returning back without orders, in such a manner as they had done. And then, we proceeded forward."[32]

Enos and his men arrived back in Cambridge in late November. He was arrested on Washington's orders and charged with "quitting his commanding officer without leave." The court martial, which was heard by military friends of the colonel, lacked testimony from Arnold's side and ended in Enos's acquittal. But his days in the army were numbered. He arrived back in Washington's camp with well-fed troops and a reputation as a deserter. He was shunned, and in little more than a week he resigned and bowed out of the Revolution.[33]

On Friday, 27 October, Arnold had not yet heard about Enos's treachery. As Dearborn was cursing the coward, Arnold crossed down from the Height of Land into Canada with a party of seventy and encountered the first direct evidence that there was hope for his mission. During a day of tough travel, he met the small scouting party he had sent north. It was returning from Sartigan, the first French Canadian settlement of note. In his diary, Arnold reported good news conveyed to him by a scouting party led by Steele: "He left Sartigan the 22nd and says the French inhabitants appear very friendly and were rejoiced to hear of our approach."[34] Steele said that the defences were lax and that Governor Carleton was still in Montreal.

Late that afternoon Arnold's group reached Lake Mégantic and rowed three miles before camping. At the camp they met another scouting party that had been sent ahead days before but had become lost because they did not follow Arnold's instructions. As he waited for them to be brought to his camp, the tired Arnold wrote letters to Greene, Enos, and Washington. To Greene and Enos (of whose treachery he still had not heard), it was a familiar plea. The roads are decent, the trail is marked, the supplies are needed. "Pray make all possible despatch."[35]

In his letter to Washington, Arnold noted their slow progress, reported that he had heard of the American victory at St John, and announced that, rather than wait for Enos to come from the rear, he would take five boats and fifteen men and carry on to the French community of Sartigan where supplies could be procured and sent back. He ended with a concise description of their arduous journey, riddled with praise for his men and an admission that the maps on

which he made his plans were flawed: "Our march has been attended
with an amazing deal of fatigue, which the officers and men have
borne with cheerfulness. I have been much deceived in every account
of our route, which is longer and has been attended with a thousand
difficulties I never apprehended. But if crowned with success and con-
ducive to the public good, I shall think it but trifling."[36]

He ended the long day by sending a note back to commanders who
were following him through the Great Carrying Place, telling them he
was going forward and would send back provisions within three days.
He warned them about taking the wrong turn out of the portage, as
the scouting party had done. The inviting-looking brook would in fact
take them into a swamp "out of which it will be impossible for you to
get."[37] Despite his clear warning and detailed instructions, most of the
army took the wrong turn anyway and got trapped in a dead-end
swamp. Their error, as we shall see, put the entire army in peril and
cost Dearborn's Newfoundland dog his life.

On Saturday, 28 October, Arnold almost lost his own life. The day
began early. He sent messengers back with his letters and ordered fifty-
five men forward on foot. At 7:00 A.M., he left with fifteen men in four
boats and a birchbark canoe, resolved to make it from the lake into
the Chaudière River and down the river to French communities where
provisions could be purchased. Arnold, in the canoe, reached the
north shore of the lake first and pulled ashore to build a fire and wait
for the slower bateaux. At 11:00 A.M., the group entered the
Chaudière River, "which is very rapid, full of rocks and dangerous."[38]
With baggage strapped into the boats, they became caught in the
current and headed downstream at a speed Arnold estimated at eight
to ten miles per hour. Fifteen miles along, they hit some rapids that
tipped three boats. All arms and provisions in the boats were lost and
the three canoes were smashed to pieces against the rocks. Six men
were thrown into the water and almost drowned.

It looked like another disaster as the drenched men, Arnold among
them, crawled onto shore, their supplies diminished. Only later did it
become clear that Providence had in fact intervened. Just ahead in the
river was a waterfall that, had they gone over, would have killed them
all. The chastened men camped for the night, now reduced to rations
of a half-pound of pork and two ounces of flour per man for the five
days Arnold expected it would take to reach a town.

The next day, Sunday, they travelled with the remaining boats and
one canoe, the canoe was soon damaged on the rocks and had to be
abandoned. All the men clambered aboard the two bateaux and

headed down the Chaudière, making forty miles in the face of a cold Quebec wind. The next day, 30 October, after a number of portages, they came to their first French Canadian house and sent back supplies, including oxen and two horses, which were driven by Canadian herdsmen hired by Arnold. "I have now sent forward for the use of the detachment," he wrote, "[five oxen and two horses] and 500 pounds of flour by Lt Church, Mr Barrin and eight Frenchmen and shall immediately forward on more, as far as the falls."[39]

Meanwhile, the troops back in the wilderness had become lost in the swamp and wandered for several days without food. By 28 October, starvation was a cold breath on their necks. The men began to boil harnesses, moccasins, bark – anything that might provide some taste and nourishment. Capt. Simeon Thayer, commander of a company of foot soldiers, saw his men "taking up some rawhides that lay for several days in the bottom of their boats, intended for to make their shoes or moccasins in case of necessity, which they did not then look into so much as they did their own preservation." They cut the pieces and boiled them, "living on the juice or liquid that they soaked from it for a considerable time."[40]

John Henry, in his later memoir, wrote of the troops marching through the bush in single file, afraid to step out of line in case they were left behind. Henry's shoes fell apart and he wrapped bark around his feet. "Every step taken, the heel of the foot slipped out of the shoes. To recover the position of the front of the shoe, and at the same time to stride, was hard labor and exhausted my strength to an unbearable degree. You must remember that this march was not performed on the level surface of a parade but over precipitous hills, deep gullies and even without the path of the vagrant savage to guide us."[41]

Private George Morison of the Pennsylvania Rifles later wrote about those awful days. Men fell as they walked but their comrades were fearful of stooping to help lest they themselves fell. "At length, the wretches raise themselves up ... wade through the mire to the foot of the next steep and gaze at its summit, contemplating what they must suffer before they reach it. They attempt it, catching at every twig and shrub they can lay hold of ... their feet fly from them ... they fall down ... to rise no more."[42] While this description was dramatized by a survivor trying to impress his post-Revolution contemporaries, the suffering and deprivation he describes are not far removed from the horrors described by other diarists.

For many of the soldiers who kept diaries, 1 November seems to have been a low point, a day during which hunger drove men to do the almost unthinkable. For days, the food, when there was food, had been awful. Dr Isaac Senter wrote in his diary that some had been trying to boil food in bad water. "No sooner had it gone down than it was puked up by many of the poor fellows." He found men eating candles, "which were used for supper and breakfast the next morning by boiling them in water gruel." For almost two days, "our bill of fare consisted of the jawbone of a swine destitute of any covering. This we boiled in a quantity of water but with little thickening constituted our sumptuous eating."[43]

On 1 November, a group of hungry soldiers decided they had had enough. Dearborn's Newfoundland dog had been with them for the full trek, a month and a half, and undoubtedly had become a pet, an army mascot. Senter said he was a poor dog "who had hitherto lived through all the tribulations [and] became a prey for the sustenance of the assassinators."[44] They grabbed him and butchered him. Simeon Thayer told the story with an air of sadness in the writing. "We observed at a little distance a sergeant and 10 or 12 men around a fire, towards whom we wade up and saw with astonishment that they were devouring a dog between them and eating paunch, guts and skin, part of which they generously offered to us but did not accept of it, thinking that they were more in want of it than what we were at that time."[45] Dearborn's diary entry about his dog was forlorn and to the point. He notes it was a day of long travel in leaky boats with no food. After thirty miles on the river and on portage "we went on shore and encamped. Here, I saw some of the footmen who were almost starved. This day, Capt. Goodrich's company killed my dog and another dog and eat them. I remain very unwell."[46]

If only they had waited one day, the dog would have made it into Canada.

On 2 November the first of the cattle sent back by Arnold arrived for the troops. The nearly starving Senter described a vision of "horned cattle, four-footed beasts, rode and drove by animals resembling Plato's two-footed featherless ones."[47]

Years later, John Henry remembered that day. He and his comrades boiled moccasins, hoping for some nourishment from the broth. They later stumbled upon those who had met the oxen and gorged. The next day, he reported that they came upon men still eating. It was not a pretty sight. "One of the eastern men, as we came to the fire, was gorging the last bit of the colon, half-rinsed, half-boiled. It may be said he ate with pleasure as he tore it as a hungry dog would tear a haunch of meat."[48] Others ate owls and drank broth.

On 4 November the ragged troops stumbled out of the wilderness and into Quebec, where they found the house. Arnold had found earlier. He had left money and instructions that his troops be accommodated. Three days before, he had sat at Sartigan to write a note to Major Meigs: "You may let each captain have about twenty or thirty dollars out of the money I gave you, as I suppose they will want a little pocket money for present use, and to supply their men. Keep a particular account of what you deliver and to whom."[49] Considering later complaints about Arnold's bookkeeping, these were very precise instructions. Much of the money was from his personal funds.

The day the army arrived in Canada, young John Henry fell ill, a victim of privation. Arnold gave him money and asked a French Canadian family to nurse him back to health. Only 675 men made it out of the wilderness, two-thirds of those who had left Cambridge less than two months before. The rest had been lost to hunger and disease but also, and mainly, to desertion and the cowardice of Roger Enos.

Randall described a joyous scene as this ragtag army emerged onto the flat land of the Chaudière Valley after their nightmare trip through the wilderness. "The French Canadians all but overwhelmed the Bostonnais with their generosity as they staggered into the settlements along the Chaudière."[50] They sold them cattle and bread and listened to their tales of hardship.

When he was healthy enough to march, Henry expressed amazement at the cozy houses he passed. "These things created surprise, at least in my mind, for where I thought there would be little other than barbarity, we found civilized men in a comfortable state, enjoying all the benefits arising from the institutions of civil society."[51] Still, they were not as free as the Americans, he figured.

The troops moved quickly along the Chaudière River towards the St Lawrence and the Fortress of Quebec. They were housed with French peasants who were being paid cash to feed and care for the hungry, ill-clothed invaders. The river was more forgiving. The terrain was less hilly.[52]

7

Quebec Awaits

For the advance party racing towards Quebec while the army straggled on behind, the trek north through Quebec along the Chaudière was leisurely enough to allow Arnold to get back to his letter writing. On 7 November, from St Mary's, he wrote to his friend John Manir in Quebec City. "We have been very kindly received by the inhabitants who appear very friendly, and willing to supply us with provisions." The strategy was to make it as far as the St Lawrence as quickly as possible, and then to attack the fort at Quebec. "I am fearful of their being reinforced from Montreal, which may possibly put it out of my power. In which case, I intend to march for Montreal."[1]

Late that night a messenger brought a letter to Arnold from Richard Montgomery informing him that the fort at St Jean had fallen to the Americans and the troops were moving towards Montreal. "I heartily congratulate you on your success thus far," he wrote back to his thirty-eight-year-old American fellow revolutionary and commander. He offered a glimpse of what his invasion force had endured. "I was not apprised or even apprehensive of one half of the difficulties we had to encounter, of which I cannot at present give you a particular detail," he wrote. "Can only say we have hauled our batteaux over falls, up rapid streams, over carrying places, and marched through morasses, thick woods and over mountains, about 320 miles, many of which we had to pass several times to bring our baggage."

He praised his soldiers and offered very muted criticism of Enos, who had deserted and stranded close to seven hundred fellow soldiers without medical supplies or provisions. He also reported that some of his letters had been intercepted by the British, who had reacted by destroying all the canoes on the south shore of the St Lawrence River to prevent the river crossing by the invaders. Arnold said the problem would be overcome by the use of twenty birchbark canoes owned by Indians who had joined the Americans, supplemented by canoes he expected to be supplied with by the Canadians. "I am informed by the French that there are two frigates and several smaller armed vessels lying before Quebec and a large ship or two lately arrived from Boston. However, I propose crossing the St Lawrence as soon as possible and if any opportunity offers of attacking Quebec with success, shall improve it."[2] Otherwise, he would march his army to join Montgomery in an assault on Montreal.

The trip through Quebec was uneventful (other than reports of a few troops gorging themselves on peasant fare and becoming sick) and by 11 November Arnold's army of more than six hundred had gathered on the south shore of the St Lawrence, across from the Plains of Abraham, Wolfe's Cove, and the walls of the Fortress of Quebec. He assembled forty canoes and waited for a dark, calm night on which they could make several trips across the river without arousing the suspicion of two British ships anchored nearby – the *Hunter* and the *Lizard*. Finally the weather cooperated and before dawn on 14 November, Arnold was able to move close to five hundred men across the river before a British frigate heard the noise and sounded an alarm. "We fired into her and killed three men," he reported in a letter to Brigadier General Montgomery at Montreal.[3]

Several days earlier a resident of the fortress, possibly Lt Gov. Hector Crahamé, heard the news that the invasion force had arrived and wrote an excited letter to the British government: "There are about 500 provincials arrived at Point Levi, opposite the town by way of Chaudière across the woods. Surely, a miracle must have been wrought in their favor. It is an undertaking above the common race of men in this debauched age. They have traveled through woods and logs and over precipes [sic] for the space of one hundred and twenty miles, attended with every inconvenience and difficulty to be surmounted only by men of indefatigable zeal and industry."[4]

In fact the American army that straggled onto the fields before Quebec was ill clothed, poorly armed, and gaunt from the trek through the wilderness. Although more than six hundred strong, it was hardly a formidable fighting machine. Yet it was an army whose very existence on those snowy fields inspired the Americans to the south and enthralled the seasoned fighting men and politicians of Europe. Arnold's accomplishment in getting them there was quickly noted. In

Europe, the young commander was lionized as the "Hannibal of America" and heroic poses of a figure, purported by its artistic creators to be Arnold, were published. Sir Henry Clinton, commander of the British forces, was also impressed. As he made private note of the invasion, Clinton described it as an enterprise "which for the boldness of the undertaking and the fortitude and perseverance with which the hardships and great difficulties of it were surmounted will ever rank high among military exploits."[5]

When word reached Philadelphia, congressmen set aside their doubts about Arnold's bookkeeping to sing his praises. Eighty-five years later, the feat was still celebrated even as its hero was denounced. "The history of the movements of that expedition, from [Maine] to the French settlements near the St Lawrence, is one of the most wonderful on record," said the author of an otherwise derogatory feature on Arnold in the November 1861 issue of *Harper's New Monthly Magazine*. "For thirty-two days, they traversed the wilderness through marshes, over cliffs, among tangled thickets, up and down rapid rivers and through snow, ice and mud. Their sufferings were terrible and their endurance wonderful."[6]

Arrayed as they were before the fort and ready to lay siege, Arnold was confident. "By the best information, they are in the greatest confusion [in the fort], very short of wood and provisions, much divided and refused provisions from the inhabitants and if blocked up by a superior force, must, as soon as the frost sets in, surrender."[7]

That night, Arnold suffered his first setback of the siege when the British captured one of his sentinels and learned from him the plans for an attack. The British burned some houses outside the walls of the fort that the Americans could have used for shelter during the siege. Any element of surprise was lost. Still, the invasion was going better than even Arnold imagined as he camped at Covil Place, just over a mile west of the fortress.

A little more than a hundred miles east, Montgomery's invasion was exceeding expectations. He had led an army north up the traditional invasion route through Lake Champlain, along the Richelieu River. He had captured Fort Chambly, which was understaffed with British soldiers who received little help from the locals. With the weapons and gunpowder captured at Chambly, Montgomery moved on to Fort St Jean and laid siege. On 3 November, the poorly defended fort surrendered. Among the British soldiers taken captive was John André, a dashing young soldier and poet who would become a key figure in Benedict Arnold's defection less than five years later.

Montgomery then marched on to Montreal and despite the earlier fiasco involving Ethan Allen, Quebec governor Guy Carleton thought the situation was doomed and he fled the city in disguise. On 13 November, just as Arnold was making final preparations to cross the St Lawrence to begin the siege and the final assault, American troops marched into Montreal and occupied the city. On a British ship in the harbour, they found Thomas Walker in chains and freed him.

A week before, Carleton had predicted the fall of Montreal and he was not optimistic about the future of British defences at Quebec. "The prospect at Quebec is not much better," he wrote to London. "Accounts say B. Arnold is on the Chaudière with twelve or fifteen hundred men. We have not one soldier in the town and the lower sort are not more loyal than here."[8]

By "the lower sort," of course, the aristocratic Carleton meant the French habitants. The message to London underestimated defences in Quebec, as he soon found out, but it also illustrated the pessimism with which British commanders viewed their chances of saving Canada from the onslaught of American rebels.

On 14 November from his camp before the walls of Quebec, Arnold sent an officer with a white flag towards the city. He hoped to take the town without a fight. The envoy carried a letter to Hector Cramahé, lieutenant governor of Quebec and the man in charge of the fort in Carleton's absence. In the letter, Arnold described the two-pronged invasion plan, told Cramahé the defenders did not stand a chance, asked him to surrender, and threatened death and destruction if it came to a battle. "On surrendering the town, the property of every individual shall be secured to him but if I am obliged to carry the town by storm, you may expect every severity practised on such occasions and the merchants who may now save their property will probably be involved in the general ruin."[9]

Cramahé responded with his own tough message: his troops fired on the envoy, bringing a protest from Arnold. The American commander was also informed that the rebel sentry captured by the British was being kept in irons. Again, Arnold accused the old French Canadian soldier of violating the ethics of war: "As I have several prisoners taken from you, who now feed at my own table, you may expect that they will be treated in the same manner in future as you treat mine."[10]

The defenders, it appeared, were digging in for a stout defence. Several times, Arnold tried to lure the troops out for a pitched battle, but to no avail. It was just as well. Arnold's army could not have held its own in any pitched battle. On 18 November he carried out an inspection of his forces and quickly realized how ill equipped and unprepared they were. It was the beginning of bad news. "Upon examination, great part of our cartridges proved unfit for service and to my great surprise, we had no more than five rounds for each man and near one hundred guns unfit for service," he reported to Montgomery as he pleaded for troops and supplies to be sent east from Montreal. "Add to this, many of the men [are] invalids and almost naked and wanting everything to make them comfortable."[11]

He had no more than 550 ill-equipped troops available to fight, so when he heard that a force might come out of the fort to fight, he moved his men back twenty miles to Point aux Trembles in late afternoon, 19 November. He asked for basic survival supplies – six hundred pairs of coarse yarn stockings, five hundred yards of wool for pants, one thousand yards of flannel for shirts, caps, and mittens, three hundred blankets, powder, shot, sugar, and rum. This was an army in need of the necessities as it faced the prospect of a winter siege. To make matters worse, Arnold had spent most of the money he brought to Canada. "My hard cash is nearly exhausted," he wrote to Montgomery. "It will not be sufficient for more than ten days or a fortnight and as the French have been such sufferers by paper, I don't think it prudent to offer it to them at present."[12]

Still, Arnold and the Americans remained optimistic. Montgomery was marching east and the two armies surely would be able to starve out the fort. "Had I been ten days sooner, Quebec must inevitably have fallen into our hands, as there was not a man then to oppose us," Arnold wrote to Washington. "However, I make no doubt Gen. Montgomery will reduce it this winter, if properly supported with men, which in my opinion cannot in the whole be less than two thousand five hundred, though it may possibly be effected with a less number. The fatigue will be severe at this season and in this inclement climate."[13]

In retrospect, it is clear that Arnold harboured a naïve hope that Congress would continue to support the invasion with fresh troops, supplies, and money. When he was given his instructions in Cambridge the previous September, Washington had suggested that the fate of the Revolution rested on the success of the northern invasion. Arnold, a political neophyte, can hardly be blamed for assuming the politicians understood that and supported Washington's urgency. But he was wrong. Congress during these days was indecisive, given to long debates that resulted far more in rhetoric than in tangible support for the war effort.

In fact, Congress was filled with armchair generals intent on waging war from the relative safety of their congressional meeting-rooms. Political intrigue was their weapon. In a letter to his wife Abigail, John Adams lamented that his ill health prevented him from marching to the front. "I, poor creature, worn out from scribbling for my bread and my liberty, low in spirits and weak in health, must leave others to wear the laurels which I have sown, others to eat the bread which I have earned." He added: "Oh that I were a soldier. I will be. I am reading military books. Everybody must, will and shall be a soldier."[14]

Arnold, in the meantime, wasn't reading military books and dreaming of glory. He was creating military history and living in battlefield conditions that gave the lie to many of the rosy illusions about military glory that made the rounds of Philadelphia taverns and debating halls. Yet on those snowy November days as Arnold sat in his headquarters on the plains west of the Quebec harbour, writing letters, reporting his situation, and asking for help, he was optimistic. All that thwarted American control of Quebec was the fortress at Quebec City. Governor Carleton was on the run. The Americans stood confident before the city. Arnold's army was about to be reinforced. To the brash young commander, American victory seemed assured. There would indeed be a fourteenth colony.

Along the thin red line of Quebec's defenders, there was little certainty that American optimism was misplaced. Inside the fortress, the British were dispirited and fearful. What is worse, they lacked the leadership and steadying hand of Guy Carleton, who was separated from his troops by Arnold's American forces.

On Sunday, 19 November, British fortunes began to change. On that day, Carleton completed a gamble that became one of the turning points of the American campaign to capture Canada. Disguised as a *habitant* in a woolen cap, blanket, and sash,[15] sitting in a small boat wending its way down the St Lawrence from Montreal, guided by French Canadian locals and British soldiers in disguise, Carleton had slipped past the American forces to arrive at the Quebec fort and take command. Good luck attended him as he made his way undetected past the Americans, who rashly failed to search every passing boat.

Carleton also benefited from a simple act of good timing. As he made his desperate bid to reach the last fortified British outpost that was not in American hands, those he was trying to elude were also in something of a panic, having been forced to retreat twenty miles upriver from the fort to await supplies and reinforcements. As Carleton made his way down the river, he and his party may well have seen the Americans in retreat. He would not have understood why, but the veteran soldier and accomplished military strategist would have recognized instantly that the American setback, temporary as it undoubtedly was, would give him a period of grace in which to organize his defences.

Carleton was lucky to have been given a second chance. In large measure, his predicament was of his own making. He had failed to anticipate the extent and seriousness of the American threat, and the previous year, without thinking it through, he had sent more than half his soldiers south for the defence of Boston. "Carleton had failed to stop the Americans because he could not raise an army to repel the invaders," said one of his biographers. "He had not foreseen armed confrontation. He had not allowed for the possibility that once hostilities broke out, the rebellious colonists might try to take over Quebec. He had made a big mistake in sending Gage 800 infantry – half his military strength – in the fall of 1774."[16]

The man who was later credited with saving Canada through quick strategic thinking and who was elevated, in the final days of the war, to the post of commander-in-chief of all British troops in North America also overestimated the support that was forthcoming from the French habitants. He had imagined replacing the trained British troops sent south with a fighting force of locals. There were few takers. Sixteen years before, the habitants had clearly taken sides with the French forces fighting the British invaders. This time, it was different. "In 1759, French Canadians were fighting an invader with a different language, religion and culture. In 1775, one group of Englishmen was feuding with another group."[17]

In his fifty-second year – a relatively advanced age for an eighteenth-century military leader still in active service – Carleton was an enigmatic character. To begin with, he was Irish. Born poor in Ulster, Carleton carried himself with an aristocratic air. Although aloof, he inspired loyalty and sometimes devotion from his followers. He was contemptuous of the American rebels, yet he also viewed them with some compassion as simple misguided compatriots who had been misled by democratic demagogues and who would return to the fold of the British Empire once they had played out their youthful folly.

He was a tall handsome man whom history has tagged as looking a bit like George Washington. He was most often described as "aristocratic" and "aloof," serious and stern. General James Wolfe, with whom he had served at Quebec in 1759 and who played a key role in advancing the career of the young Ulsterman, called him "the grave Carleton."

In England, his military mentor the Duke of Richmond described him as "distant and reserved in manner." He was to prove himself an able leader when fortune called, and an able political and administrative governor of Quebec once the fighting was over.[18]

Once he arrived inside the fort that cold Sunday afternoon, Carleton quickly grasped how desperate the situation was. For months the British had been receiving warnings and intelligence about the American invasion. Privately, an air of pessimism and defeatism had settled over the defenders. They imagined the invaders to be well armed and determined. They imagined that the English-speaking traders in Quebec were working for the invaders as fifth columnists. They suspected that the French-speaking habitants, subjects of the British Crown for only a dozen years and far from assimilated, were at least sympathetic to the invaders and maybe even collaborators or active partisans. Inhabitants of the garrison often appeared to assume defeat, even as British leaders concocted fantastic schemes for saving Quebec, including the use of thousands of Russian troops to be sent by the tsar to aid his British ally.

Yet for all the bleak prospects that awaited him inside the fort, Carleton was determined to make the best of the situation he inherited. His presence had an immediate impact, according to historian Hilda Neatby. "If Carleton's thoughts were depressing, they were not paralyzing," she wrote. "His calm or cheerful manner, his energy and confidence, were remarked on from the moment he arrived at Quebec."[19]

That may have been partly because of a packet awaiting him from London with the news that he had been commissioned commander-in-chief of Quebec. Arriving as it did just after Carleton had lost three of the colony's four forts to the enemy, the commission was wreathed with a bit of unintended irony, but for this ambitious military officer it was also a welcome sign that London recognized his military and political skills. "I cannot enough express my gratitude for this mark of favor and confidence His Majesty has been graciously pleased to honor me with," Carleton wrote on 20 November to Lord Dartmouth, the British cabinet minister in charge of the North American colonies.

Still, he could not help but add a note of pessimism about his situation. The man who had worked so hard to finesse the Quebec Act through Parliament as a way to pacify the new French Catholic colony had to admit that it did not appear to have had that effect. "Nor can I enough lament the blind perverseness of this people who frustrate all His [the king's] paternal intentions for their own protection, interest or happiness by an unprecedented defection without even pretending the least cause of complaint ... Besides this base desertion of the Canadian peasantry, which renders impractical any scheme for their own defence founded on the provincial strength alone."

Carleton ended his message to the home government with a dire prediction. "The severe weather is far advanced, we have so many enemies within and foolish people, dupes to those traitors, with their natural fears of men unused to war, I think our fate extremely doubtful, to say nothing worse."[20]

The day before Carleton sent his letter, Hector Crahamé was in the fort, in charge of defences and waiting for the arrival of his commander. In the hours before Carleton unexpectedly arrived, having eluded the American besiegers, Crahamé wrote his own letter to Dartmouth, voicing similar fears: "The enemy without is not so much to be dreaded as their numerous friends within the town."[21]

Why were these two military leaders so pessimistic, given the wretched state of the American army waiting outside the gates?

There are several possible explanations. They were ill informed. They did not realize how truly vulnerable, unprepared, and ill equiped the American troops were. They overestimated the number of American troops coming north and the congressional resolve to do what had to be done and to commit what resources had to be committed to capture Quebec. They overestimated the resolve of French Canadian peasants to join the ranks of the "liberators," misjudging their scepticism about both sides. But perhaps most important, they were reflecting the defeatist panic that seemed to have settled over the British commanders and leaders during that revolutionary autumn of 1775.

As early as the beginning of August, British spies were reporting that the restless thirteen colonies planned an invasion north. On 6 August, Lord Dartmouth had received a secret report from spies in the Boston area, warning that as many as seven thousand Americans would be invading Canada, with "better than half the Canadians having promised to join their forces."[22] That warning was not passed on to Carleton until September.

By then, it was not news to the commander of British forces in Canada. In fact, three months earlier, on 26 June, he had sent a note to Dartmouth telling him of early rumours of a rebel attack through the woods, although the route and the seriousness of the rumour were not known. It is unlikely the Kennebec route would have been considered a potential invasion path.

In London, the news from the colonies during the summer of 1775 was almost uniformly bleak and none more so than news of American victories on the road north. First there was Ticonderoga, then St John, Crown Point, and the rumours of a full invasion into the poorly defended but strategically important Quebec colony. When he first heard about the loss of Ticonderoga, Dartmouth lamented the "backwardness of the Canadians" in not rallying to the benign British side. But he promised a vigorous British response and hoped that the show of strength would convince the French Canadians to stay loyal. "I trust that the resolution here to act with vigor and the knowledge of measures intended for exerting ourselves on the side of Canada ... will have a good effect and inspire more confidence."[23] It was a soothing message, accompanied by news of Carleton's promotion to Canadian commander-in-charge. Of course, Carleton had left for Montreal by the time the letter arrived on the next supply ship and he did not receive the news until 20 November when he was back inside Quebec's walls.

Meanwhile, on Aug. 14, Carleton had written Dartmouth about the growth of support for the American cause inside Quebec. Militias to defend the colony had been organized at Montreal and Trois Rivières, but the peasants were not very cooperative. They had been receiving propaganda from the rebels. Many had been "corrupted, some by more immediate intercourse with the rebels upon their borders and others by the friends of the rebellion residing amongst us."[24]

This flow of troubling news, moving slowly back and forth across the Atlantic Ocean by packet boat, produced several desperate strategies by the government in London. Despite Carleton's distrust of the local Indians as allies ("They are not to be depended upon, especially by those who are in a weakly condition,"[25] he wrote to London during the summer), the government decided to try to buy them off with gifts and guns. In August London dispatched a shipment of bribes worth £2,541 – more than five hundred rifles with walnut stocks, clothing and blankets, utensils, laced beaver hats, bullets, barrels, and pipes. They were, Carleton was told, "presents to the Indians in America."[26]

The deepening panic in London also produced one of the strangest British responses in the history of its uneven and bumbling political and military response to the growing North American crisis – the Russian card. During the summer of 1775, in search of an ally who would ride to the rescue in early 1776, the British government opened negotiations with the Russian government. At one point, it appeared that the Russians would throw tens of thousands of troops into the defence of British North America. Had that happened, it is an interesting historical speculation whether the Russians would have been willing to leave, once the job was done. The Russian empire was growing. It had already intruded into the North American sphere with Russian possession of Alaska. Did the Russian government imagine the British invitation to intervene an easy way to establish a permanent influence in the eastern and southern reaches of the continent, which had long been the commercial and colonizing preserve of the French, British, and Spanish?

The first private British acknowledgment that Russia was being courted came in a letter of 8 September 1775 from Dartmouth to Carleton, informing him that the Russian empress had offered "the fullest assurances of every assistance for suppressing the present unnatural rebellion in the colonies, which the safety and security of her own dominions will admit." The note was sent to alert Carleton that he should prepare some plan to use and accommodate an influx of foreign soldiers that would dwarf the existing army:

In consequence of these assurances, application has been made for a corps of twenty thousand infantry and we hope to be able to send to North America as early as possible in the spring a very considerable body of these auxiliaries. If the ideas of the plan of operation for the next year which have been suggested shall be adopted by Maj. Gen. Howe, it is most probable the greatest part of the Russians will be sent to Quebec and therefore, you will not fail to consider of every preparatory arrangement that may be necessary upon a supposition that we shall not be disappointed in a measure which at present has every promising appearance of success.[27]

As it turns out, the alliance with Russia never did materialize and Britain turned to German mercenaries for their foreign support. In fact, Carleton never did receive the instruction to begin planning for thousands of Russian troops. There was a mix-up in mail going to the transatlantic packets and the letter was not sent as intended. It was just as well. Carleton had his own galaxy of problems to deal with, including some unease about the troops he had under his command and real doubts about the loyalty of the population that he was supposed to protect behind Quebec's walls. He hardly needed to deal with an influx of Russian troops whose political masters probably harboured broader political ambitions than simply helping Britain retain its control of much of North America.

In the tense days before Carleton's arrival, several crucial decisions had already been made about the defence of Quebec. On 11 November the leaders of the garrison decided to block British subjects from leaving the province and several British ships in the harbour that normally would have weighed anchor before freeze-up were asked to stay for the winter as a show of support. Sailors from the ships were offered three pounds sterling each to enlist.

On 16 November they did a head count and identified 1,116 defenders – six Royal Artillery, two officers, and 186 marines from the ship *Lizard*, 133 officers and private seamen from the ships, 68 from a sloop anchored in the harbor, 50 from a second ship, 74 from a merchant ship stranded by the order not to depart, 80 carpenters, 200 British militia stationed at the fort, and 300 Canadian volunteers. Another 11 officers and 132 privates from Newfoundland were expected and in fact arrived within days.

They also did an inventory of supplies – 800 bushels of peas, 406 quarter-barrels of butter, 55 tons of biscuit, 1,500 barrels of wheat, 1,950 barrels of flour, and some rice. The commanders figured these supplies would last until spring, when new supplies could arrive once the ice broke in the harbour. On 16 November, emboldened by this sense of security, the commanders held a council of war at which they decided not to give in to the rebel demands that they surrender and "to defend the town to the last extremity." As noted earlier, they also decided to deny the besiegers shelter by burning houses on the outskirts of the fort, "which may afford shelter to the enemy."[28]

In essence, the defenders decided to have no communication with the rebels and to remain inside the walls. They would resist the temptation to bring the confrontation to a head by leaving the fort to confront and try to defeat the enemy on the Plains of Abraham. In that, they were refusing to repeat history's mistakes. Sixteen years before, General Montcalm had marched his French troops from inside the safety of the fort's walls, lined up against the Redcoats led by James Wolfe, and suffered the defeat that lost France the continent. The British descendants of Wolfe's army were not about to expose themselves in the same way, despite constant intelligence reports of American weaknesses.

The defiant tone of the decision to stick to the front fit nicely into Carleton's own view of how to deal with the rebels. In late October, faced with a growing threat that the rebels would capture Montreal where he was organizing the defence, Carleton was adamant. "I shall return no answer nor enter into any correspondence with rebels," he wrote. "I shall treat all their threats with a silent contempt."[29] Later in the war, he would show compassion for the rebels as wayward brothers, a compassion that left the historical impression that Carleton was an indecisive military leader. He showed none of that indecision when he arrived at Quebec.

Once inside the fort and in charge, Carleton quickly assessed the strengths and weaknesses of his situation. His strengths were obvious – he had the troops and supplies to hold out until spring while the Americans had been weakened by their invasion ordeal and by their lack of money and effective weapons. The weaknesses of his position were equally obvious – the walls of the fort were in a state of disrepair; not all its defenders were there of their own free will – the seamen whose ships were commandeered had no choice – and not all the residents of Quebec could be trusted. Moreover, in the event of a battle, the garrison had inadequate medical supplies. An urgent letter had been sent on 17 November to London by garrison surgeon Adam Mabane, pleading for supplies: "None have been sent since 1760, nor are there any hospital stores of any kind belonging to the King in this town. Instruments of every kind are much wanted. It is impossible without knowing the number of men that will be sent to the relief of Quebec to make out a list of the quantity of medicines which may be necessary or of the stores which should accompany them."[30]

Carleton acted quickly. He ordered the local carpenters to begin to repair the walls of the fort and on 22 November he issued a proclamation aimed at ridding the fort of American sympathizers. Anyone who would not take up arms against the rebels should leave "under the pain of being treated as rebels or spies, if therefore they shall be found within the said limits." The fifth columnists had until December to leave the town. "A number of British merchants, Adam Lymburner at their head, retired into the Island of Orleans, to Charlesbourg or to other places where they had villas, to await the result and hail it with a cry of 'God Save the King or the Congress forever!,' according to the circumstances."[31]

Among the small band that left the safety of the garrison for the uncertainty of life with the besiegers were twenty-nine merchants and their families, including John McCord, Zachary Macaulay, and Edward Antill. One thing they had in common, other than close ties to the thirteen colonies, was that the fur trade was not their main business, though it was at the time the dominant economic activity of the colony and the main tie to the traditional French Canadian economic culture.

This fact has led some Canadian economic nationalists to describe the pro-American dissenters as outsiders, merchants with an eye on profit and a political agenda that included democracy but who did not take into account or express sympathy for the political sensibilities of the French peasant class. Historian Donald Creighton, trail-blazer in economic nationalism, biographer of prime ministers, and proponent of the argument that early Canadian history was shaped by the demands of a relatively simple staple economy, was a leading advocate of the view that economics are the best prism through which to view the decisions taken during the 1775 invasion. "It was the men whose business activities were least attuned to the distinctive commercial system of the north who went over to the enemy," he wrote in 1937 of the merchants who accepted Carleton's invitation to leave rather than take up arms against the American ideals of democracy and early capitalism.[32]

Once Carleton had purged the town of the heretics, untrustworthy, and faint of heart, he and his garrison settled in to await the inevitable attack. Since the defenders would not venture out, the besiegers had to attack. The advantage clearly lay with the British. It was a bitterly cold winter, best endured behind the wind-breaking walls of the city. The area was shrouded with one of the deepest snow blankets in years, drifting almost to the tops of the garrison walls. The American storm-troopers still had to exist in bitter conditions with few supplies. They ate whatever they could hunt for themselves or buy from local peasants. The army was chronically short of money and supplies, including warm clothing.

Time was also on the side of the British. The rebels had a limited opportunity for attack since they knew that, come spring, the harbour would be open and fresh British troops could arrive with supplies. There had to be a winter attack if the American invasion was to be successful.

The American commanders had another, even more serious, timing problem. The American army of the day, which was not meant to be a standing army, was organized around the rule that soldiers, whether volunteers or conscripts, were obliged to serve for just one year at a time. The rule also catered to those revolutionary soldiers who were farmers: while they were off fighting, their farms lay fallow and the food supply of the fledgling nation, and the Revolution, was diminished. At the beginning of the fighting, there was an assumption that soldiers would be called to duty near their homes, allowing them to slip home for planting and then harvesting. A foreign invasion, taking soldiers hundreds of miles away from home, had not been anticipated.

The result was that, as Arnold and Montgomery contemplated their limited options during that bitter snowy autumn of 1775, they were constantly aware that at year's end, many of their troops would be freed from their one-year obligation to the army and would inevitably head home to their farms and families in the southern colonies.

Thus, it was an uneasy, vulnerable army of invasion that settled down outside the walls of Quebec, and many soldiers were more interested in keeping themselves safe until they could go home than in attempting death-defying heroics on the Plains of Abraham.

For both sides, there was one great unknown in the guessing game that would determine the future of Canada – the attitude of the French Canadian population. While the two English armies were squaring off, the French Canadian majority for whom they were fighting was going through its own revolution, complete with competing factions, a conflict between theology and self-interest, and a complex intermingling of politics, history, opportunism, and class warfare.

Superficially, at least, both sides were vying for the support of the French Canadians. The Americans took the rhetorical, political route, issuing proclamations aimed directly at the peasants, promising them freedom and democracy. The invaders were to treat the French as friends, not enemies, Washington had made clear to both Montgomery and Arnold. "We are your friends, not your enemies," said a letter from the Continental Congress distributed through Quebec parishes. "These colonies will pursue no measures whatever but such as friendship and a regard for our mutual safety may suggest."[33] In his letter sent with the invading armies, Washington wrote that the American soldiers were there "not to plunder but to protect you, to animate and bring forth into action those sentiments of freedom you have disclosed and which tools of despotism would extinguish through the whole creation."[34]

At first, the American invaders had reason to believe their appeals had fallen on fertile ground. In many cases, the troops were welcomed by the habitants. The sick were taken in and nursed back to health. Some young men pledged to join the invading army. In southern Quebec, which first saw the spectacle of Arnold's army staggering out of the bush, there was even an early boost for the reputation of the Americans because of some bad translation. "Many of the soldiers wore canvas shirts and somehow, the word became mangled in the translation and word spread through many parishes that these invaders were invincible in part because they wore shirts of sheet iron (*tole*), rather than shirts of canvas (*toile*)," said an unnamed diarist of the time. "The Canadians who saw them first reported that they were a hardy race, not sensible of cold, being *vetu entoile*. The report spread. The word *toile* was changed to *tole*. Then, the rumor ran that the Bostonnais were all covered with sheet iron."[35]

The American military leaders felt confident enough to send back word to Philadelphia that hundreds of French Canadians were anxious to join the invasion force, if money could be sent north to pay them.

For their part, the British took a less democratic, more feudal approach in their appeals for French support, or at least neutrality. Carleton, having won support from the French landlords and clergy for the features of the Quebec Act that guaranteed the property rights of the seigneurs and the religious privileges of the Roman Catholic church, appealed to these Establishment allies to impress upon their humbler countrymen the obligations and subtleties of their own self-interest under British rule. The Church, under the signature of Monsignor Jean Olivier Briand, issued a directive to parishes instructing parishioners to oppose the American rebels. "Your oath and your religion impose upon you the solemn obligation to defend your king and country to the utmost of your power … There is no question of carrying wars into the farther provinces. All that is asked of you is that you lend your aid to repulse the enemy and to withstand the invasion which threatens this province."[36]

These appeals to the French habitants reeked of political hypocrisy. Privately, both sides in the conflict held them in contempt. When the habitants did not rise up against the Americans, Carleton privately accused them of "corruption and may I add the stupid baseness of the Canadian peasantry."[37] It was in part a bit of pique by Carleton, who was disappointed that his hard-won agreement to make Quebec the only British possession where Roman Catholicism was allowed did not win universal French Catholic loyalty. It also reflected the upper-class British view that the French Canadians were, in Lord Dartmouth's dismissive description, "backward." In effect, they did not know their place. There was also a strong anti-Roman Catholic bias built into the attitudes and even the language of the British upper classes.[38] As a group they were not likely to view the French Canadians with respect, even as they appealed publicly for their loyalty.

The Americans, despite their public professions of brotherly love, were no more sympathetic. Many grew up hating the French as the traditional enemy of the Mother Country. Benedict Arnold, for example, had been taught as a boy "that they [the French] were the hated enemy, the murderers of babies and women."[39] The history of the North American colonies was littered with tales of raids, battles, and

atrocities between soldiers and traders from the French Catholic northern colonies and the English Protestant southern colonies.

Added to that was an American fear that the French would export
their Catholicism and anti-democratic traditions south, as well as an
unease that the British would use them as shock troops to tackle the
rebels. This led revolutionary and congressional leaders like John
Hancock to suggest that American-style liberty should be forced upon
Quebeckers, even if they did not seem willing to embrace it voluntarily
or fight for it themselves. Hancock urged an attack on the fortress of
Quebec because it would "greatly facilitate the entire reduction of the
deluded malignants in that province to liberty."[40]

This was far from an expression of sympathy and admiration for
potential brothers-in-arms. It showed a profound contempt for those
the Americans were proposing to liberate.

The French Canadian community, meanwhile, was thrown into volatile
turmoil by the backdraft from the American Revolution. The invasion,
the competing propaganda campaigns, and the demand that they
choose sides created what Quebec historian Gustave Lanctot has called
"a political and religious crisis" in the province.[41] It pitted peasant
against landlord; the Church, farmers, and traders against the aristocracy; neighbours against each other. It threatened to undermine the
progress that the French language, religion, and legal customs had
made under the Quebec Act. And in the end, it revealed a pragmatic
commercial streak among the French that alienated and enraged the
British, Americans, and the traditional Quebec French Establishment.

In good measure, the turmoil was the result of changes that had
taken place within Quebec society since the British conquest sixteen
years before and the political and diplomatic transfer of Quebec into
the British Empire in 1763.[42]

When French rule ended, Quebec was very much a traditional European feudal society. The military leaders, bishops, and landlords were
the power élite. There was a small artisan and commercial class but it
was too small to be a political or cultural counterweight. The bulk of
the population was rural and most depended on farming and the fur
trade for their living. Relations between the seigneur and the peasant
as land steward were orderly and peaceful. Relations between the priest
and the peasant as parishioner were based on obedience. University
of Toronto scholar Allan Greer has described this dual relationship as
a "subtle sort of peasant unfreedom." The peasant understood his

obligation to the landowner, including submitting a portion of his produce as payment. The message was reinforced when he went to church, which, "with a large number of fiefs of its own, was no enemy to seigneurial tenure and it tended to preach submission and respect for feudal obligations."[43] In many areas of Quebec, the church demanded one-twenty-sixth of the annual grain harvest, in addition to fees for services, pews, funerals, and the like.

In the early years of the Conquest, several things contributed to the weakening of this traditional society. The Roman Catholic church became unofficial and while not driven underground, it lost the authority of being the state church. The habitants began to question it, challenge it, and – most devastating of all – ignore it. This had the side-effect of weakening the hold of the landlords as well, since they were allies of the Church.

An even greater erosion of the feudal economic system occurred because of relative prosperity in the province, and the growth in the mercantile economy. "After 1760, the province had 15 years of complete peace, farmers were no longer called from their farms (to work on other landlord lands), and favorable weather resulted in a series of good or excellent crops."[44] They discovered a ready market for their surplus with the English traders who had moved north from the thirteen colonies or west from Europe to take advantage of the post-1763 opportunities that a new British colony offered. They sold produce, received cash, and used it to buy household goods and implements from the traders or their agents.

With these developments, the peasants developed an independence of thought and action that they had not had under the French *ancien régime*. It was encouraged by the traders who were influenced by the democratic and egalitarian philosophies taking hold in New England in support of an elected assembly for Quebec and a diminution of the power of the traditional élites. The traders demonstrated the weakness of the ruling authorities by openly promoting and distributing American propaganda and by collecting and shipping one thousand bushels of grain south to rebels enduring the British blockade of Boston in 1774. The peasants undoubtedly took note.

The result, according to Lanctot, was the development of a form of egalitarianism that, while not as aggressive as in New England, still marked Quebec off from its former self. "This spirit of equality, which surprised both newcomers from France and travelers from other lands, was the result of certain factors in the environment: the habit of self-sufficiency, the autonomy of militia companies, the absence of privileged classes, the comparative poverty of the seigneurs and the contrasting prosperity of the very well-to-do peasants living like minor noblemen in France."[45]

Carleton sensed this. In a letter of 4 February 1775 to General Gage outside Boston, he suggested that the French Canadian habitants could no longer be counted upon to obey their superiors. The post-Conquest government had been so lenient, and the traditional author-ity system so eroded, that the habitants had "in a manner emancipated themselves and it will require time and discreet management likewise to (return) them to their ancient habits of obedience and discipline."[46]

Yet by using the Quebec Act that year to try to win the support of the élites and the clergy through reimposition of religious and seigneurial privilege, Carleton fell into the trap of expecting the habitants to follow their leaders: "His political ideal for the command he held was the soldier-aristocrat's ideal of order, obedience and 'subordination from highest to lowest,'" wrote Donald Creighton. "Inevitably, he came to see what a soldier-aristocrat wished to see in Quebec society – an insignifi-cant group of transient merchants, an influential landed gentry, and an overwhelming majority of simple, untutored, biddable peasants."[47]

On some level, the French Canadian peasants should have been susceptible to American liberation theology. The seeds of radical thought had been planted in what might have been the fertile soil of a conquered people. Yet there are reasons why it did not immediately produce a harvest of revolutionary converts. In many ways, the Quebec that the American soldiers marched through still resembled the Quebec of an earlier age. It was a close-knit rural society. The houses were wooden and cramped, created in the "*pièce-sur-pièce*" style of squared logs piled horizontally, secured by joints or posts at the cor-ners. The larger dwellings measured roughly thirty feet by twenty-five feet. Downstairs there were two or three rooms; upstairs was storage and sleeping quarters for the children. Farm buildings in the back were roofed with thatch.

Most habitant houses were heated by a box stove, although the cook-ing was done on an open fireplace. The houses were cramped, stifling, crowded, and smoky. But "they were warm and well-equipped for activ-ities such as cooking, eating, sleeping, socializing and craft work. They were built for the basic security and comfort of family members, not for projecting an impression of status. Above all, the buildings them-selves, as well as their contents, were for the most part made by Habi-tants for Habitants."[48]

It was a society in which most people married young and produced many children, one-quarter of whom would not live to celebrate their first birthday. The water supply was often polluted by run-off from the humans or the farm animals.

The vast majority of habitants could not read or write, and this illiteracy worked against the invading Americans, with their sheets of liberation propaganda. In the 1750s and 1760s, parish records indicate that fewer than ten percent of the men of Quebec could write. This meant that for news and public opinion, the habitants largely depended upon the priests or educated gentry, who supported the *status quo*, or word-of-mouth tales that were not always reliable. The first printing press was not established in Montreal until 1776 and the first influx of skilful printers did not come until the Loyalists fled north after the Revolution.[49]

The level of illiteracy had a profound effect on the ability of the demagogues of democracy to radicalize Quebecers, as they had radicalized the more literate New Englanders with tracts denouncing tyranny. "The possible implications of changing levels of popular literacy go well beyond the realm of ideologies and politics," wrote Allan Greer in a study of literacy rates in New France. "It has often been claimed that illiterate societies are more resistant to change, less open to influences beyond the immediate community than are literate societies."[50]

In the early days of the invasion, however, the Americans could be forgiven for believing that they were among friends in the Quebec countryside. They were greeted warmly, often fed and nursed back to health and supplied with goods sold by traders and habitants who were more than willing to have dealings with the enemy. Despite a warning from some bishops that anyone cooperating with the rebels would be denied the sacraments or even excommunicated, many locals had discarded their "ancient habits of obedience" and acted as allies. "The Habitants welcomed them, sold them supplies and services and a number took arms on their side."[51]

In the end, perhaps several hundred French Canadians took up arms for the invaders. As many joined the British defenders. Most decided to sit it out, waiting to see who won.

Historians have long speculated about why the recently conquered French Canadians did not take the American invasion as a chance to stand up to their British conquerors. Had they done so, the American

chances would clearly have been significantly better. The British
defenders were few and isolated. A province in revolt, fuelled by American promises of freedom and democracy, would have tested, and perhaps defeated, the British defences. Cramahé, Carleton's second-in-
command, had already warned London about the consequences if
Quebec fell into enemy hands. "Two battalions in the spring might
have saved the province," he wrote in November 1775. "I doubt
whether twenty would regain it."[52]

With the opportunity to throw off the British occupiers so close at
hand, why did the French Canadians not jump at it? Both British and
American leaders lamented what they saw as the French tendency to
do what they had to do to stay out of the line of fire, to support
whichever side appeared to be winning, and to disappear when they
were proven wrong. Quebec historian Gustave Lanctot offered an
explanation: "True Normans, shrewd and argumentative, the Habitants
meant to remain neutral in the struggle and masters of their own
province. They had no intention of going off to be killed either for
the English or the American cause."[53]

It was also clear that many French Canadians had heard and understood the hypocrisy in the American message – the invaders appealed
to the discontent among French Catholics while privately denouncing
their religion, their attitudes, and their language.

Noting the booming economy that had helped the rural areas after
1763, the arguments of the élite and Church against the invaders, and
the British concessions in the Quebec Act, historian Dominique Marshall
posed a reasonable question: "If the peasants were not economically
unhappy or feeling tremendously oppressed, what would be their moti-
vation to join a revolution or an invading army that was going to throw
their world into chaos?"[54]

For most habitants, the obvious answer was that they were not interested. It was different for merchants and others who were involved in
the commercial system. Quebec residents with something to sell were
happy to deal with the invaders, as long as they had Yankee gold to
spend. "I have this minute arrived here and met my express from the
French inhabitants who, he tells me, are rejoiced to hear we are
coming and that they will gladly supply us with provisions," Arnold
wrote in a message to those of his troops who had not yet reached
Quebec.[55] It was true. The French proved only too happy to sell goods
to the invaders, at least in the early weeks of the invasion when the
prospects for victory looked good and the American money was presumed to be valuable.

Of course, contact with the Americans did not mean success for every Quebec merchant. Richelieu Valley trader Samuel Jacobs, one of Arnold's commercial contacts in the years before the invasion, was an example. Jacobs, a German Jew, had arrived in Quebec after the Conquest of 1759 as a supplier of the British troops. He settled in St Denis and established a thriving trading business, buying supplies from local farmers and then dealing them to travelling traders like Arnold. Jacobs was willing to deal with the Americans in the early days of the invasion, undoubtedly counting on his friendly relations with one of the leaders of the invasion as an entrée to what looked like a lucrative new customer base.

Problems soon began as Montgomery's army moved into Quebec through the Richelieu Valley in the autumn of 1775. At first, the Americans seized a boat Jacobs was having built at St Charles and used it to transport their own supplies. Then, when they arrived at Quebec City, the Americans commandeered a schooner Jacobs owned. It was filled with merchandise, which the Americans seized. To make matters worse, some of his traditional Canadian customers took advantage of the breakdown to refuse to pay their debts.

The result was that Jacobs, an influential local figure with traditional ties to the New England traders and no real reason to oppose them, became a bitter enemy. "The undermining of the established order would, along with the seizure of the two vessels, account for the hostility of Jacobs, who otherwise should have had more reason to sympathize with the 'Bostonnais' than with his French Canadian neighbors," wrote historian Allan Greer, who profiled Jacobs in a study of rural Quebec life.[56]

The merchant's story had a happy ending. When the British army reoccupied the Richelieu Valley in the summer of 1776, Jacobs became a supplier to British troops and grew prosperous in the process. He died in 1786 a rich man, owner of a thriving trading business and many area farms.

On the whole, the American invaders expected an outpouring of support and hundreds of eager recruits from among habitants. But they mistook commercial eagerness for political support and in the end few French Canadians joined the cause. Most were content to stand on the sidelines, waiting to see which side would triumph. "As long as the fate of the country was uncertain, they would maintain an attitude of friendly but passive sympathy towards the army of occupation."[57] During the early months of the invasion, enthusiastic neutrality was the order of the day for most of the French population.

More than a century later, prominent Quebec nationalist and journalist Henri Bourassa explained the French Canadian refusal to join the American invaders as follows: "It was all very simple," he wrote. "We had to choose between the English of Boston and the English of London. The English of London were further away and we hated them less."[58]

The truth of that became clearer the longer the American occupation of Quebec continued.

8

The Battle for Quebec

When Benedict Arnold led his troops across the river to the plains before Quebec fortress, he had a simple plan. "The town is very short of provisions but well fortified," he reported to George Washington in a letter of 8 November 1775. "I shall endeavor to cut off their communication with the country, which I hope to be able to effect, and bring them to terms, or at least keep them in close quarters until the arrival of Gen. Montgomery, which I wait with impatience."[1] This letter was intercepted by the British.

Arnold had several weeks to wait, during which time he tried to lure the British out to fight, then discovered he was ill equipped to fight anyway and retreated with his men twenty miles west of the fortress to Point-aux-Trembles. There, on 3 December, "to my great joy Gen. Montgomery joined us with artillery and about 300 men."[2] Within hours, the combined force marched back before the walls of the city and began to plan the assault on the fort, "which has a wretched, motley garrison of disaffected seamen, marines and inhabitants, the walls in a ruinous situation and cannot hold out long." Arnold willingly relinquished his command to Montgomery.

By all historical accounts, Arnold respected Montgomery and was happy to take orders from him. The two men got along well. Arnold admired Montgomery's decisiveness, charisma, and experience. Montgomery appreciated his junior's character, natural leadership ability, stamina, bravery, optimism, and strategic thinking. "Richard Montgomery was Benedict Arnold's model of what a soldier should be and in December, 1775, the two were like brothers," wrote historian Willard Randall. "In the company of able leaders who appreciated him, like

Montgomery, Washington and Schuyler, Arnold not only never got into trouble but always played the cheerful subordinate."[3]

On 5 December, from their new position of strength within sight of the walls, the Americans posted soldiers on all roads around the town, effectively cutting it off from any help from the countryside. Two days later, they sent a woman into the city. As Carleton later told the tale: "The 7th, a woman stole into town with letters addressed to the principal merchants, advising them to an immediate submission and promising great indulgence in case of their compliance. Inclosed [*sic*] was a letter to me in very extraordinary language and a summons to deliver up the town. The messenger was sent to prison for a few days and drummed out."[4]

The next day, Arnold approached the walls with a white flag and another appeal for surrender. The British would not accept the letter and sent him on his way. Carleton was being true to the heritage of his Ulster past where, eighty-five years before, a group of Protestant apprentices had closed the gates of Londonderry rather than submit to the Catholic forces of King James II. For months they held out inside the walls, suffering from starvation, disease, and deprivation. Their slogan was "No surrender." In the end, the siege of Derry was lifted by the Dutch prince William of Orange. It became a defining moment in the collapse of the Catholic claim to the English throne.

Inside the walls of Quebec, Carleton and his troops were equally adamant there would be no surrender to the American pretenders. On 6 December, a confident Montgomery tried to convince Carleton that his cause was hopeless. "I am well acquainted with your situation," he wrote in a message sent into the city, "a great extent of works in their nature incapable of defence, manned with a motley crew of sailors, the greatest part our friends, of citizens who wish to see us within their walls and a few of the worst troops who ever called themselves soldiers." He also told Carleton he knew the garrison's supplies were limited. "I am at the head of troops accustomed to success, confident of the righteousness of the cause they are engaged in, inured to danger and fatigue and so highly incensed at your inhumanity, illiberal abuse and the ungenerous means employed to prejudice them in the minds of Canadians that it is with difficulty I restrain them till my batteries are ready."[5]

This clearly was as much propaganda, bombast, and intimidation as it was truth. The American army was already having problems. It was not as large or as well equipped as Montgomery would have wanted. There were quarrels among the men as some, including the Virginia riflemen, set about looting and stealing, contrary to Arnold's and

Washington's orders. "The person of a Tory or his property became fair game," wrote John Henry after soldiers ransacked the house of a prominent British defender that lay outside the walls of the garrison. He had fled inside for protection. The next day, there was another plundering, local habitants having directed the Americans to their landlord enemies. Henry said that after that trip, during which a farm was "stripped," plundering ceased. "It is a solemn truth that we plundered none but those who were notoriously Tories and then, within the walls of Quebec."[6]

Meanwhile, some men, spurred on by Arnold's enemies in the army, refused to serve under him and wanted to be transferred to other commanders. And as the days passed, of course, increasing numbers of men were nearing the end of their commitment to the army and looking forward to midnight 31 December, when they could leave for home without being accused of desertion and risking an American bullet in the back. Henry noted the restlessness among his fellow revolutionary foot soldiers. "Many of the New England troops had been engaged on very short enlistments, some of which were to expire on the first of January, 1776. The patriotism of the summer of '75 seemed almost extinguished in the winter of '76."[7]

Just as seriously, death had begun to stalk the American encampment. Smallpox, one of the great killers of the day, made an appearance in early December as the weather turned warmer and rainy. "The smallpox is among them," noted a diarist inside the fortress. "'Tis a fatal disorder in an American constitution. They die of mere apprehension. They are a dispirited people when attacked by sickness."[8] In this case, despite the dismissive view from an enemy observer, the Americans were not falling sick and dying from "apprehension" but from a disease that in those days was usually unstoppable.

An American victory against the fort, therefore, was still far from certain, despite Montgomery's bravado and the various commanders' efforts to figure out the best plan of attack.

On 9 December the British fired on the American camp, inflicting one casualty. "The enemy's fire did us no harm except killing an old French woman ... administering a spirituous potion to one of our lads," noted the army doctor, Isaac Senter.[9] The next day the Americans fired back, sending forty-three shots over the walls into the fort. They did no damage. Then the weather worsened as the wind shifted from south-west to north-west, blowing in cold air that turned the rain to snow and the wet streets into "sheets of ice" inside the town. "There was no stirring without creepers," wrote an anonymous diarist inside

Quebec.[10] On 15 December a drummer led two Americans wrapped
in blankets to the walls, where they demanded a meeting with Carleton
to offer him one last chance to surrender. The British guards ordered
them away and with them went the last hope for a bloodless end to
the siege.

The next few days featured a sporadic exchange of gunfire with no
real impact. The weather remained bitterly cold and windy. The anonymous diarist could only gloat from the warmth of his house. "Wind
at west, very cold," he wrote on 20 December. "Nothing remarkable
happened last night. If this weather continues, Mr Montgomery will
find it difficult to eat his Christmas dinner at Quebec ... it is reported
that he swore 'he'd dine in Quebec or in Hell on Christmas Day.' We
are determined that he shall not dine with us and be his own master
... The weather is very severe indeed! No man, after having been
exposed to the open air but for 10 minutes, could handle his arms to
do execution. One's senses are benumbed. If they ever attack us, it will
be in mild weather."[11]

For the next few days, there were a series of false alarms, rumours
of attack, and tension. "Everything was remarkably quiet last night,"
wrote the diarist on Christmas Day. "We saw lights in every quarter,
which we took for signals."[12]

For both sides, it was a waiting game. The British awaited the American
attack. The Americans were waiting for a cloudy night when the moon
was obscured so that they could attack under the cover of deep darkness.

Remarkably, just when the decisive moment arrived is a matter of
historical dispute. Conventional wisdom places it after nightfall on
31 December 1775 and into the early hours of the new year. Thus,
Willard Randall writes: "December 31 at 8:00 P.M., a gale was coming
and in Ste Foy, soldiers were being told to be ready at midnight." At
2:00 A.M., they were ready to march and at 5:00 A.M. the first clash
between attackers and defenders began.[13]

Benedict Arnold, in his battlefield letters, indicated otherwise. His
first report, sent to Gen. David Wooster, who replaced Montgomery as
the military commander at Montreal, was dated 31 December. He said
that the clash had started the previous evening. Lest that be considered
an error, he sent a second letter on 2 January that talked of his earlier
letter "three days since."[14] It seems likely that the battle actually began
a day earlier than it is dated in most historical accounts, in the midst
of a fierce snowstorm that obscured the moon but also piled up the
drifts, soaked the American guns and powder, and made their advance
through deep snow slow and difficult. An attack on 30 December

would make sense, since many soldiers clearly planned to leave and head home the next day at midnight when their enlistment expired.

The American plan was to carry out a "pincer" movement. Montgomery would lead a troop of men along the shore of the St Lawrence at the base of the cliff – a point called Cape Diamond– fighting past several guard towers on the narrow road and then climbing the road from Lower Town into the streets of the city on top of the hill, on the eastern side of the fortress facing the St Lawrence. Meanwhile, Arnold would feign attacks on several of the gates in the wall that stretched across the west side of the Upper Town and then attack through a gate at the north end of the Lower Town wall. Inside the fortress, the two American forces would meet.

The plan, concocted by Montgomery and quickly passed on to the British defenders by spies and deserters, was a disaster. The weakest part was Montgomery's assignment. The British were alerted, the church bells rang in the night, and guards were at their posts by the time the first American soldiers struggled into view through the snow. The young American soldier John Henry described it later as a fierce night. "The storm was outrageous and the cold wind extremely biting," he wrote. "In this northern country, the snow is blown horizontally into the faces of travelers on most occasions. This was our case."[15]

In 1972 the American author Michael Pearson told the story dramatically and with literary licence as he described a bitterly cold, windy night with a fierce snowstorm blowing over the tense community:

At 4:00 A.M., the officer of the guard, Capt. Malcolm Fraser of the Royal Highland Emigrants, trudged along the wall with his body bent before the gale, on his routine rounds. As he approached the posts at the southern end of the walls, he saw what looked like musket flashes on the heights but he was puzzled because he could not hear any shots. He questioned the sentries facing Cape Diamond, which overlooked the St Lawrence, and they said they had seen the flashes for some time. He moved back along the wall and asked the guards at the next post about the lights. "Like lamps in the street," was how one man described them. Fraser guessed that they were lanterns and that the rebels were forming for attack. He ordered the alarm.[16]

There followed a scurry of activity and as some of the Americans began to shoot, their positions were exposed. Defenders, recently roused from their beds, returned the fire. A line of men, led by Arnold, was seen passing along the north of the town, along a path that would lead into St Roch on the outskirts of Quebec. On the other side of the town was the sheer cliff of Cape Diamond. The road along the base of the cliff leading up the hill and into the town was guarded by a blockhouse that had been a brewery building. It was defended by a battery of three-pound guns and close to fifty men – Quebec residents, seamen, and one Royal Artillery officer in charge. Out of the darkness of the night, they saw men trudging towards them from the west, almost single file as they struggled through the snow and ice. Thomas Ainsley, a customs officer serving as a militia captain, was among the defenders. They held their fire until the Americans made a run for the blockhouse. "The gunners put their matches to the touch holes and the explosions as the guns went off in those confines were deafening. The musketeers squeezed their triggers and swiftly reloaded. 'Our musketry and guns,' Ainsley wrote, 'continued to sweep the avenue leading to the battery for some minutes. When the smoke cleared, there was not a soul to be seen.'"[17]

There were, however, thirteen bodies bleeding in the snow, General Montgomery's among them. Aaron Burr organized a retreat. Half the pincer had been severed.

The other half fared a little better. They attacked the St Roch Gate and a fierce fight ensued. Many of the rebels actually breached the wall and gained access to the town. Arnold was not among them. He was hit in the right leg after more than an hour of intense fighting. As he was carried back through the line, he urged the Connecticut troops to continue the attack. "Hurry on, boys. Hurry on."[18]

Henry Dearborn was with a group of close to a dozen attackers who became lost in the confusion of that night. When they finally found themselves near some British defenders, he tried to shoot but discovered his gun was wet and useless. The powder and flint were wet. It would not fire. They had to retreat and eventually were captured. At one point during the night, Dearborn stumbled upon the scene of the wounded Arnold being carried from the front, blood streaming from his leg. "When I arrived at St Rock's, I met Col Arnold wounded, borne and brought away by two men," the soldier wrote in his diary. "He spoke to me and desired me to push forward ..."[19]

Daniel Morgan, a Virginia rifleman, took charge of the troops who had entered the town and led them for several hours of combat through the streets until, near dawn on 31 December, the Americans were trapped and surrendered. Morgan's men had entered the attack with paper banners attached to their hats proclaiming: "Liberty or Death." Most of them that night were blessed with neither.

The attack had been a failure. The last, best chance the Americans had to capture a fourteenth colony disappeared on that snowy, bloody night at Quebec. It was a complete victory for the British defenders. Although accounts vary, the most credible tally is that as many as one hundred Americans had been killed, while 426 men, including most of the Kennebec marchers, were taken prisoner. As many as one hundred New York troops took advantage of the expiry of their army obligation to abandon their comrades and head for home.[20]

The prisoners were herded into warehouses, to be kept under guard until the siege was lifted. Young John Henry was one of them. Like most, he was released the following autumn and sent home. He had followed Arnold, and then Morgan, into the streets of Quebec and once in prison he became feeble and ill. He never totally recovered and played no further significant role in the Revolution.

Rhode Island soldier Capt. William Humphrey was also taken prisoner, claiming in his diary that with a blanket and some straw, he was made "very comfortable" in captivity. He lamented that surviving the march through Maine only to "bring me to this place to be made a prisoner ... I think to be no great favor." Still, the dead and wounded had sacrificed for "a glorious cause."[21]

The day after the battle, Montgomery's body was found at the base of the cliff. He was carried into the town, to a house on what is now Rue St Louis, and buried a day later with full military honours by his adversary and one-time military ally Guy Carleton. In modern-day Quebec City, a plaque a few blocks west of the Château Frontenac Hotel marks the spot where Montgomery's body rested, in the house of one Jean Gaubert, before burial.

On 31 December, in their camp outside the walls of Quebec, the Americans were filled with the bitter after-taste of defeat and confusion about what really had happened the previous night. Hundreds of troops had not returned from the battle. The American force in the camp numbered approximately eight hundred, half of them French Canadian militia. What had happened to Morgan and the men Arnold had left inside the walls? Were they prisoners or had they captured part of the town?

At a building known as "the general hospital" where the wounded were being treated, a defiant Arnold lay in pain. With Montgomery's death, he had inherited leadership of the tattered and demoralized troop force before Quebec. In the days ahead, he would sometimes doubt himself or privately express pessimism about the venture. But in the early hours after the débâcle, there was no public display of fear or doubt. Through those dark hours, Arnold's leadership abilities came to the fore. As usual, he led by example.

The tone was set within hours. In the camp, there was a fear among the survivors that the British would emerge from the walls to finish the previous night's work. Aides around Arnold, including Dr Senter, wanted to move the headquarters and the commander away from a vulnerable position within sight of the walls. The defiant commander would hear none of it. Nor would he consider proposals that his leg be amputated. "We entreated Col Arnold, for his own safety, to be carried back into the country where they [the British] would so not readily find him out, but to no purpose," Senter recorded in his diary. "He would neither be removed nor suffer a man from the hospital to retreat. He ordered his pistols loaded with a sword on his bed, adding that he was determined to kill as many as possible if they came into the room."[22]

In a letter to Washington, Arnold later described the decision as a matter of tactics rather than bravery. "I could not approve the measure as it would undoubtedly have made unfavourable on the minds of the Canadians, and induced them to withdraw their assistance, which must have ended in our utter ruin. I therefore put the best face on matters and betrayed no marks of fear."[23]

In fact, within a week, Arnold was recovered and confident enough to write to his sister Hannah and his sons back in Connecticut that all was well. "I have no thoughts of leaving this proud town until I first enter it in triumph," he wrote. "My wound has been exceeding painful but is now easy and the surgeons assure me will be well in eight weeks. I know you will be anxious for me. That Providence which has carried me through so many dangers is still my protection. I am in the way of my duty and know no fear."[24]

In the immediate aftermath of the defeat, one hundred of Arnold's surviving troops and officers marched east to the safety of occupied Montreal. "It was with the greatest difficulty I could persuade the rest to make a stand," Arnold later told Washington. "The panic soon subsided. I arranged the men in such order as effectually to blockade the city, and enable them to assist each other if attacked."[25]

A few days before, on the bleak day of 31 December, Arnold, lying in pain in a hospital bed, wrote a letter to Gen. David Wooster, the American commander who had replaced Montgomery in Montreal and who was, in effect, the new commander of the Northern Army.

The letter was a remarkable feat of clear thinking and accurate reporting. The plan of attack the previous day had been changed, Arnold wrote, because of information leaks to the enemy. Instead of simultaneous attacks on upper and lower towns, Montgomery had decided that there would be two attacks on Lower Town, coming from different directions. Arnold was assigned an assault on St Roch's gate and breached it but came up against a two-gun battery. After a brave, hour-long defence by the British, it was captured. "With the loss of a number of men, we carried it."

Arnold was one of the casualties and was carried to the hospital "where I soon heard the disagreeable news that the General was defeated at Cape Diamond, himself, Captain Macpherson, his aide-de-camp and Captain Cheeseman killed on the spot." After Arnold was wounded, he lost contact with troops. They took a second barrier but were attacked from behind by British troops. "The last accounts from my detachment, about ten minutes since, they were pushing for the Lower Town. Their communication with me was cut off. I am exceedingly apprehensive what the event will be. They will either carry the Lower Town, be made prisoners or cut to pieces. I thought proper to send an express to let you know the critical situation we are in ..."[26]

He said he was passing command to a subordinate while he was confined to bed and asked that Congress be informed so that help could be sent. "The loss of my detachment, before I left it, was about two hundred men killed or wounded." Arnold added a postscript to his letter to Wooster. "It is impossible to say what our future operations will be until we know the fate of my detachment."

On 2 January his worst fears were confirmed. Maj. Return Meigs, taken prisoner, was sent out of the garrison with a white flag to collect the personal effects of the other prisoners. He told Arnold that all the missing had been either captured or killed. While General Carleton was claiming that American casualties exceeded one hundred, Meigs said he thought there were no more than sixty killed and wounded. The remaining three hundred or so were prisoners.

This led Arnold to send the following casualty report to Washington and Congress on 14 January:

The brave and amiable General Montgomery, killed; Capt. Macpherson, his aide-de-camp, killed; Capt. Cheeseman, First Battalion Yorkers, killed; Capt. Hendricks, Pennsylvania Riflemen, killed; Lieut Humphreys. Virginia Riflemen, killed; Lieut Cooper, Connecticut, killed.

Col Arnold, wounded in the leg; Maj. Ogden, in the shoulder; Capt. Lamb of the Train, in the head; Capt. Hubbard, slightly; Capt. Topham, slightly; Adjutant Steel, slightly; Quartermaster Taylor, slightly.

Non-commissioned officers and privates killed and wounded, about sixty – names unknown. The whole detachment, prisoners, except Captains Smith, Burr and Hopkins, seven subalterns and about two hundred privates, sick and on command.[27]

The attack on the Quebec fortress had been a bloody disaster. Now Arnold faced the unhappy prospect of convincing his dispirited and battered men to maintain a winter siege almost certain to fail without Divine, or at least political, intervention. Once again, his leadership mettle would be tested.

9

Siege and Retreat

As Arnold took stock, it became clear that the British defenders were far from his only adversaries. He lacked resources and men; he faced disease and harsh winter conditions; he had evidently lost local and political credibility with the failure of the attack; and he had to battle a morale problem in what was left of his army. He also had to deal with Gen. David Wooster, in charge of the troops in Montreal and the most senior American commander in Quebec since the death of Montgomery.

Wooster was an unlikely military commander. He was a veteran of the Connecticut militia with little experience in the field, sixty-five years old, overweight and tired, with a fondness for the bottle. He had little use for Arnold, the brash young commander who had humiliated him less than a year before in Connecticut by demanding the keys to the weapons cache so that the Connecticut militia could march to Boston. Now the two were supposed to work together and Wooster, though more than a hundred miles from the action, was in charge. He would be of little help, despite Arnold's increasingly desperate pleas. He had little stomach for getting closer to the action or for helping those on the front line. He may even have taken pleasure in seeing Arnold's star tarnished.

Wooster certainly knew about the plight of the troops outside Quebec. Three days after the attack, Arnold sent a second letter to Montreal, pleading for reinforcements. A measure of desperation was creeping into the plea. He had just four hundred Americans and the same number of French Canadians. He was short of guns, food, troops, and money. There were troop defections and he needed reinforcements. "Many of the troops are dejected and anxious to get home and some have actually set off. I shall endeavor to continue the blockade while there are any hopes of success. For God's sake, order as many men down as you can possibly spare, consistent with the safety of Montreal, and all the mortars, howitzers and shells that you can possibly bring. I hope you will stop every rascal who has deserted from us and bring him back again."[1]

He said the besieging force had no more than five hundred pounds in cash and just twenty barrels of salt pork – hardly enough to last the army a few weeks at small rations. "If any can be spared from Montreal, I think best to bring it down and all the butter."

He asked Wooster to urge Congress to send at least eight or ten thousand soldiers north to "form a lasting connection with this country." He complained of his "excessive pain," said he would not be back to full capacity for two months, and urged Wooster to come from Montreal to take charge. "Many officers here appear dispirited. Your presence will be absolutely necessary."[2]

Little came of this appeal. On 4 January he wrote again from his sickbed, noting that many of the French Canadians who had joined were not armed. He needed weapons from the main force at Montreal, as well as "three or four hundred pair of snow shoes, a few barrels of sugar for the hospital and fifty light shovels." He also reported more personnel problems – one captain was being sent back under arrest for sabotaging the force by igniting some powder barrels. Colonel Nicholas was being sought for deserting. "I hope you will think it necessary to send back every soldier who has deserted from us under the pretense of his time being out."[3]

That evening, a French Canadian who had fought for the Americans and been captured, and who had then feigned conversion to the British cause, was sent out of the fort with instructions to incite the French countryside to rise up against the Americans. Arnold reported this in a letter to Wooster, along with an urgent warning that the besieging army was out of lead for bullets. In a rare moment of public self-doubt, he begged Wooster to replace him. "The burden lies very heavy on me, considering my present circumstances. I find myself unequal to the task. My wound is in a fair way and less painful." He said the front was quiet and he hoped that Carleton was afraid to venture out to test their strength. "I pray God they may not, for we are in a miserable condition to receive them."[4]

After a week, having heard nothing from Wooster, Arnold scrawled a note to Congress, explaining his poor writing by the fact that he was "confined to my bed with my wound and a severe fit of the gout." It was an optimistic letter, considering Arnold's state, filled with information and regret about Montgomery's death and the defeat of 31 December, yet brimming with confidence that if Congress sent help, the mission could still be salvaged. "I beg leave to recommend the sending of a body of at least five thousand men, with an experienced General, into Canada as early as possible and in the meantime, that every possible preparation of mortars, howitzers and some heavy cannon should be made." His plan was that by mid-March, fire could be directed towards the town to set alight some of the buildings inside the walls and force the garrison to negotiate.

Arnold insisted the garrison was weak. Fifteen hundred troops were there to protect a total population of four thousand and many of those troops were untrustworthy, or else Carleton would have counterattacked. The French would welcome the Americans, but they were under the discipline of the British. Meanwhile, the American besiegers kept up their guard duty, despite harsh conditions, a lack of supplies, and almost no cash to buy more. "Their duty is exceedingly hard. However, the men appear alert and cheerful, though wanting many necessities which cannot be procured here."[5]

On 12 January Arnold learned that Wooster would not come from Montreal to replace him but would send an officer instead. He would assign no more than two hundred soldiers from Montreal, claiming the remainder were needed to defend the town, which was not under attack. Arnold decided to hire French Canadians into the army, not as volunteers but as paid soldiers with the same status as the Americans. It was the first time foreigners were integrated into American forces and it was done by Arnold without congressional approval. He believed that he had no choice.

On 23 January one hundred men arrived from Montreal with the promise of sixty more to come. The next day, Arnold wrote again to Congress that while the British garrison was strong, he thought it could be taken with support from the south in the form of money, men, and arms. "Our finances are low," he wrote. "We have been obliged to beg, borrow and squeeze to get money for our subsistence."[6]

Over the next weeks, Arnold watched anxiously as events conspired against his troops. Smallpox increasingly took its toll in the camp. The British tried several times to capture American guns by venturing out past the city walls. Domestic political intrigues continued to plague Arnold, both in Quebec and back home. Congress continued to send out signals that it would not send the thousands of troops he believed were needed. His enemies in Congress and in the army often won praise that should in part have gone to Arnold. Meanwhile, the peasants increasingly refused to accept American paper money for the food and supplies Arnold's army desperately needed.

There was the occasional piece of good news to keep Arnold's spirits up. On 27 February he received a letter of praise and support from Washington. The commander-in-chief repeated his assertion that what happened in the frozen fields of Quebec would determine the fate of the Revolution. Arnold, in typical fashion, replied by deflecting any praise to his troops and to his God. "The repeated successes of our raw, undisciplined troops over the flower of the British army, the many unexpected and remarkable occurrences in our favor, are plain proofs of the over-ruling hand of Providence and justly demands our warmest gratitude to Heaven, which I make no doubt will crown our virtuous efforts with success."[7]

In the same letter he told Washington that his own health was better, despite continued discomfort and obvious impairment. "My wound is entirely healed and I am able to hobble about my room, though my leg is a little contracted and weak. I hope soon to be fit for action." But as he wrote optimistically about his own health, Arnold was dealing with a crisis that threatened to destroy his little army more surely and swiftly than British bullets. Up to one hundred of his men were sick with smallpox. Eventually he authorized the inoculation of troops, against army orders. Arnold brushed aside the rules and ordered doctors in Montreal to attempt the then new and very controversial technique of vaccination. It saved scores of lives. Other troops, under different leaders, were not so lucky.

He also had to deal with insubordination as his old nemesis John Brown showed up with more than one hundred men from Montreal insisting that he be promoted from his rank of major. Arnold knew that this was a long-standing dispute, unresolved by Montgomery before he was killed. Brown had been accused of pilfering British supplies when the fort at Sorel was captured. It was, Arnold wrote to congressional president John Hancock, "a great scandal of the American army" that had damaged the image of the invading army. He would not promote Brown until the issue had been resolved; he noted that Montgomery had taken the same position before he died. By insisting that Montgomery had promised a promotion, Brown was in effect putting words in the mouth of a corpse who could not correct the record. Arnold told Hancock that Brown and others in the same boat would likely plead their cause to Congress. He wanted all the facts known and asked that his letter be shown to Brown so that he would know the accusation.[8] Considering the trouble that Brown had caused Arnold over the years, Arnold's insistence that Brown be given a chance to defend himself before the politicians was a remarkable act of restraint by a commander living and working under duress on the front line.

Meanwhile, Arnold's troops had reason to be disgruntled. No reinforcements were coming from the south. While officers in the field were not being promoted, some of those who had deserted the previous autumn with Enos were back in the army and had been promoted. The Quebec troops were cold, "illy-clad and worse paid."[9] Arnold took his plea for a replacement directly to Washington, since Wooster would not respond. "In short," he wrote, "the choice of difficulties I have had to encounter has rendered it so very perplexing that I have often been at a loss how to conduct matters."[10]

Four years later, as Arnold stood before an army court-martial hearing in a tavern in Morristown, New Jersey, to answer charges that he had abused power, he recalled those bleak days on the fields before Quebec. They were an example of his willingness to risk his life to defend America and the revolution, he told the military judges and the twelve army officers who made up the jury. "But for the lack of support from Congress, he could have taken the whole province."[11]

Back in Philadelphia, news of the Canadian defeat came as a shock to Congress, which was still dithering about how far to go in its defiance of Britain even as Arnold put his life on the line and colonial soldiers died in Quebec for the cause. Nonetheless: "One of the heaviest blows to the morale of Congress and of patriots everywhere was the news of the unsuccessful Canadian expedition which had been launched in early fall amid high hopes. The two-pronged invasion ... had been wasted by sickness, bitter cold and rugged terrain."[12]

The congressional response was to authorize more troops for the invasion, approve new inducements for Canadians joining the force, and write a new appeal to Canadians for their support. Approved 24 January by Congress and issued under John Hancock's signature, the appeal thanked Canadians for the support already shown and pledged continued American effort:

The best of causes are subject to vicissitudes and disappointments have ever been inevitable. Such is the lot of human nature. But generous souls, enlightened and warmed with the sacred fire of liberty, become more resolute as difficulties increase and surmount with irresistible ardour every obstacle that stand between them and the favorite object of their wishes. We will never abandon you to the unrelenting fury of yours and our enemies. Two battalions have already received orders to march to Canada, a part of which are now on their route. Six additional battalions are raising in the United States for the same service and will receive orders to proceed to your province as soon as possible. The whole of this army will probably arrive in Canada before the ministerial army under General Carleton can receive any succours. Exclusive of the forces before mentioned, we have directed that measures be immediately taken to embody two regiments in your country.[13]

Since there still was a need for more cooperation, the Americans also pleaded with the French peasants to create some elective, democratic bodies to represent them: "We advise and exhort you to establish associations in your different parishes, of the same nature with those which have proved so salutary to the United States, to elect deputies to form a provincial assembly and that said assembly be instructed to appoint delegates to represent them in this congress. We flatter ourselves to hold in view the happy moment when the standard of tyranny shall no longer appear in this land and we live in full hopes that it will never hereafter find shelter in North America."[14]

Inside the walls of Quebec, Carleton was indecisive. He was too unsure of his own strength and the American's weakness to venture out in an attempt to finish off the rebels. Instead he hunkered down, authorized a few half-hearted and unsuccessful forays to capture American guns, and waited out the winter. Arnold reported that there were defections from the British garrison and complaints about the cold, the lack of food, and the grim prospects within. Yet he was not strong enough to attack.

In mid-February the British government was still unaware of the events of 30–31 December. Carleton received a message that reinforcements were on the way – soldiers and provisions enough to sustain the existing force while it tried to retake the fortress "in case it should have fallen into the hands of the rebels."[15] The government was sending three thousand British troops and five thousand Germans.

By late March the first reports had reached London of the unsuccessful attack and Lord George Germain sent a message to Carleton: "The defeat and repulse of the rebels at Quebec on the 31st of December was a great and happy event and I am commanded by the King to express to you the sense His Majesty entertains of your service on that important ... and of the services of all those who distinguished themselves on that occasion."[16] Still, London was taking no chances. If the reports of success were in error, then enough force was being sent from

London to capture Quebec, Germain said, or at least to cut it off from the rest of the rebellious provinces.

Outside the walls of Quebec, the brutal Canadian winter of 1775–76 continued to plague Arnold and his forces. Arnold was still battling his own pain. Though he had been promoted in January to brigadier – general in recognition of his exploits at Quebec, Congress still refused to match its fine words with reinforcements or weapons or money. The local population remained indifferent; Smallpox spread among his troops along with insolence and insubordination. And, of course, there was the weather: "Feb. 9, snow drifts 20 feet high"; "March 24, the weather is intolerably cold"; "March 25, northwest wind extremely cold."[17]

In mid-March, the meager American forces were deployed in a thin arc in front of the walls of Quebec, trying to deter or intercept deserters who might attempt to bargain with the British by offering information about the sorry state of Arnold's army. Arnold, meanwhile, pleaded in vain with the local French Canadians to come to the aid of the invasion: "The peasants, however friendly disposed, thought it too precarious a juncture to show themselves in the capacity," noted Dr Sentor early in the new year. "And those nigh rather retreated back into the country than give any assistance."[18]

The habitants, in fact, were beginning to turn on the Americans. The cautious welcome of the autumn and the benign neutrality of the winter was turning into sullen indifference or even active hostility. In the spring, Massachusetts-born Moses Hazen, a Quebec farmer and American collaborator who became a commander of American and Canadian troops, offered a brutal assessment of the lack of sympathy felt for the invaders by Quebec's commercial and opinion leaders. "With respect to the better sort of people, both French and English, seven-eighths are Tories who would wish to see our throats cut and perhaps would readily assist in doing so."[19]

What had happened?

At the time, both British and Americans concluded that the answer was largely political. The French had little ideological commitment to either side. They were politically pragmatic, interested only in supporting a winner. Had the Americans shown the strength to defeat the British, or had Congress proven itself willing to send the resources that were needed to win at all costs, the French Canadians might have been more willing to take a risk. Early on, most of the peasants were willing to support the Americans, particularly when they were "over-running the country," as Quebec historian Alfred Burt wrote in 1933. "Then, the big battalions from the south vanished and the Canadians saw that the Americans were not almighty. Their new-found friendship had been quite fortuitous, for there had been little or no mutual understanding and it quickly dissolved when the Habitants discovered that the invaders could not win salvation for them. They realized that the difference between revolution and rebellion was the difference between success and failure and they wished to avoid the sad fate of rebels."[20]

There was also the increasingly arrogant behaviour of the Americans. Historian F.X. Garneau, one of the first to analyze the invasion, wrote as early as 1846 that the Americans invited some of the hostility themselves by treating the French as inferiors rather than comrades. Habitants who had joined the American cause found themselves playing "a secondary, even a subservient part."[21] This perception would have been transmitted through the colony.

Likewise, the antics of General Wooster, the aging, bigoted soldier who held American command of Montreal and Quebec in the early months of 1776, did not help. He arrested priests and merchants and closed Roman Catholic churches, showing little tolerance for anyone who would not openly support the Americans. He was insensitive to the delicate balancing act many Quebeckers were living and even expressed contempt. "There is little confidence to be placed in the Canadians," Wooster wrote early in the year. "They are but a small remove from the savages and are fond of being of the strongest party."[22]

There were also economic reasons for the falling out between the American invaders and those they said they were liberating. The invaders had little money. Despite constant pleas from Arnold, Congress did not send gold coin north and the American army of liberation quickly became an army of occupation, confiscating habitant property and insisting that Quebec merchants and farmers accept paper currency issued by Congress, even though it had no real value and a bad reputation. Early Quebec hopes that the Americans would be a commercial opportunity were dashed on the shoals of American poverty and arrogance, including some looting.

By the end of April, Congress finally began to take the Canadian invasion plan seriously, sending north Maj. Gen. John Thomas – the hero of Boston who had driven the British army from the city using cannon captured in May at Ticonderoga by Arnold and Allen – to take over the Quebec City siege and to push Wooster out of the picture. A force of five thousand was sent north to try to bolster the invasion force. A group of prominent colonials, including America's most famous son, Benjamin Franklin, was sent to Montreal with a printing press to produce propaganda and the assignment of figuring out what could be done to entice Quebec into the Revolution. Franklin, then nearing seventy, was the toast of America and Europe for his inventions (such as the efficient heat-retaining "Franklin stove" and the harmonica), his discoveries (including some rudimentary experiments with electrical energy), his writings, and his brilliant mind. The delegation from Congress also included Charles Carroll of Maryland, a French-educated bilingual Catholic who was reported to be the wealthiest man in the colonies; Samuel Chase, another rich Maryland Protestant merchant; and John Carroll, a Jesuit priest who later became the first Roman Catholic archbishop of the United States.[23]

When they arrived at the Montreal wharf on 29 April 1776, they were met by Arnold, who had been granted his wish to move from the command at Quebec to Montreal. He was an elegant and gracious military commander on his well-groomed horse. The visit of the luminaries from head office began on a grand note, although the featured guests were barely up to the ceremony, which became a test of endurance. Franklin, clearly the star, emerged from the boat wearing a marten cap he had purchased during the trip. It had been a long, tiring journey for the old man, who had left New York City on 2 April and subsequently travelled by road, boat, and ox-cart. At one point Franklin wrote to a friend: "I am here on my way to Canada, detained by the present state of the lakes in which unthawed ice obstructs navigation. I begin to comprehend that I have undertaken a fatigue that at my time in life may prove too much for me so I sit down to write a few friends by way of farewell."[24]

Franklin and his party survived the journey, although the old man developed a painful case of boils while in Montreal. He and his fellow congressional ambassadors were treated to the greatest pageant that Arnold could offer in his rudimentary northern outpost. When their boat docked in Montreal, there were military honours and a cannon salute before Arnold escorted their carriage to his headquarters. John Carroll recorded what happened next: "Being conducted to the general's house, we were served with a glass of wine while people were crowding in to pay their compliments, which ceremony being over, we were shown into another apartment and unexpectedly met in a large assembly of ladies, most of them French. After drinking tea and sitting some time, we went to an elegant supper which was followed with the singing of the ladies, which proved very agreeable and would have been much more so if we had not been so much fatigued with our journey."[25]

Over the next several days, this pleasant mood turned sour as Arnold briefed the congressional delegation on the problems with the Quebec invasion. Primarily the invasion force needed money. Franklin offered £353 out of his own pocket, but Congress had sent nothing. Arnold estimated that debts to Quebec merchants and supporters who had supplied goods on credit totalled thirty-five thousand pounds.[26] The lack of hard currency had turned the Americans into thieves, demanding provisions for worthless paper currency and turning the locals against them. Franklin and his fellow commissioners recommended that Congress send twenty thousand pounds in hard currency or withdraw the army from Canada. Withdrawal seemed the only logical course.

Arnold also told the delegates about sickness among the troops, lack of supplies, problems with discipline, and the short enlistment period. Franklin's report back to Congress drew a response from John Adams, in a letter to wife Abigail: "Our misfortunes in Canada are enough to melt an heart of stone. The small pox is ten times more terrible than Britons, Canadians and Indians together. This was the cause of our precipitate retreat from Quebec ... There has been want approaching famine, as well as pestilence. And these discouragements seem to have so disheartened our officers that none seem to act with prudence and firmness."[27]

Among those who fit that grim assessment was Maj. Gen. Thomas. He was sent north as a hero to take over the Canadian campaign, propelled by flattery from congressional leader John Hancock. "The situation of Canada being of the greatest importance to the welfare of the United Colonies," Hancock wrote, "the Congress have been anxious to fix upon some general officer whose military skill and courage and capacity will probably insure success of the enterprise. In Maj. General Thomas, they flatter themselves they will not be disappointed."[28] After the Montreal reception for Franklin and the other commissioners, General Thomas headed east to take over command of the forces outside Quebec. He found a disaster in the making – an army of just under two thousand, half of them sick with smallpox. Thomas made the situation worse. The disease also appeared in Montreal but Arnold ignored the conventional wisdom of the day and ordered his troops to inject themselves with a bit of smallpox in order to create an immunity – an early form of inoculation. This was opposed by the powerful Puritan church on the grounds that it interfered with God's plan of who would die and who would not. Arnold, devout as he was, showed himself willing to challenge God's judgment. In doing so he saved his small troop guarding Montreal from the ravages of the disease.

Thomas, his military commander, heard of this, overturned the order, and threatened death to any soldier caught inoculating himself. In mid-May Thomas himself caught the disease. By the beginning of June he was dead.[29] The Franklin commissioners had watched Thomas in action in early May and judged him "totally unfit to command our army."[30] The hero of Boston turned out to be less than a great general or leader of men, though he had been promoted over Arnold despite the latter's impressive record.

By May Arnold was convinced that the siege of Quebec was hopeless. British reinforcements, certain to arrive in the spring when the harbour opened, would present the Americans with impossible odds. Against the judgment of his superiors, Arnold advocated that an orderly retreat be planned and executed. "I am content to be the last man who quits the country and fall, so that my country may rise," he wrote to General Schuyler in defence of his argument that the colonial army should quit Canada before it was driven out. "Let us not all fall together."[31]

Arnold had not arrived at this defeatist attitude without several serious attempts to break the fortress of Quebec. In mid-March there had been an attempt by the several hundred American prisoners inside Quebec to free themselves and open the gates. They had worked for weeks, turning scythes and iron barrel hoops into weapons. The plan was that they would break out, capture parts of the town, and then open St John's Gate to allow Arnold's troops in. Arnold was kept aware of the plot and encouraged it. It was discovered by British guards at the last moment when they heard the racket of prisoners trying to open a door frozen shut by ice. The prisoners were shackled and the British tried to turn the failed escape plan to their advantage. Carleton tried to lure Arnold in by feigning the break-out and encouraging him to believe the plan was working. Arnold sensed something amiss and kept his troops at their stations. The trap failed: "Arnold would not be out-foxed."[32]

The prisoners from then on had few amenities and spent the rest of the winter and much of the next summer confined, trying to cope with lice, scurvy and other diseases. "No man knows what it is to be a prisoner till they are made prisoners," Capt. William Humphrey noted unhappily in his diary on 6 June.[33] He was released shortly after but it was August before he made it home to Providence, Rhode Island. Little more than a year later, he re-enlisted in the revolutionary army for the duration of the war.

Several times in April, the Americans tried to lob red-hot cannon balls over the walls of the fort, hoping to start fires that would force evacuations, or at least demoralize the population. In all cases, the balls fell harmlessly into the garrison. The final American attempt to break the defence came on 3 May when a ship was set ablaze and sent into Quebec harbour, hoping to strike and burn the British ships at anchor, causing panic and surrender. Considering that British supply ships filled with fresh provisions and men were just days away, it was a desperate and hopeless gesture that fizzled out when the ship was sunk by British fire from the garrison before it could do any damage.

The die was cast. The American siege was hopeless. The invasion was all but over.

The end for the Americans in Quebec came in a flash of Red Coats who marched from the ships that arrived off Île d'Orleans on 6 May. Thomas, so soon to contract smallpox, knew the British reinforcements were coming and in fact, on May 5, had convened a council of war at which a decision was taken to organize a retreat. He was too late and too slow. The British ships were just over the horizon and there were no plans for an orderly retreat. When the British reinforcements came ashore, they were quickly joined by troops from inside the fort as they marched towards the American lines.

The rebels fled in disarray, leaving behind weapons, arms, supplies, and even the sick and wounded. In a dispatch to London, Guy Carleton described the scene. The arrival of the troop ships had raised British spirits and made the beleaguered defenders bold. They had

marched out of the [gates] of St Louis and St Johns [*sic*] to see what those mighty Boasters were about. They were found very busy in their preparations for a retreat, a few shot [*sic*] being exchanged, the line marched forward and the plains were soon cleared of those plunderers, all their artillery, military stores, scaling ladders, petards, etc. were abandoned ... Thus ended our siege and blockade during which the mixed garrison of soldiers, sailors, British and Canadian militia with [help] from Halifax and Newfoundland showed great zeal and patience under very severe duty and uncommon vigilance, indispensable in a place liable to be stormed, besides great labor necessary to render such attempts less practical.[34]

It was a blot on the reputation of the American army and a disgrace in Arnold's eyes. He had seen the end coming and had urged an orderly retreat to preserve what could be saved of the army, as well as the dignity and reputation of the force that he had miraculously shepherded through the Maine wilderness and then kept together and motivated as a besieging force after the disaster of 31 December. Now his men were running away in disarray, sometimes stealing supplies along the way. Hundreds of sick and wounded Americans were abandoned to their fate in a shocking display of undisciplined self-interest. To a proud army leader who valued discipline and bravery above all else, it was a disgrace.

Seeing the scope of his victory, Carleton rose above the bitterness of the past winter to make a remarkable gesture of reconciliation and humanity. On 10 May he issued a decree whereby his soldiers had to help the feeble Americans abandoned by their comrades. They were suffering "diverse disorders" and were "in great danger of perishing for want of proper assistance," Carleton said when ordering his captains to take time from the chase to search out helpless rebels and take them to hospitals where they could be nursed back to health. "I hereby make known to them that as soon as their health is restored, they shall have free liberty to return to their respective provinces."[35]

In Montreal, news of the British landing and the American retreat arrived within a day of the appearance of the Red Coats. The congressional commissioners were still there, trying to figure out whether the invasion could be salvaged. The reports from Quebec quickly convinced them it was over and a decision was made to send the ailing Franklin, weakened by painful attacks of gout, back to Philadelphia.[36] He took the wife of collaborator Thomas Walker back with him. In Philadelphia, his news was greeted with shock by politicians who had never understood how overextended and underfinanced the Quebec invasion really was, and by ordinary citizens who had assumed that the "liberation" of Canada was merely a matter of time. "Word of the retreat left the colonies stunned and disbelieving," wrote the historian Robert Hatch. "Citizens wanted to know what had gone wrong, who was to blame, why more had not been done for the under-supplied and woefully-handicapped army."[37] To answer the question, Congress needed only to look into its collective mirror.

On the ground in Quebec, the British rout of the Americans was compete. On 31 May Arnold sent to Maj. Gen. Horatio Gates a blunt assessment of the disaster. Gates was travelling north to take over command of the American army in Canada. "Neglected by Congress below, pinched with every want here, distressed with the smallpox, want of generals and discipline in our army, which may rather be called a great rabble, our late unhappy retreat from Quebec ... our credit and reputation lost in a great part of the country, and a powerful foreign enemy advancing upon us ... there are so many difficulties we cannot surmount them."[38] His use of the term "rabble" to describe the troops he had been so proud of gave away his anger over their unruly retreat and the débâcle that had taken place.

The final scene of the invasion was played out on 13 June on the shores of Lake Champlain when the last American left Canadian soil with the British in pursuit. In May Arnold had rejected a proposal from his superior, Gen. John Sullivan, that the Americans make a last stand at Montreal. Instead, he planned an orderly retreat, expecting to catch up to Sullivan's fleeing troops near Chambly or St Jean. He received permission from the remaining congressional commissioners to seize supplies from Tory merchants if they would not sell for congressional currency. Arnold promised payment later and had the supplies transported to St Jean, where they were supposed to be labelled according to the merchant from whom they were taken and then stored for the American army. But Chambly commander Moses Hazen was in the midst of a feud with Arnold and refused to obey the order. He left the supplies untended on the banks of the Richelieu River and they were looted. Arnold had him charged with negligence. Hazen fought back with his own accusations and his enemies later charged that Arnold had organized and benefited from the pilfering. The incident eventually became part of the litany of suspicions about Benedict Arnold's behaviour.

Once he reached St Jean and saw the chaos, Arnold took charge. He had organized a defiant retreat strategy, both in Montreal and St Jean. He had his troops take what was needed and then burn anything that could be used by the pursuing British, including bridges. This "scorched earth" tactic was unconventional at the time but has since become an effective strategy of armies forced into strategic withdrawals. To his admiring subordinates, Arnold was signalling that despite the fiasco outside Quebec, this was not a defeat but a strategic retreat. He was not conceding anything to the British.[39]

At St Jean, he set up a guard to delay the advancing British while most of the army boarded boats to head south, down the Richelieu to Lake Champlain and at least temporary safety. Key parts of St Jean were set ablaze. Then, members of the guard troop pushed off from shore, leaving just Arnold and an aide, Capt. James Wilkinson. In a dramatic gesture, the two waited until the British troops appeared in the distance, shot their horses so the British could not use them, and clambered into a boat to head south. Arnold pushed the boat from shore, the first American to invade Canada and the last to leave.[40] His many critics would later condemn this as grandstanding.

The defeated, hungry, and weakened American army made its way down the Richelieu River and into Lake Champlain. Within days, the troops reached Fort Ticonderoga where the sick were separated from the strong and where the army leaders faced the complicated question of what to do next. Clearly, they were no match for the strengthened British forces that undoubtedly would be pursuing them down Lake Champlain in the hope of ending the rebellion that summer. Should they make a stand or continue retreating? The American leaders were divided. But Arnold had a plan. Its brilliant execution gave the young general a reputation for bravery and leadership so lustrous that none of his detractors, could then or later, deny it. In the terrible and bloody weeks that followed the retreat from Canada, Arnold converted his little ragtag army into America's first fighting navy. In the process, he probably saved the Revolution.

Behind British lines where there was much rejoicing about the victory in Canada, there was also a premonition about the threat posed by Arnold. In late June, upon hearing the news from Canada, Secretary of State Lord Germain sent a dispatch of congratulations to Carleton tinged with regret. "I am sorry you did not get Arnold for of all the Americans, he is the most enterprising and dangerous."[41] Still, Carleton received high praise. "I am happy to have it in command from the King to inform you that your sovereign highly applauds the spirit, discretion and manly perseverance which you have manifested in the defence of that important place," Germain wrote. The reinforcements should be strong enough to conquer the rebels and "to reduce the Canadians to lawful obedience."[42]

Later, there would be questions about Carleton's tactics during those crucial weeks. If he had more aggressively pursued the retreating Americans, his troops might well have been able to capture the entire northern army, which could have changed the course of the American Revolution. "His firm and effective stand at Quebec was duly praised and won him as reward the red ribbon of the Knight of the Bath," wrote Hilda Neatby. "But George III and the ministers who honoured him were not entirely blind to the fact that the success of the American retreat added one more to the list of Carleton's errors and miscalculations."[43] It probably explains why Carleton was not chosen that summer to lead the British invasion force south out of Canada. The command went to a nominally more junior officer, Gen. John Burgoyne.

In Philadelphia and elsewhere in the American colonies, there was much speculation among politicians about the causes of the fiasco. Samuel Adams suggested that the political indecision that delayed the issuing of the Declaration of Independence was part of the problem. A clear break with Britain before the invasion would have impressed the French peasants. "If this declaration had been made nine months earlier, Canada would be ours today," he said after independence was declared on 4 July 1776.[44]

Congress began an inquiry into the causes and many turned to the delegation that had visited Montreal in April. Charles Carroll wrote of the lack of money and support from Congress, illness, and finally, hostility from the French once the hard currency ran out and some American soldiers began to steal or mistreat the local population. In June General Washington was ordered by Congress to investigate what had happened and to punish those soldiers convicted of cowardice, plundering, or other crimes.[45]

For most of the French Canadians and English Quebecers who were left behind, life returned somewhat to normal. There was some lingering resentment about the American stealing and the huge debt owed to local businessmen and farmers. The clergy and landlords beat a path to British offices to remind them that they had been loyal. Some, like the Richelieu Valley trader Samuel Jacobs who appeared earlier as a supplier to the first American invaders, resumed his trade with the occupying British soldiers. After spring 1776, his area around St Denis became an armed British camp and a staging ground for troops heading south to fight the rebels. Jacobs became wealthy supplying the British army with rum, food, and other provisions.

In large part, life resumed its medieval European pattern, with the landowners and Church in charge and the British as relatively benign occupiers. Carleton gave the peasants a chance to re-establish their apolitical security through a return to the previous life rhythms. He understood that their pervasive neutrality had deprived the Americans of a force that could have tipped the balance. It would be more than half a century before rebellious, democratic winds blew through the Quebec countryside again, fanned by a fiery establishment landowner named Louis-Joseph Papineau.

There was one group of Quebecers for whom life did not, and never would, return to "normal" – the collaborators who threw their lot in totally with the Americans and left the province with them, rather than remain behind among hostile neighbours. Many of them spent their savings and gave up their property for the American cause. Despite a congressional promise in 1776 to cover the debts run up by the northern army, many of these unfortunate souls ended their lives in poverty, in a foreign land. Some Canadians were compensated. Many were not.

Their stories are told in two-hundred-year-old petitions that lie in congressional records, appeals to the Board of War, which had the power to rule against the petitioners or to send their pleas to Congress with a recommendation for action.[46] In many cases, Arnold interceded on their behalf with Congress to try to win compensation. In many cases, Congress was too impoverished, inept, or politically constipated to make quick decisions. The allies who gave up everything for the cause often ended up as some of the most pathetic victims of the invasion.

At one point, in a statement of 10 February 1784, the congressional Board of War recognized the debt of gratitude owed by the newly independent United Colonies to their Canadian allies but did not extend it to an obligation to pay financial compensation. The statement was signed by James Monroe, later a president. The Canadians joined the cause after being promised American protection and friendship, he wrote. At the same time, they had understood the risks. The potential reward was freedom, the potential loss was everything, "the exertion of every individual was the effect of a voluntary choice" and the states had no obligation to compensate for losses. Still, many had suffered and while there was no legal obligation, their experience "entitles them to the gratitude and attention of these states and from motives of humanity as well as policy, it is advisable to give them such compensation as will relieve their distress."[47] Those generous words did not put food on the table for many former Canadians who believed that the new nation owed them something.

The most prominent petitioner was Thomas Walker, the Montreal trader and rabble rouser who had exceptional credentials for American gratitude. A former American who had moved north to Montreal in the early 1760s, he had spied for the Americans, raised money for them, been mutilated by British soldiers, and then imprisoned; he had raised funds to send to Boston after news of the Bunker Hill defeat seeped north, entertained Benjamin Franklin and the other commissioners at his home, turned over his house to Arnold as a headquarters, sent his wife south with Franklin for safety when the invasion was collapsing, and generally risked life, limb, and ear for the cause of the Revolution. By the beginning of 1785, Walker was trying to scratch out a living as a merchant in Boston and he sent a plea for help. He outlined his sacrifice and his situation "so that a compensation may be made him for his great and manifold losses and sufferings, in his early and steady adherence and exertions in the favor of liberty; in a way and manner suitable to his present circumstances and consistent with the dignity, honor and justice of Congress."[48] There is no record of a congressional decision nor of any American help.

James Livingston claimed to be "the first in Canada who took up arms in favor of the United States." He joined the army, raised and led a force of Canadian volunteers, and lost his Canadian business and property for his troubles. In April 1784 he still was complaining to Congress that he had received no compensation even though some other Canadians had received "considerable sums."[49]

William Holton was a Quebec City hat maker who was sympathetic to the Americans, jailed on suspicion of providing supplies to Arnold, and expelled from the city; he joined the American army and was wounded. His petition of 26 June 1776 was not answered.

Jonathon Eddy was one of fifty-six Nova Scotians who refused to fight the Americans and were expelled. They moved to the United States but by 25 February 1784 were desperate enough to petition Congress. "At the opening of peace, they now find themselves destitute of a home for their retirement, of property for their support and of all hope of assistance but from the justice and humanity of your honorable body."[50] Despite support from John Hancock and Samuel Adams, a congressional committee set the plea aside.

At the end of the Revolution, John Halstead, who had served as deputy commissary general to Arnold, was in New York in financial trouble. He wrote that in the mad retreat, he had lost vouchers owing to him worth more than $1,379. By 1784 he had been paid just four hundred dollars. He had borrowed money to get back to Canada to try to claim some property, but he needed money to support his family. It took Congress four years to issue a non-committal reply[51].

Of all the stories in the congressional files, none is more heartbreaking than that of Father Louis Lotbinière. In his late fifties at the time of the invasion, he was one of the few Catholic priests to side with the invaders. He paid a price. On 3 February 1787, the seventy-one-year-old former cleric petitioned Congress for help. He was ill with gout and rheumatism, poor, and hungry. "Would to God that I had never known either ... General Montgomery or Arnold in Canada. I would not now starve with hunger and cold for not being paid according to the convention made between Gen. Arnold and me 26 January, 1776 and ratified in Congress assembly 12 August, 1776, for long my life ... to indemni [sic] me for having lost my parish of 1,200 bushels of all grains, lordship, two horses at Quebec." Father Lotbinière complained that the Treasury department would not honour the 1776 agreement to compensate him. "I hope, gentlemen, it will not be so [that he die from cold and hunger] and your bowels will be moved at my situation, as I am very old and my sight being to put out."[52]

There is no record of congressional compassion, since by then memories were fading, finances were tight, the individual states were claiming more powers, and many congressmen were suspicious of the deluge of pleas for help from people without receipts to prove their loss and supportive evidence to prove their service. For wretches like Father Lotbinière, supporting the American Revolution had been a losing gamble.

In modern-day Quebec, there are few reminders of the American invasion of 1775–76 and the almost successful campaign to make Canada the fourteenth colony in revolt against the British Empire and its arrogant imperial ways.

There is a river and a hotel named for Arnold near the Quebec-Maine border. There is Auberge Benedict Arnold in Saint-Georges, which in Arnold's day was called Sartigan. Lying sixty miles south of Quebec City in the Beauce region, the motel boasts the "Arnold and Maude" dining-room (whoever Maude was) where you can "discover General Arnold's menu, savour a meal and become part of history."

In Quebec City itself, there is a plaque on the site of the rue St Louis house where Montgomery's body was taken after his fatal wound during the attack. There is a plaque on the front wall of the Chateau Frontenac to commemorate the defenders of the city:

This tablet is erected by permission of His Majesty King George V, Commander-in-Chief of the Royal Fusiliers, by the regiment: To the memory of the officers and men of the Royal Fusiliers who defended Quebec in 1775 and 1776 under Sir Guy Carleton and who, with the help of detachments from the Royal Navy and merchant shipping, the Royal Artillery, Royal Emigrants, English and French Canadian militia and volunteers held the fortress and the city secure during a siege of 164 days throughout the rigors of a Canadian winter, against a numerous and enterprising enemy.

For the most part, the rest of contemporary Quebec and Canada are silent on the nine months that could easily have extended American control into the northern Canadian colony and changed dramatically the nature of the French-English relationship that eventually evolved into Canada.

10

Heroics and Enemies Within

Through the eyes of many American historians, the summer and autumn of 1776 were crucial seasons in the American Revolution, one of its turning points. It could easily have collapsed. Revolutionary forces were weak and disorganized, little more than three thousand strong. The colonial politicians in Philadelphia remained indecisive and quarrelsome, making the crucial and fateful decision to declare independence but still proving unwilling to throw the full resources of the emerging country into the fight. The British, having driven the Americans out of Quebec, were strong and advancing.

Military historians argue that the Revolution was saved from collapse that year by two factors: excessive British caution in taking advantage of their superior position; and the heroic efforts of a small band of American fighters who built a small fleet of ships on Lake Champlain and for two days battled a much larger British fleet sailing down the lake to attack the heart of the Thirteen Colonies. Benedict Arnold was the head and heart of that epic American naval battle.

The commanders of what increasingly was being seen as a British war effort rather than a campaign to quell temporary unrest had a strategic plan for 1776, a plan they thought would end the uprising. Its two most important engagements were to take place in the northern theatre. A force would capture Long Island and New York City, a strategic port and in those days America's second largest city with twenty-five thousand residents. A second force would push down from Canada through Lake Champlain and the Hudson River to connect with the army occupying New York City. "The object of these two attacks was to seize this line and cut New England off from the rest of the colonies," wrote military historian Joseph Mitchell. "The British planners felt certain that if the colonies in revolt could thus be divided into two parts, the rebellion would be crushed."[1]

The August attack on Long Island was a success. After a bloody battle, the American defenders fled. The British forces occupied and held the island until the end of the war. Eight years later New York City was the staging ground for the evacuation of Loyalists to Canada. In retrospect, the one strategic British mistake in that successful assault was that the victorious army allowed the American troops to escape, leaving them free to fight another day. As they had in Canada, the British seemed reluctant to pursue the retreating Americans too aggressively lest they close a door to future reconciliation.

Meanwhile, on Lake Champlain that summer where the second stage of the British plan was to unfold, there was a naval arms race. The British set about at Fort St John to assemble a lake fleet for the southward invasion. The Americans also authorized construction of a fleet but only after much dithering, political intrigue, and mischief making by ambitious army men with a grudge against Arnold. Since spring, Arnold had been arguing that the Americans should take a stand against the British on Lake Champlain. By the beginning of July that argument had been won and Arnold was put in charge of building a small fleet, but the road to that decision was tortuous and politically dangerous for him. Many of the controversies that marred the summer haunted him for the next four years and helped to convince him that his best option was to embrace the British. In 1776, though, the British were his sworn enemies and Arnold was anxious to assemble a navy on Lake Champlain to confront them.

There were a number of road blocks. His commander on the lake, Maj. Gen. Horatio Gates, was jealous of Arnold's take-charge attitude. Gates was also an ally of some of Arnold's enemies in Congress and the army. He often undermined, delayed, and obstructed Arnold's efforts during that frustrating summer. Congress contributed to the delay by refusing or dragging its feet on Arnold's repeated requests to send the men, money, and carpenters needed to build and staff the boats. There were intrigues on the lake as some officers tried to take advantage of the confusion to build up their own spheres of influence and power.

The most ominous development, however, was an attempt by some of Arnold's political enemies to have him tried before a court-martial for "looting" goods during the retreat from Montreal. These were the supplies Arnold had taken from Montreal merchants with the approval of members of Franklin's commission. They were taken with the promise of future payment and sent to Chambly where Moses Hazen was in charge. The supplies were meant to sustain the retreating Americans, who had left most of their goods behind during their chaotic flight from Quebec City. At Chambly, commander Hazen was in a battle with Arnold and had refused to guard or retrieve the supplies dumped on the shore. In the days following, they were looted.

Arnold, who blamed Hazen, ordered him arrested and charged with negligence. Hazen found friends in Congress, allied himself with Arnold's enemy John Brown, and turned the tables. A congressional committee travelled to Ticonderoga to investigate Arnold's behaviour in Canada. Hazen accused him of seizing and looting the supplies for his own gain, whereupon Gates ordered Arnold to attend a 26 July court-martial hearing. The court was evidently biased. It listened to Arnold's detractors, refused to listen to his key defence witness, and generally seemed weighted against him. After a week, knowing that time was wasting, Arnold lashed out at the politically driven military court. When challenged, he refused to apologize and was ordered arrested. Gates finally realized that this had gone too far and dissolved the court-martial. He wrote to Congress that he could not afford to arrest Arnold because he was too valuable. "The United States must not be deprived of that excellent officer's service at this important moment."[2]

Despite these obstructions, Arnold's plans to create a navy on Lake Champlain took shape that summer in the shipyards at Skenesboro, New York, at the southern end of the lake. In five weeks during July and August, a little fleet was built. Arnold designed a fast, manoeuvrable forty-eight-foot gondola and oversaw its construction. Congress and governments of the individual colonies delayed the process by arguing over who would pay, how much they should pay to attract qualified men, and whether there should be a continental navy to stand independent of the small navies of the individual coastal colonies. It was a time when individual colonies had not reconciled the growing pressure to cede some power and jurisdiction to a central government. It was a tension that would plague the United States throughout its first seventy years, fuelled by recurring states' rights movements. It was not until the decisive civil war of 1860–65 that the issue was settled.

By mid-August 1776, a fleet of ten ships – schooners, gondolas, galleys, and bateaux – had been built. More were promised as congressional and colonial support began to flow, but with reports of British movement Arnold could wait no longer. He led them out of port and up Lake Champlain to confront the British, leaving instructions that the new constructions should be sent north as they were ready. He would need all the reinforcements he could get.

As Arnold departed, playing the role of commander of the little fleet, he wrote a scathing review of his own forces: "We have a wretched motley crew in the fleet, the marines the refuse of every regiment and the seamen, few of them ever wet with salt water."[3] Without enough volunteers, some in fact had to be conscripted into service and he knew they were far from reliable. Still, Arnold struck out with this tiny American navy, knowing he would be badly outgunned and yet hoping to slow the British down, to give Washington more time to prepare his defences. Typically, as work neared completion in the shipyard, Gates had written a report to Congress taking most of the credit for the fleet and leaving Arnold little of the glory.[4] Arnold would earn that glory within weeks, not through political intrigues but in the heat of battle.

The American fleet that floated north through the last two weeks of August was a strange mixture. Arnold was in the lead ship, the two-hundred-ton *Royal Savage* with twelve guns. The schooner *Revenge* had eight cannon and ten swivel guns. The schooner *Liberty* had eight guns. The sloop *Enterprise* had ten guns. There were six fifty-nine-foot gondolas, designed by Arnold to carry up to forty-five men. The rowing galleys were still being built. By the time of the battle, the American force would be supplemented by the row galley *Washington* and Arnold's flagship, *Congress*.

In contrast, the British fleet sailing south carried nine thousand men in 624 vessels, including Indian war canoes with troops and some well-armed men-of-war assembled at St John.[5] Arnold knew the size and progress of the British invasion fleet through an intelligence network he established that autumn, after sailing north almost to the Canadian border and dispatching spies. He also developed an audacious plan of defence that was brilliant in its simplicity and courageous in its defiance of orders from his superiors that he operate only a defensive campaign. The plan was obvious. He could not subject his tiny armada to the firepower of the British in open water. The British would have to be tricked into fighting on his terms.

The battle began in the early morning of 11 October. Through a ruse, the British ships were lured into the American trap. Arnold had lined up his ships from the tip of Valcour Island to the New York shore. The ships were attached to the bottom by cables which allowed them to be winched broadside to fire, and then turned north-south with the current to reduce their target surface while the guns were reloaded.

A fierce day of fighting ensued. At one point a cannon ball from an American gun arced between Governor Carleton and his younger brother Thomas, knocking them both down and rendering Thomas unconscious and bleeding from his ears from the percussion. Thomas may have remembered that close call a decade later when, as governor of New Brunswick, he was Arnold's political leader.

Arnold clearly proved himself a better military commander and tactician than Guy Carleton, who would later be his commander-in-chief. Through his telescope "Sir Guy Carleton could see Arnold darting from gun to gun, rowing to nearby ships to direct their fire."[6] By the end of the day, the British had not broken through the American line and they had taken a pounding. Many of the British ships were damaged. Scores of British soldiers were dead from the withering fire. On the American side, most of their ships were damaged or out of commission. Most of their gunpowder was gone. Another day of direct battle would be suicide.

Arnold's officers believed they had done what they could and that now was the time to make a strategic retreat. As he had in the Maine wilderness, Arnold denied the possibility of disaster and, through a combination of praise and encouragement, convinced them that they stood to gain by staying put. He had a plan to float the damaged ships silently through the foggy night, past the British ships and into a bay where repairs could be made. His enthusiasm and bravery won the day. "In a few minutes, Benedict Arnold could whip up enthusiasm in his officers in a way that few other leaders in the revolution ever equalled. His determination and his reckless courage were infectious. Men who dragged themselves into a meeting came out fired with a vigor that carried them into the frenzy of battle."[7]

On 12 October the winds prevented the British from catching the Americans, who were now seven miles down the lake and licking their wounds. Arnold's daring escape led to lingering questions among British contemporaries and historians about Guy Carleton's military abilities.

There followed one of those exceptional days when the course of history is changed. On 13 October the British fleet met its match. Arnold had scuttled some of his badly damaged ships and concentrated his remaining troops on the few that were seaworthy. The American situation was hopeless but Arnold was determined to fight to the end. The British attacked and, after several hours of pounding, had reduced the American fleet to several gondolas and the *Congress*, commanded by Arnold. It was surrounded by British ships that blasted away for more than five hours. On a blood-slicked deck, Arnold refused to concede defeat, at times firing the guns himself. Finally, he gave the British the slip one more time, manœuvring the ships into a shallow bay where the British could not follow, abandoning and then burning them. Arnold then led nearly 150 wounded, bloody and exhausted survivors twenty miles to Crown Point, which he ordered abandoned and burned, and then marched on to Ticonderoga, enduring almost three days and nights without sleep or food. It is almost impossible to imagine the stamina that was required.

The British fleet – damaged, embarrassed, and delayed – decided it was too late in the year to continue its invasion south and returned north to winter quarters in Canada. Arnold, after a rest, rode south into another year of political controversy and intrigue. The world, and his contemporaries, were in awe. "No man ever manœuvered with more dexterity, fought with more bravery or retreated with more firmness," wrote army doctor James Thatcher.[8] Arnold had achieved "a remarkable action of great strategic importance."[9] Joseph Mitchell, an historian of revolutionary military leaders, goes further. "The Americans, by building a fleet on Lake Champlain, thereby forcing the British to take time to build a larger one, thus delayed the invasion of Upper New York by a year. It may well be true that the year saved at Lake Champlain ... saved the Revolution."[10] Even Arnold's sometimes less-than-supportive military bosses were impressed. "It has pleased Providence to preserve General Arnold," Gates wrote to Schuyler afterwards. "Few men ever met with so many hairbreadth escapes in so short a time."[11]

It was a pattern for Arnold throughout the war. He was a daredevil, seemingly protected by Providence, as if a greater force kept him from mortal harm on the bloody ship decks of Lake Champlain. He was a fearless military leader who chose to lead by example, as he did through the invasion and siege of Canada. He was a leader of men who believed decisive action, rather than political intrigue, would triumph.

After his heroics at Valcour Island, Arnold went home to New Haven to try to get his faltering, neglected business affairs in order and to see his sister Hannah and his three sons. Even away from the war, however, he was dogged by politics, intrigues, and demands. At home near the Connecticut waterfront, Arnold learned that Congress had promoted to the rank of major-general five officers of lower rank than himself and with less experience and fewer accomplishments to their names. Arnold was offended. He suggested to Washington that he could serve only as long as he could do so with honour. It seemed like a thinly veiled threat to quit the army. Yet in April 1777, Arnold showed how incapable he was of stepping aside from the conflict and how crucial his presence was for the rebels.

At home in New Haven, Arnold received word that a British force had invaded Connecticut. His old commander and nemesis David Wooster was the main defender and acquitted himself well, but it seemed to be a losing cause. Arnold rushed to the scene, rallied Connecticut men to form an army of defence, and established a barricade at Ridgefield. The British attacked with superior force and while they succeeded in breaching the barricade, they were delayed and battered seriously enough to retreat the next day. Despite a counterattack led by Arnold, the Red Coats made it back to their ships, but the defence had been both heroic and effective. Wooster was killed in the action.

Arnold once again seems to have been kept alive by divine intervention. His horse was shot and Arnold was thrown to the ground, with his foot caught in the stirrup. "An alert enemy soldier leaped down from the rocky ledge and ran at him, bayonet at ready. Arnold extricated his pistol in the nick of time, shot the man dead, disengaged himself from the stirrup and followed his men down the main street of Ridgefield through a shower of small and grape shot."[12]

Congress, which had so recently snubbed him, heard of his "gallant conduct" and presented Arnold with a new horse, named Warren.[13] The American warrior was far from mollified. By July he was offering to resign his commission, only to be persuaded yet again by George Washington that the army and the nation needed him. Arnold was ordered north to help defend against a British invasion, delayed the year before because of his heroics but now in full force down Lake Champlain. Arnold was given a northern commission. His ego demanded that it be backdated to February, to cover the period for which his reputation was in dispute. Congress vetoed the proposal in a vote of sixteen to six. Despite yet another political rebuke, Arnold went north.

In contemporary America, an upstate New York monument perched on an incline in Saratoga National Park, surrounded by a wrought-iron fence close to the Hudson River and at one of the most famous spots of the Revolution, is as good as it gets for the memory of Benedict Arnold. His name is never mentioned but his spirit and story are everywhere.

The commemorative monument was erected in 1887 by the Saratoga Monument Association, in tribute to the soldier who was widely credited with winning the day at Saratoga, a chaotic, brutal day that Americans believe changed the history of the world. It features a bronze relief of a single military boot. "In memory of the most brilliant soldier of the Continental Army who was desperately wounded on this spot, the sally point of Burgoyne's great western Redoubt, 7th Oct., 1777, winning for his countrymen the decisive battle of the American Revolution and for himself, the rank of major general." There is an accompanying painting of a soldier on a horse, charging up the line of battle, shouting encouragement to his men in the face of enemy fire.

The name that could not be written, the "most brilliant soldier of the Continental Army," was Benedict Arnold, who sealed his place in American mythology on the fields of Bemis Heights. At the site, details of the engagement have been packaged for tourists, reduced to historical sound bites as modern travellers drive the nine-mile route through the battlefield, stopping here and there to read the signs, to listen to audio tapes that purport to describe what it was like on that day more than 220 years ago, where the battle lines were drawn.

The area was the scene of skirmishes for three weeks before the decisive engagement. The first skirmish happened in mid-September at Freeman's Farm, a site near the river, in the path of the advancing British army. John Freeman and his son had abandoned the farm that year to fight for the British. The rebels occupied the farmhouse, waiting for the Red Coats to appear. As 19 September dawned, American troops were in possession of the farm and used the Freeman farmhouse as a base from which to fire at the advancing British and their German mercenaries. Through the day, the field changed hands several times. At one point, Arnold led a charge across the field against the British and stopped their attack, but as the action unfolded there was little support from American leaders and a superior British force won the day. The Americans retreated to the nearby Bemis Heights to await the main British march south towards Albany.[14]

A visitor these days can look down from a hilltop onto Freeman's Farm and listen to an American National Park Service commentary that describes the divided society that was the thirteen colonies, the uncertain outcome of the struggle, and the importance that American mythology has conferred on these few acres of field and forest:

Many historians believe that the destiny of our newborn United States of America was decided here, in the fall of 1777. Relive those dramatic moments in your mind. Replace the modern road with twisting wagon ruts. Picture trees, larger, the forest ... The clearings dotted with tree stumps. It's a humid summer afternoon. A frontier farmer on horseback appears ... "How long since John and his son went to Canada? A month? It could be a year by the look of his house. Corn's ripe for picking. Wonder if John had a part in the fighting at Ticonderoga. Some call them traitors, John, his son McBride and the other Tories. It seems a mite harsh. But what must it be like to turn against your friends, even your kin? But if they win, it will be John's turn to gaze at my deserted farm. Oh well, time's past for talking."

The first mention of Arnold in the Saratoga signage comes in a reference to 7 October, the decisive day. In the time following the engagement at Freeman's Farm, the Americans dug in on the nearby rise called Bemis Heights and the British amassed a larger army as troops marched in from the north. They set up camp on Freeman's Farm.

Both sides had their problems. For the British, it was logistics and the vulnerability of their army of invasion. Bemis Heights was a steep hill with a commanding view of the plain running beside the river. The British could not march past on the way to Albany without being cut down by American fire. They had to attack. British commander Gen. John Burgoyne, encamped in the area, realized he was running out of food and was outnumbered by the rebels. He had his troops harvest some local corn. Prospects were not the best. The Americans were blessed by good position and plentiful troops – eighty-five hundred had arrived to dig fortifications on the heights. But they were cursed by short supplies and politics. So many troops had arrived that they were short of musket balls and tents. An appeal went out to patriots in Albany to melt down the lead from their windows to make musket shot.[15]

The political tensions were less easily remedied. As usual, Arnold was at the centre of the controversy. Not for the first time, he was locked in a bitter dispute over tactics and strategies with the commander of the American forces, General Gates. Arnold had arrived on the northern front to find the usual in-fighting in full flight. A British force of eight thousand soldiers – Canadians, Indians, and German mercenaries – was moving south. Gates was lobbying to replace Schuyler as commander of the northern army and Arnold arrived with a cloud over his head because he was one of Schuyler's allies. Maj. James Wilkinson, once an aide to Arnold in Canada but now an enemy and an influential aide to Gates, viewed him with suspicion. In August Arnold acted decisively to lift a British siege at Fort Stanwix, inland in New York's Mohawk Valley. His success made Gates, who had been dithering over what to do about the siege, look bad.[16] What's more, Arnold would not renounce his friendship with Schuyler.

Arnold's success in driving the British from Fort Stanwix freed the entire American force to face Burgoyne as he led his troops south along the river. Gates was in charge on the American side, joined by such veterans and former Arnold colleagues from the Quebec campaign as Henry Dearborn and Daniel Morgan. Officially, Arnold was second-in-command at Saratoga and he chose Bemis Heights as the logical location for the American fortifications. But the divisions between the two men went far beyond personality and politics. Gates was a cautious traditional soldier. Arnold was an audacious flexible military gambler. Gates thought the best strategy was a good defence – dig in strongly and wait for the British to attack and be repulsed. Arnold, as a veteran of the Indian wars, the Maine march, and the battles for Quebec and Lake Champlain, believed that the Americans should aggressively harass the British forces from the forests in an eighteenth-century form of guerrilla warfare. Gates's caution was never more evident than the day at Freeman's Farm when the battle was there to be won. Arnold gambled by leading a risky charge to stop a British advance, but when he expected reinforcements from the rear to rout the enemy, none came. He stormed to the rear, found Gates in his tent, and demanded reinforcements. Gates took the demand as insolence and essentially put Arnold under house arrest in his tent. The American forces were mired in confusion and ended the day retreating to their position of strength on Bemis Heights. Arnold was furious. Gates was unforgiving. In his dispatch to Congress describing the day's battle, he gave Arnold no credit for his leadership and initial victory.

The toll that day was dreadful. The Americans lost ten percent of their force of three thousand to death or injury. The British lost six hundred. The most devastating description of the politics of the day came from military historian Joseph Mitchell: "The American hero of the battle, Benedict Arnold, with 3,000 men had almost won Freeman's Farm. General Gates had sat in his tent with 4,000 men standing by, just listening to the sounds of battle."[17] Whatever the military merits of the day, Arnold clearly lost out in the political fall-out. Gates decided he was insubordinate and stripped him of his command. Arnold asked to be allowed to visit Washington and Gates gave him a pass, letting it be known that Arnold was asking to leave the army. Officers, in defiance of Gates, circulated a petition asking Arnold to stay. He stayed but remained confined to his tent.[18]

On 7 October 1777, a bright autumn day, several thousand men were gathered near Saratoga, preparing for a battle that determined the fate of the Revolution. The British fortifications were on the Bal-carres Redoubt, a hillside not far from the American lines. Two hundred yards of sniper cabins and log fence guarded the British right flank. Canadian volunteers guarded two cabins as part of the defensive works. Burgoyne sent close to two thousand troops and volunteers outside his camp to harvest corn. They were spotted and attacked by troops led by Quebec campaign veterans Dearborn and Morgan. The battle was on.

The troops charged in wave after wave. The Americans made several unsuccessful attempts to breach the redoubt, which would have given them access to the main British force. Gates listened to the sound of battle from his tent but did not assume command. Nearby in another tent Arnold, a virtual prisoner, paced and listened. Finally he could stand no more and despite orders to remain out of sight, he strode from his tent, saddled and mounted his stallion, and rode to the front.

Here, heroic legend takes over. A soldier who watched events unfold later called Arnold "the very genius of war."[19] The heart of the story is that Arnold arrived to take command of a force of men attacking a British fortification. He seemed oblivious to the danger, obsessed by the need to win, exhilarated by the chance to fight again. The first fortification fell. As the afternoon wore on, several American attempts to capture the second fortification, the Breymann Redoubt, had been repulsed. Arnold rode between the two lines, sword in hand, urging his men on. Inspired by this wild, charismatic figure, they surged forward and captured the redoubt.

Descriptions of the battle of 7 October 1777 that established the exalted nature of Arnold's accomplishments are exhilarating. Arnold is portrayed as a dashing horseman "wearing an American major general's uniform" riding onto the battlefield to the cheers of the men. "Benedict Arnold had been completely unable to sit quietly in his tent, listening to the noise of battle. With no authority whatever, he swept onto the field. Every man in the American army must have known that Gates had divested Arnold of his right to command but here was the leader they wanted to follow."[20] Elsewhere he is described as a "madman" who demoralized the enemy and energized his own troops. "Arnold appeared at once deranged and exhilarated, barrelling downhill on his big horse, his sword flailing." Some troops heard him shout: "Come on now boys. If the day is long enough, we'll have them all in hell before night." And in the heat of battle, he rode between the two lines to inspire his troops. "Both armies held their breath as he lashed his foam-flecked horse the entire length of the British line amid sheets of grapeshot, musket balls, cannon shells ... Arnold raced its length, leaning over his horse's mane as he charged right across the British line of fire. Miraculously, neither man nor mount was hit."[21]

Soon, his luck ran out. Arnold had a horse shot out from under him by a wounded German Hessian and was then struck in the leg by a musket ball, which shattered the same bone that had been damaged at Quebec. He was carried off the field an invalid, but his frenetic heroism had won the day and the British retreated.

Arnold, the wounded hero of Saratoga, spent more than three months in hospital fighting proposals to amputate his leg. He eventually regained some use of it. He was honoured by Congress and finally returned to New Haven to a hero's welcome.

Burgoyne, meanwhile, retreated to Saratoga where a swelling American army of twenty thousand surrounded him. On 17 October he surrendered six thousand troops and the weapons of the invasion, marking one of the most decisive American victories. Events at Saratoga

had reversed the tide of the revolutionary war. After Arnold's rearguard victory at Valcour Bay and his shocking attacks at Saratoga, the British would never again mount a major offensive against the Americans from the north. The defeat of Burgoyne's army was all Benjamin Franklin in Paris needed to convince the French that the Americans would not only stand and fight but, with military and financial help of European allies, could ultimately defeat the British ... Arnold's bold tactics had bought a new nation time to build an army, even if they had left him, at age thirty-six, partially crippled with one leg shorter than the other and a pain that never completely went away.[22]

They also left him with enemies inside the American forces and Congress who would play a large role in Benedict Arnold's undoing. Congress was particularly in the thrall of his critics. The politicians listened to complaints about his brashness, his inattention to bureaucracy, his aversion to politics. They withheld promotions, started investigations, spread rumours alleging cases of Arnold's self-serving money making, humiliated him, and, in the worst cut of all, fell over themselves welcoming the neophyte nineteen-year-old French nobleman Marquis de Lafayette to the cause, immediately giving him the same rank as Arnold. The appointment of Lafayette and other Europeans to senior military positions during the Revolution was not just a problem for Arnold. It caused a stir that prompted resignations and threats of resignation from Generals Nathaniel Greene, Henry Knox, and John Sullivan, among others.[23]

For Arnold, the proud and vain American warrior, it was a slap in the face. He had earned his rank in the breach and felt he deserved better than the late-arriving European stars. And he had experienced first hand the problems of dealing with arrogant but inexperienced Europeans who were seeking glory in America. During the frantic days on Lake Champlain in 1776, Arnold had to deal with, and find detours around, the incompetence of Jacobus Wynkoop, a Polish officer who had been given a commission by Congress as commander of the lake. Now, a French teenager was handed a high rank on a silver platter merely for showing up.

The American leadership, and particularly Benjamin Franklin, were infatuated with all things French. And, of course, there was the possibility of drawing France into the war against Britain. Lafayette's presence and the deference he was paid by American military and political leaders rankled with Arnold for the rest of his career in the American revolutionary army. As the historian Willard Randall put it, "The Continental Congress made few worse judgments than it did in the matter of Benedict Arnold's rank and seniority, and few with more tragic and far-reaching consequences."[24]

The American leadership's love affair with Lafayette made for some comic-opera moments, few more ego driven than the madcap plan in early 1778 to launch a winter invasion of Canada as a way to give the Frenchman some military credentials and to reward various of Arnold's old enemies, such as Moses Hazen, with a chance to do what the general could not do two years earlier. Arnold, still a towering figure in the army and a man who knew the challenges of a Canadian invasion, thought it an ill-conceived venture and did what he could to discourage it. When the invasion collapsed, its sponsors did what they could to place the blame on Arnold and his nay-saying. In fact it collapsed under the weight of its own contradictions and lack of planning. It was a campaign motivated by the quest for glory rather than results.

Planning began in late 1777, after Lafayette had let it be known in Europe that he would use his recently acquired commission in the American army to lead an invasion of Canada.[25] He chose Gen. Moses Hazen to be his northern point-man in organizing the men, the supplies, and the invasion from a base in Albany.

On 17 February Hazen wrote to his commander that he had enough supplies for three thousand soldiers for sixty days, enough time to capture Canada. He was being overly optimistic. Two days later John Barclay, chairman of the revolutionary committee in Albany, asked Hazen for help in assembling five hundred sleighs that he had located in three counties. He worried that things had been left so long that by the time he assembled the sleighs and the feed for the horses, it would be too late to invade.

That same day, Gen. Thomas Conway, the senior American commander, reported that despite the enthusiasm of the leadership, there were too few men, too few supplies, and too little hope to allow the invasion to proceed. "The intelligence from Canada is not encouraging."[26] Besides, the men of the invasion army had not been paid for five months. They were demoralized.

Meanwhile, the venerable Philip Schuyler, former commander of the northern army, had weighed in with a letter to Conway on 17 February denouncing the plan that he had initially embraced. "My hopes of success were founded on the supposition that a competent force would be employed and that my superiors were well aware that in a service so severe, in the most inclement season of the year and that on a march partly through a country thinly inhabited and partly through a desert, the troops ought to be well equipped." Instead, he found an undersized force, few supplies, and little preparation. "It is much to be lamented that those expectations have not been realized and that the laudable intentions of Congress are unhappily frustrated."[27] It is difficult not to imagine this as a none-too-subtle payback by Schuyler, who had watched in the past as his political enemies worked the corridors of Congress to undermine him and his allies, Arnold among them.

When he arrived in Albany, Lafayette was shocked to find his plan and his army in shambles. He complained in a letter to the local revolutionary committee that Hazen had done a poor job of preparing for the invasion, which might now have to be called off. He said he felt "deceived" because news of the venture had already been published throughout Europe and he had understood that he had Arnold's support.[28] Hazen, the quartermaster-general, of course tried to deflect the blame from himself and to place it on his enemy, Arnold. In a letter to Gates, Hazen laid the groundwork for his own exoneration. "I am now greatly hurt at the thoughts of the Canada expedition being laid aside," he wrote. "I am also sorry for the Marquis. His disappointment is great and mortifying."

Then he spun his conspiracy theory. "I am convinced there has been great pains taken by some ill-minded people to fix the failure of this expedition on the quarter-master general's department, holding up as I conceive the difficulty or rather, as they term it, the impossibility of my being able to provide carriages and forage necessary for the expedition."

He argued that he did not think the sleighs and provisions had to be assembled first. He imagined he was being set up by an old enemy. "Gen. Arnold has taken the command at this place and he has countermanded the orders which I gave in the course of my duty and also has ordered the cloathier-general to issue cloathing I procured at Boston by his orders only."

There was, of course, no proof that Arnold was behind the débâcle. Hazen himself suggested that the obstacles were irrelevant to the 366 men he had assembled. "They are so warm for the expedition that they would consent to go almost naked into Canada. I wish I could see as much forwardness in the other troops."[29]

As a veteran of the earlier Canadian campaign, Hazen knew better. This was political exaggeration. Near-naked troops in a Canadian winter campaign were dead troops. This was private propaganda, aimed at keeping Arnold the villain in Gates's mind.

11

Politics and Treason

To understand Arnold's treatment at the hands of his own emerging country, it is useful to consider some of the tensions that swept through the revolutionary forces of the day. Far from the simplified image of a unified, single-minded people struggling for liberation, the revolutionary forces were a morass of conflicting personalities, ambitions, loyalties, and agendas. Benedict Arnold was far from the only soldier to be shunned, belittled, and harassed by the politicians and the political generals. His case is merely the most famous because it had the most drastic outcome.

Through the last half of the 1770s, the Continental Congress was a weak, quarrelsome entity, short of money and authority but determined to play a role. With jealous colonies unwilling to transfer too much authority to the central body, the gathering of politicians at Philadelphia was more a caricature of a government than the real thing. One of the few real powers congressmen had was control over promotions and pay within the fledgling continental army. The politicians jealously guarded their political control over the military, believing that an independent army was a stage on the road to tyranny. They were resentful of military leaders like Arnold who bristled at political orders issued by those who were safely away from the battle front. They were distrustful of brash, independent, aloof men like Arnold who thought so little of Congress and politicians that he spent no time lobbying for their support. Military historians generally agree that Congress often made a botch of it, promoting politically astute but militarily suspect men like Horatio Gates and David Wooster while overlooking or even persecuting decisive military leaders and strategists like Arnold and Daniel Morgan of Virginia.

Gates, in particular, has fared poorly in the historical record despite his prominent roles as leader of the Northern Army in 1778 and the Southern Army in 1780. He was a favourite of John Adams, who used his influence in Congress to promote Gates's career. One military historian has dismissed him as a "politician-general" who took credit for victories won by others, including Saratoga; whose main battles were fought in the political trenches against fellow officers; and who directed American troops into various disasters, proving "beyond a shadow of a doubt that he was completely incompetent."[1] Meanwhile, more worthy military men like Schuyler and Morgan withdrew from the war at crucial moments rather than live with the political decisions of Congress that Gates and his allies helped orchestrate.

In Congress and among the revolutionary forces, there were also class divisions. Some saw the Revolution as an attack on inherited privilege and a fight for democracy (at least for white adult males). They resented those they saw as the privileged rich, whether plantation owners like George Washington of Virginia, estate owners like Philip Schuyler of New York, or businessmen like Benedict Arnold of Connecticut and James Wilson of Pennsylvania. Yet the reality for many of these businessmen was that the war was draining or entirely wiping out their fortunes. Arnold's trading business had all but collapsed and he often used his own money to buy provisions for his men when Congress was too slow in granting funds, or refused to do so. When these officer-businessmen tried to organize their commercial affairs to make some money from the war effort – as many civilian politicians were doing – they were looked on with suspicion and often accused of using their positions for personal gain. Military historian Roger Spiller has noted: "Like many other officers, [Arnold] was particularly angry about civilians who profited from the war while he was rebuffed and accused of financial chicanery when trying to settle accounts with Congress and other civil agencies."[2]

In fact, by 1779 Arnold was telling Washington that he was broke, even though he had joined the cause four years before as one of Connecticut's wealthiest men. He had used much of his personal fortune to finance the Canadian invasion, yet Congress still had not paid the bills he had submitted, often challenging them because Arnold did not keep proper receipts. For three years, like most of the army, he had not been paid. Still, he had expenses that ranged from providing housing and paying staff to entertaining official visitors; all the while he watched inflation devalue his Continental currency.[3]

In addition to financial and political aggravations, the mix in that revolutionary stew included personality conflicts. In an era of heroic events and powerful personalities, one man's advance or fame was often perceived as coming at someone else's expense. By all accounts, Arnold's demeanour alienated many, even as it attracted people who, like George Washington, saw in those same personality traits the ingredients of decisive and charismatic leadership. Arnold had some powerful and persuasive enemies. John Brown had been an adversary from the earliest day of the war, an ally of Ethan Allan and a bitter Arnold rival after he was refused promotion during the Quebec campaign. Horatio Gates was an enemy, in part because Arnold was a friend of some of Gates's rivals and in part because the two men were vying for military glory from the same battles. In reports back to Congress, Gates consistently downplayed or denied entirely Arnold's battlefield triumphs. Later, Arnold also locked horns with Joseph Reed, the powerful, ambitious, and politically devious chairman of the Philadelphia council who saw Arnold as a rival for power and influence in the city.

The combination of political intrigue and personality clashes, so distant from revolutionary principles and battlefield heroics, undermined Arnold's faith in the cause, some historians have suggested. It was not the specific reprimands and setbacks that drove Arnold to contemplate treason: 'Far more important was Arnold's sense that human frailty had ruined the republican cause."[4] The main weapon at the disposal of his political and military enemies was the military court. In many ways, they did more damage to Arnold than the thousands of British, Canadians, and Germans who faced him and tried to kill him over the course of his career as a soldier of the Revolution.

The trouble started after his first engagement at Fort Ticonderoga in 1775, when Massachusetts politicians had accused him of failing to account for funds. As noted earlier, the need to clear his name hung over Arnold through that summer as Washington contemplated the prospect of appointing him to lead the audacious invasion of Quebec. That invasion, and in particular the disorganized retreat, brought more allegations of theft of property and appropriation of congressional funds. It is remarkable that in the summer of 1776, as Arnold struggled to build a fleet and plan the defence of Lake Champlain, he was distracted by a court-martial hearing instigated by John Brown. Although the bare bones of the 1776 court-martial were described earlier in the narrative, they warrant a brief retelling as part of the unending war against Arnold from within.

Brown, the young lawyer, felt aggrieved by Arnold's refusal to promote him in Quebec. He was outraged when Arnold justified that decision in part by accusing Brown of overseeing the stealing of supplies from British officers captured at Sorel. Brown counter-attacked with the charge that Arnold had stolen, for his own use, goods confiscated in Montreal. On 26 July 1776 a court-martial was convened at Fort Ticonderoga, presided over by Colonel Enoch Poor. Arnold was summoned to account for himself and riled the presiding officers by showing little deference and by citing politics and jealousy as the forces behind the charges. Poor was neither a fan nor friend of the beleaguered Arnold, favouring instead the infamous Roger Enos, who had deserted Arnold in the Maine wilderness. Poor badgered Arnold through the hearing. Arnold was unbending, contemptuous, and arrogant in turn. Ultimately, Gates dissolved the hearing without a verdict because he did not want to lose Arnold. It was an omen of what lay ahead.

That same summer, Arnold ordered the arrest of Moses Hazen for failing to guard the stores sent from Montreal to Chambly, where they were pilfered. Hazen, once an Arnold ally in Quebec but now in the John Brown camp, was acquitted in a court-martial after suggesting that Arnold was the thief. Arnold exploded with invective against the court, was ordered to apologize, and refused. He was ordered arrested but that was overturned by Gates.[5] Although there was no proof that Arnold had benefited personally, his critics through the years have steadfastly contented themselves with assuming that something was amiss. Even if he wasn't guilty that time, his flawed personality and greed meant that he could have been.

Even after the brilliant battle at Valcour Island, Arnold's critics persevered. One of the judges in the Hazen court martial showed his bias by suggesting to Congress that, rather than praise and promote Arnold for stopping the British fleet invasion, he should be criticized for losing the American fleet and essentially mishandling the battle. "You may have heard that a few days ago, we had a fine fleet but General Arnold, our evil genius of the north, has with a good deal of industry got us clear of it."[6]

Arnold went back to Connecticut for the winter, threatening, as he often did, to quit the army rather than take the political abuse and accusation. Then came his heroics during the Danbury raid, a promotion from Congress to major general, and a plea from Washington to join the northern defence against the advancing British.

Still, Brown carried on his campaign against Arnold. After the Quebec campaign, he had joined Hazen in suggesting that Arnold's performance had been more self-serving than heroic. They twisted his life-saving smallpox inoculation program into a dangerous decision to spread smallpox among his own troops. On 12 May 1777 Brown returned to the issue of greed with a published article meant to be circulated among the nation's political class. "Money is this man's god and to get enough of it, he would sacrifice his country," he wrote, making a charge that Arnold's critics would see as prescient, considering later events.[7]

To try to lift the cloud surrounding his valuable soldier, Washington referred to Congress and the Board of War the issue of whether Arnold had profited from the Quebec campaign. Once again, the proud soldier, who had recently returned from New Haven and the grim reports of his disappearing fortune and business, had to stand before politicians and try to convince them that he was not in the war for profit. Brown did not appear as the accuser and the charges were dismissed, although some congressmen said they were still unhappy that much of the money Congress had advanced for the Quebec campaign had not been properly accounted for by the general. Arnold's standard answer was that others beneath him in the chain of command had been responsible for keeping the accounts and it was an impossible book-keeper's demand properly to receipt every dollar spent in the heat of battle and invasion. "Arnold was a whirlwind soldier who could not be bothered with keeping track of small expenses," wrote one historian. "He spent what had to be spent and figured the amount up later. Let civilians supply what soldiers needed … this attitude led to constant battles with accountants and suspicions about his personal gain."[8] He also regularly noted that Congress had yet to reimburse him for the personal funds he used to keep his men fed, clothed, and armed.

In the aftermath of the Battle of Saratoga, Arnold was a partially crippled, increasingly embittered man. Washington did not want to lose him and yet realized he was not physically fit to return to the front. He appointed him military governor of Philadelphia. In hindsight, it was this unfortunate appointment that largely sealed Arnold's fate. Arnold and the revolutionary leaders of Philadelphia were like oil and water. Washington's attempt to favour his old comrade with an easy job while he healed was a monumental error in judgment. It put a man of action behind a bureaucratic desk. It exposed the politically inept Arnold to the force and fury of Philadelphia politics, with its large Tory class and antagonistic, radical Pennsylvania Council led by Joseph Reed. It brought out Arnold's conservative side as he found the monied class of Philadelphia better company than the suspicious, ambitious radicals.

It gave Arnold a chance to make some money by dabbling again in business deals – deal making frowned upon by the radicals. It exposed Arnold to continuing allegations from his enemies about the sins of his past, all gleefully published in the *Packet*, a newspaper controlled by the radicals that always neglected to mention that Arnold had been cleared of all charges, or certainly had never been convicted.[9]

All of this drove Arnold even closer to the Tory class of businessmen and Loyalist sympathizers who had collaborated with the British when they occupied the city and were now making their peace with the revolutionary occupiers. They admired Arnold for his commercial acumen and his sense of class values and occasion. Like them (and like most of the revolutionary leaders), he was a selective democrat at best. They also fêted him for his military exploits and legendary bravery, considering him something of a revolutionary star in their midst, which was more than the local revolutionaries did. For all these reasons Arnold was less than hostile to the local Tories who were so despised by the radicals. He argued that he was governor of all Philadelphia, not just the friends of Joseph Reed.

Then there was Peggy Shippen, a woman who still excites speculation about her role in Arnold's decision to betray the Revolution. Peggy was a theatrical, flirtatious, and beautiful eighteen-year-old Tory when she met Arnold. He was a widower twice her age with three young sons and solid credentials as an enemy of the British. It made them a strange match. Arnold was the military governor appointed by the revolutionary forces. Despite his cane and limp, he was an impressive figure and the scourge of the old order. She was the daughter of Judge Edward Shippen, the product of old money, high-class presumptions, and a background in the British colonial system. Peggy Shippen regularly entertained British officers during their occupation of the city and one of them – the dashing and artistic John André – painted a famous portrait of her, with sparkling eyes and hair piled high in the style favoured by upper-class ladies of the day.

Yet the Shippen family also had its rebel connections. Peggy's father's cousin William was a prominent revolutionary and chief of the medical department of the continental army. Judge Shippen was a longtime friend of the slave-owning patriarch George Washington and the general had known Peggy from her childhood.[10] Edward survived the Revolution and became chief justice of Pennsylvania in later years.[11]

Arnold met Peggy in mid-1778 and began to spend more time at the Shippen household, wooing her and trying to win over her sceptical father. In September 1778 he proposed to Peggy after asking for her father's blessing. His letter to Edward seeking his daughter's hand offered a hint that the revolutionary warrior was tiring of the conflict after more than three years. "Our difference in political sentiments will, I hope, be no bar to my happiness. I flatter myself the time is at hand when our unhappy contests will be at an end and peace and domestic happiness be restored to everyone."[12] Despite their political differences, Edward Shippen consented and his daughter married Arnold on 8 April 1779 in Philadelphia.

By then Arnold was clearly considering dropping out of the fray. In late 1778 he was contemplating the purchase of a large tract of land in New York State that was being offered at a bargain price by some admirers. He seriously considered it before political intrigue forced him back to Philadelphia to defend his reputation against new charges by the radicals.

Meanwhile, Peggy Shippen was becoming part of Arnold's problem with the radicals. The marriage added to their suspicions. Peggy had a Tory outlook and high-level British and Loyalist contacts, which Arnold later used. This has led some Americans to insist that she was behind Arnold's later treason.[13] But while many Americans like to imagine Peggy as the evil influence who turned Benedict's head, it also is true that she showed no particular political involvement in future years. Instead, she gave unbending support to her husband and her marriage. She had fallen in love with and married a hero but ended up spending most of the rest of her life married to a political leper, a man despised by many, often in debt, and an anti-hero to those who had once praised him. Her loyalty to Arnold meant she had to be physically separated from her family. Yet despite her disappointed dreams, Peggy never deserted him nor publicly doubted him but presented the perfect portrait of a loyal and loving wife.

Peggy the vivacious teenager quickly began to produce children for Arnold, five in all. By 1795 she had had her fill of child bearing. "For my own part, I am *determined* to have no more little plagues, as it is so difficult to provide for them in this country," she wrote to a friend from her home in London, England.[14]

In the romantic winter of 1778–79 all that was in the future as Arnold found himself falling in love with the young Peggy Shippen while continuing to fend off the jealousy and damaging allegations of his supposed allies in the cause of independence. He was growing weary of politics and harassment. As he returned from New York to Philadelphia in February 1779 to face accusations from the Pennsylvania council and Joseph Reed, he wrote a letter to Peggy that showed a weary side: "I am heartily tired with my journey and almost so with human nature. I daily discover so much baseness and ingratitude among mankind that I almost blush at being of the same species and could quit the stage without regret was it not for some gentle, generous souls like my dear Peggy ..."[15] Leaving the stage, however, was not in the cards. Arnold faced the most serious charges of his long battle against the enemy within.

One of Arnold's first acts as military governor had been to proclaim martial law because of the unrest and mob violence perpetrated by pro-independence thugs against those they imagined to be Tories. This decision, typical of Arnold's style of seeing a problem and dealing with it, was seen by radical leaders as another indication of his Tory sympathies. Arnold compounded the problem by using his authority to order or approve several questionable commercial transactions. As governor, he granted safe passage to the ship *Charming Nancy* to move from Philadelphia harbour, where it had been seized and confined by local revolutionary leaders, to another harbour where it could be unloaded. He was a part owner of the cargo. *En route,* it came under British attack and took refuge in Egg Harbor. At a time when the harbour was under British embargo, he sent twelve wagons to collect guns, linen, woollens, glass, sugar, tea, and nails, which could be sold in Philadelphia. In essence, he was speculating and using his authority to try to help his business partners.

The political leaders of the Pennsylvania council thought they had him in their sights. They objected to his arrogance in strutting around Philadelphia with guards, like a British lord. They objected to his Tory friends, like the Shippens. They objected to his business connections, like his friendship with the merchant James Wilson, a signatory of the Declaration of Independence who was now suspected of using a shortage of goods to justify raising prices. Now they thought they had caught him in a clear case of violating the law and revolutionary niceties. Joseph Reed pressed charges and used the *Packet* to keep the charges alive and to keep Arnold's reputation under a cloud. Arnold asked for a court-martial hearing and again, Washington agreed to the plea as a way to salvage his friend's dignity and reputation. On 5 May 1779 Arnold wrote to Washington asking for quick justice. "Having made every sacrifice of fortune and blood and become a cripple in the service of my country, I little expected to meet the ungrateful returns I have received from my countrymen ... I have nothing left but the little reputation I have gained in the army. Delay in the present case is worse than death."[16] Washington understood and scheduled the trial for

1 June but a British troop movement up the Hudson River from New York forced him to postpone the court martial and to mobilize all available troops. Through the summer and autumn of 1779, the hearing was delayed as Washington's army faced the British threat. Arnold brooded as rumours swirled, slanders became commonplace, and his day in court was delayed, to the advantage of his accusers.

The court martial was finally set to start on 22 December 1779 at Washington's winter headquarters in Morristown, New Jersey. That morning at a tavern in a stone building with a roaring fireplace, twelve military officers sat in judgment at a long heavy wooden table. Col Alexander Hamilton, Washington's closest aide, was there. Reed and the Pennsylvania council executives sat as Arnold's accusers on one side of the table.[17] Judge Advocate Col John Lawrence read the eight charges. Arnold was allegedly guilty of exceeding authority given by Washington when he allowed the *Charming Nancy* to leave port; closing shops in Philadelphia while he had access to goods; forcing a guard to do "menial duties" (Arnold had asked him to fetch a barber); profiteering from a captured sloop, a charge already dismissed by a grand jury; using private wagons to transport goods from the *Charming Nancy*; usurping the authority of the Pennsylvania council to allow a Philadelphia woman to travel to New York to help her mother; disrespect for the Pennsylvania council; and "showing favoritism to tories over patriots."[18] The arguments, charges, and counter-charges went on for days, spilled into the new year, and eventually ended in late January.

When Arnold had a chance to defend himself, he attacked Reed as a political opportunist, justified his business dealings as the attempt of an impoverished patriot to pay the bills, and contrasted his record with that of the politicians who sat in safety in their offices, criticizing soldiers in the field. "In every hour of danger, I have always obeyed the calls of my country and stepped forward in her defence. When many were deserting her cause, which appeared desperate, I have often bled in it. The years and wounds and marks I bear are sufficient witness to my conduct."[19] While there is no verbatim transcript of the trial, another recorded version of Arnold's message to the court martial has the same tone:

When the present necessary war against Great Britain commenced, I was in easy circumstances and enjoyed a fair prospect of improving them. I was happy in domestic connections and blessed with a rising family who claimed my care and attention. The liberties of my country were in danger. The voice of my country called upon all her faithful sons to join in her defence. With cheerfulness,

I obeyed the call. I sacrificed domestic ease and happiness to the service of my country and in her service have I sacrificed a great part of a handsome fortune. I was one of the first that appeared in the field and from that time to the present hour, have not abandoned her service.[20]

Arnold then went back to Philadelphia to face increasing debt, a hostile population, and growing family responsibilities. On 19 March Peggy produced their first child, a boy. Beyond this good news, it was not a happy time. The previous autumn, with charges pending and rumours swirling, Arnold had been hassled on the streets of the city. He asked Congress for more protection but was refused. His relations with Congress and the Pennsylvania council were increasingly strained. The verdict was reached and sent to Congress and Washington in March. It was a mixed blessing for Arnold. He was cleared of most of the allegations but found guilty of misbehaviour on two counts – the first, of naving issued the travel permit for the *Charming Nancy*, and the second, of using publicly owned wagons to haul private goods from the ship. Washington, long Arnold's defender, was forced to reprimand him publicly. He did it as gently as possible in his daily orders published on 6 April 1780: "The commander-in-chief would have been much happier in an occasion of bestowing commendations on an officer who has rendered such distinguished services to his country as Maj. Gen. Arnold but in the present case, a sense of duty and a regard to candor oblige him to declare that he considers his conduct in the instance of the permit as particularly reprehensible, both in a civil and military view, and in the affair of the wagons as imprudent and improper."[21]

To add injury to insult, Congress that spring finally refused Arnold's request that he be reimbursed for thousands of dollars of war expenses paid out of his own pocket. Instead, congressmen insisted that he owed them close to nine thousand dollars for receipts not submitted on cash advances paid to him before the Quebec campaign. They refused to accept his explanation that in the heat of battle receipts were not always issued and in the chaos of retreat, many had been lost. Congress also turned down certain expense claims from his duties as military governor of Philadelphia. "In effect," wrote the historian Willard Randall, "Arnold could no longer afford to serve as an American general."[22] Hoping to help out his old comrade, Washington wrote privately that April: "As far as it shall be in my powers, I myself will furnish you with opportunities for regaining the esteem which you have formerly enjoyed."[23] Washington's idea was that he would give Arnold a new command and a new battle front where he could again cloak himself with glory and make the nation forget his minor transgressions.

What Washington did not know was that by then, Arnold already had given up on his country and its dreams of independence. He was double-dealing, talking with the British about defecting and preparing to betray his commander-in-chief. When he stood before the court-martial in the Norris Tavern to proclaim his love of country and his continued fidelity to the cause, Arnold was lying. He had decided the leaders of the Revolution were unworthy, interested in creating a country only in order to dominate it. He was uneasy about the American alliance with the French, whom he loathed and distrusted. Besides, there was strong evidence that the Revolution was faltering. In many parts of the colonies, there was popular unrest and a weakening continental army. Whether delusional or not, Arnold convinced himself that his defection would attract others to cross the line and help end the war and its privations. Great Britain, happy to end a conflict that was increasingly costly and unpopular at home, would make some concessions and the colonies would find themselves a new, more autonomous niche in the British Empire.

And of course, there was the question of money. Arnold detractors have made much of his hard-nosed negotiation with the British over money, attributing it to base greed. Base need was also a factor. He was broke or close to it and the prospects of recouping his losses in inflation-devalued continental currency were dim. He needed the money for his growing family and to rebuild his business after the war. Arnold clearly thought his defection would be worth a considerable sum to the British.

The facts of Arnold's act of treason are well known. He left a paper trail that became available to historians in the 1930s through the papers of Sir Henry Clinton, housed at the University of Michigan.[24]

As far as historians can tell, the British made the first move. It was not uncommon for leaders of the revolutionary forces to have their loyalty tested by hints from contacts on the other side about the possibility of cooperation to end the turmoil, killing, terror, and exodus of refugees that marked the conflict. Arnold would have been a natural target because of his well-publicized feuds with the radicals, his unhappiness with the political leadership of the united colonies, his Loyalist connections through the Shippens, and perhaps even the rumours of some very unrevolutionary opinions that he supposedly expressed in the drawing-room of the governor's mansion, Mount Pleasant.

In May 1779 Col Beverly Robinson, who recruited colonial Loyalists to fight for the British wrote to Arnold. As a former Virginia plantation owner, Robinson knew Washington and shared Washington's acquaintance with the Shippens. "The exhausted colonies cannot much longer sustain the unequal contest," wrote Robinson. "Every reason presses us to put an end to this unhappy discord. We must seek a reunion without shedding any more blood ..."[25] It struck a chord.

Arnold approached Philadelphia Loyalist Joseph Stansbury indicating that he was interested in talking to the British. Stansbury, who owned a glass-and-china shop and travelled regularly to New York for trade, carried the message to Clinton's headquarters on Broadway Street. He spoke to Clinton's aide and designated spy handler John André, who was familiar with Arnold. Three years before as a young British soldier in Quebec, André had been captured by Arnold's forces and held for months as a prisoner-of-war. He also knew him through Peggy Shippen, with whom André was acquainted from his days as an artistic man-about-town in Philadelphia and whose portrait he had painted. André and Clinton were obviously intrigued by Arnold's offer to discuss coming over to the British side, but they were probably also suspicious. Was this brilliant soldier-hero with impeccable revolutionary credentials really interested in working for the enemy? To test him out, Clinton let it be known that he did not want Arnold to defect. Rather, he wanted him to work as a double agent, feigning fidelity to the American cause while feeding information to the British.

To prove his sincerity, Arnold went along with the scheme, all the while trying to wring out of Clinton a promise that he would be given ten thousand pounds if he defected. Clinton balked at the sum, which was a small fortune. Yet he did not want Arnold to walk away and continued to encourage him by promising that he would be well rewarded. Arnold quickly caught on to the life of double-dealing. He took the code name Gustavus and developed an elaborate, if simple, system for exchanging coded messages with André. Both men had a copy of the book *Blackstone's Commentaries*, fifth Oxford edition, volume one. Each word in an encoded message consisted of three numbers – the page number, line number, and word number. At other times they used a code based on *Bailey's Dictionary*. Through the last half of 1779 and the first half of 1780, Arnold supplied information about troop numbers and movements that was largely innocuous and usually available to the British elsewhere.

Arnold was not the only prominent American to consider or to carry out a switch of allegiance. As fortunes ebbed and flowed, loyalties often switched with them. Ethan Allen's secret offers to the British to deliver Vermont to His Majesty is one prominent example but there were many.[26] The Revolution had never been a unanimous uprising. As one historian put it: "What had been a political controversy became increasingly a civil war."[27] In some areas, "the war became a vicious guerrilla struggle ... the devastation and the bloodshed were frightful and the British, the revolutionaries and the loyalists all bore a share of the responsibility."[28]

The conflict between friends and within families and communities was evident even in high-profile revolutionary families. George Washington's mother was a British loyalist and at times, the British thought that Washington himself could be bought with a title and a position. Revolutionary icon Benjamin Franklin produced a son, William, who was the Royal Governor of New Jersey and a prominent anti-revolutionary. His son, in turn, was an American patriot.[29]

A vivid example of the fluid politics of the Revolution occurred on 6 October 1779 when Philadelphia merchant James Wilson, an original revolutionary and a signatory of the Declaration of Independence, became an Enemy of the People. The street mobs turned on him, believing that he, like other merchants in their view, was enriching himself by hoarding supplies. They surrounded his magnificent house, threatening to ransack it and to deal with him as mobs had dealt with other Enemies of the Revolution – by tarring and feathering, beatings, and sometimes murder. Arnold, then military governor of Philadelphia, protected Wilson at gunpoint. The incident helped confirm the mob's suspicion that Arnold had become a defender of Tories and other British sympathizers.[30]

Both sides had their spy networks. Both sides had their informers. The Boston-area silversmith Paul Revere was one of the leaders of the American intelligence-gathering system. John André was one of the main spy handlers on the British side. There were spectacular cases and before Arnold, few were as high level as that of Dr Benjamin Church, director general of hospitals for the congressional army in 1775 and a close confidant of such leading Massachusetts rebels as John Adams, John Hancock, and Sam Adams. But he was also a paid informer for the British general Thomas Gage, passing on information through 1774 and 1775 on the mood of the people, their growing militancy, their military training, where arms were stored, and where fighters were congregating. For a time, the British were receiving sensitive tips from directly inside Paul Revere's intelligence-gathering network and Revere suspected Church. Finally, in September 1775, he was arrested, convicted, and imprisoned while Arnold was putting his life on the line in the Quebec invasion.

Throughout the war, suspicious eyes were cast on many leading revolutionaries, including Philip Schuyler and Washington himself. Metcalf Bowler, the chief justice of Rhode Island, defected. So did Edward Fox of Maryland, clerk of the continental treasury in Philadelphia. In 1776 Thomas Hickey tried to parlay his position as a member of Washington's guard to cut a deal with the British. He was hanged for his efforts. Even Maj. Gen. Charles Lee, second-in-command of the rebel forces, kept in touch with the British during the war, hoping a peaceful compromise could be found. In September 1777 British general Robert Howe published an offer that attracted some interest from discontented Pennsylvania rebels. "Such spirited fellows who are willing to engage will be rewarded at the end of the war, besides their laurels, with 50 acres of land where every gallant hero may retire to enjoy his bottle and lass."[31]

In summer 1780 Arnold's double-dealing became much more directed. He had decided to defect and if he could, he would deliver valuable assets to the British when he crossed sides. By then, Washington had decided that Arnold was well enough to join active duty again. Arnold had other plans. He had drawn strong British interest with a proposal to deliver West Point, a key American post on the Hudson River north of New York City. He begged off active duty and persuaded Washington to make him commander of West Point, against Washington's better judgment. It was a fort in need of repair and Arnold set about doing that, all the while trying to negotiate the best way to surrender it, for the most money. He had been dealing with André through intermediaries and his plan was to ensure that the fort's defences were down so that the British army could march in, capture the defending American troops, and disarm an important link in American defences.

On 15 September the stakes got considerably higher. Arnold received word that Washington would be passing through and spending the night at West Point on 24 September. Maybe he could deliver the American leader as well. Surely that would end the war and make him a rich hero. "General Washington will be at King's Ferry Sunday evening next on his way to Hartford, where he is to meet the French admiral and general. Will lodge at Peak's Kill," Arnold wrote in a coded message to André.[32] After a frenzy of letters it was decided that senior British officers, including Robinson and André, would sail up the Hudson River to a site near the fort where Arnold would meet them to make final arrangements. Thanks to bungling the on-board meeting was aborted. Arnold then insisted that André come onshore to meet him in civilian dress. Against protocol and the natural British caution, André agreed. The risky meeting, which stretched over several nights, revolved around money and arrangements. In the end, the disguised André was sent back behind British lines with Arnold's final offer. More bungling ensued, and the British officer was captured by three country militiamen on an isolated road near Tarrytown, just north of the safe British town of New York. André was carrying incriminating documents. The unsuspecting militiamen, seeing Arnold's name, assumed he should know and sent the documents to him. Their blunder saved his life.

What followed was high drama. Washington did not make it to West Point by the night of 24 September. Instead, he sent word that he would arrive on Monday, 25 September, in time for breakfast with Arnold and Peggy. Arnold waited anxiously, assuming that his act of treason had been arranged and the leader of the Revolution would be delivered to the enemy the next day. Washington's aide, Alexander Hamilton, arrived to say that their commander had been further delayed and that breakfast should start without him. Suddenly, within an hour of Washington's planned arrival, a messenger burst onto the scene with a package for Arnold. The general read it, excused himself, went to tell Peggy that he had been discovered, and then rode to the river and commandeered a boat to row him around the corner to the *Vulture*, where the British awaited his arrival.

Back on shore chaos prevailed. Washington had been looking forward to spending some time with Arnold "and his very pretty wife." But when he arrived at their house outside the fort, there was no sign of Arnold and he was told that Peggy was "indisposed." Expecting that the Arnolds would arrive for a late afternoon dinner with himself and his aides, Hamilton and Lafayette, Washington's Party "dispersed to their rooms. As Lafayette was dressing, Hamilton dashed in with the request that he attend at once on the commander. He found Washington trembling with emotions, a packet of papers in his hand ... 'Arnold has betrayed us. Whom can we trust now?'"[33]

They found Peggy in her upstairs bedroom. Whether through feigned or real hysteria, she convinced them that she had known nothing of Arnold's treasonous intentions and that the shock had made her crazy with fear and anxiety. The young Hamilton, smitten by Peggy, wrote that day to his girlfriend, Elizabeth Schuyler: "Could I forgive

Arnold for sacrificing his honor, reputation and duty, I could not forgive him for acting a part that must have forfeited the esteem of so fine
a woman."[34] The attempted treason quickly became sustaining fodder
for revolutionary leaders whose spirits had flagged as the war dragged
on and American colonial society became more divided and war-weary.
From Paris, where he heard the news, Benjamin Franklin wrote to
Lafayette: "His character is in the sight of all Europe already on the
Gibbet and will hang there in chains for ages."[35] Thomas Jefferson
wanted Arnold kidnapped and brought back with a price on his head.
Privately, he wrote that there would be American satisfaction at seeing
Arnold "exhibited as a public spectacle of infamy."[36] Across the colonies, there was outrage. Mobs burned Arnold in effigy and destroyed
most of the public references to his name, including the tombstones
of his ancestors and namesakes in New Haven and Rhode Island.

On the British side, Arnold may have received a cool traitor's welcome from the soldiers, as American biographers have suggested, but
his defection was seen as a coup that would hurt the rebel cause,
probably entice more defections, and perhaps help end the war. "The
defection of one of the best generals they have at this time has thrown
them into great confusion and will have most important consequences," Clinton wrote a week later to his sisters in England.[37]

Arnold's first act, once safely on the *Venture,* was to write a letter to
Peggy assuring her he was safe. Then, there was a letter to Washington
justifying his defection as an act of patriotism. "The heart, which is
conscious of its own rectitude, cannot attempt to palliate a step which
the world may censure as wrong," he wrote. "I have ever acted from a
principle of love to my country. Since the commencement of the
present unhappy contest between Great Britain and the colonies, the
same principle of love to my country actuates my present conduct,
however it may appear inconsistent to the world, who very seldom
judge right of any man's actions."[38] He asked that Peggy be spared and
be allowed to return to her family in Philadelphia, for she was "inno-
cent as an angel."

There developed a tawdry affair over the fate of John André. Washington had him tried as a spy and executed by hanging, despite pleas
from the British that he be spared, a threat from Arnold that if he was
executed American blood would flow, and a plea from André that he
be allowed to die by firing squad as a soldier, rather than be hanged
as a common spy. André has fared well in history as a sensitive tragic
figure caught in the web of Arnold's deceit, loved by Clinton, the
British, and Peggy, admired by his American captors, and praised post-

humously by Hamilton as a brave and honourable man. He is com-
memorated in London's Westminster Abbey.

Washington put a price on Arnold's head. Since the traitor stayed
in North America for more than a year, often at the front lines, it is
amazing that he was not captured or killed. It seemed as if Providence
was still watching over him as he escaped capture or death on a couple
of occasions by the narrowest of margins. Meanwhile, Arnold put a
price on his own head once he arrived in New York and met Clinton.
He was lodged at the home of Maj. Gen. James Robertson, royal governor of New York. Arnold wanted £10,000 and a commission in the
British army. He received £6,000 and a further £350 for expenses –
more than $200,000 in modern US currency. He was also made a
brigadier at a salary of £650 annually and given a stipend of £225 for
life. What he received was worth far less than the property he lost and
the debt he wrote off.[39]

After several months of agitating, Arnold was given command of a
troop that he was authorized to raise from American military defectors.
His American Legion never amounted to much but eventually Arnold
was put in charge of a force to fight in the American South. British
troops and the élite Virginia Loyalist troops of the Queen's Rangers,
led by André's good friend John Graves Simcoe, were part of his command. His assignment was to capture Portsmouth, Virginia, and, if the
opportunity arose, to attack communities lying up the James River.
Although Peggy and the children had joined him in New York, he
spent part of the winter of 1780–81 back at war, leading seventeen
hundred soldiers on a successful southern campaign. On that trek, his
troop was almost cut off and captured by a French ship but the raid
was a successful thrust into the southern colonies.[40] At Richmond, he
came close to capturing Thomas Jefferson, then governor of Virginia.
At the very least, Arnold humiliated Jefferson with the ease of his
invasion and destruction of Virginian mills and armaments despite
Jefferson's efforts to mount a defence.[41]

One frightful episode marred Arnold's tour of duty in British uniform. On a march into New London, Connecticut to destroy some
rebel armouries, he instructed his men to leave the town alone and
burn only military targets. Nonetheless, when some of the townspeople
fired on the troops, a battle ensued and the victorious British troops
torched various buildings, one of which contained gunpowder. It
exploded and much of the town was burned.

In the spring of 1781 Arnold and his family sailed from New York
to London where he pleaded with the British government to send a

large army across the Atlantic Ocean to win the war. In Britain he
discovered a country that had lost the will to continue the fight. The
Americans captured a large British force in Virginia that spring and
the war was all but over. A new anti-war Whig government took office
in London and peace negotiations were launched. Arnold's gamble
had failed. He was in a London that generally ignored him. Outside
the royal court and upper classes, few people considered him a hero.
The mood had turned against the entire enterprise of trying to coerce
the colonies into staying. Arnold seemed to represent the failed policy.
He was shunned by the Whigs and defamed by prominent politicians
like Edmund Burke.[42]

Efforts to win an army command failed, in part because the British
army was still very much dominated by upper-class officers who had
purchased their commissions. Having proven oneself in the field, as
Arnold had done countless times, was not an important qualification
for command in the British army of 1781. It was a form of class snob-
bery that the American-bred Arnold undoubtedly had a difficult time
accepting. His attempts to win a business management position in such
prominent British companies as the British East India Company were
also denied, partly because of his notoriety as a military traitor and his
position as a symbol of an unpopular military campaign, much as
returning Vietnam war veterans faced the disdain of their anti-war
neighbours in the 1960s and 1970s in the United States.

In the early 1780s Benedict Arnold found himself with no way to
support his large family in London, despite his prominent and high-
born friends. He was only in his early forties and the reward he
received for defecting, while large, was not nearly enough to allow him
to live as one of Britain's idle rich. He needed work. He needed to
find a place where an energetic, enterprising man with some capital
to invest could start anew and build a fortune. He needed a place that
was less developed and class-ridden than London, a place not unlike
the New Haven of his youth – a rough and growing seaport where a
man with self-assurance and a gambler's instinct could prosper.

By 1784 Arnold was beginning to hear tales about the new Loyalist
colony that was being built in the forests north of Nova Scotia. There
was talk of a natural harbour on the north shore of the Bay of Fundy,
where Champlain had landed and where the French had built a fort
a century earlier. There were tales of natural riches, a recently landed
Loyalist population in need of the supplies that a trader could bring,
and a rough-and-tumble sea port culture that would let the entrepreneurial cream rise to the top. By the last half of the year, Arnold was

planning to leave Peggy and the kids temporarily, hoping to build them a new home back in North America, where his family had more than a century of roots.

At least in New Brunswick, he would be free of the stolid class system and prejudice that held him back in England. He would be among others who had turned their backs on the Revolution. He would be in a frontier society where a man was respected for what he accomplished rather than for what he had done in the past, where opportunities abounded for those who would grasp them.

In November 1785, late in his forty-fifth year, he sailed from London on a merchant ship bound for Halifax. He signed on as a "supercargo," hired by the owner to take care of the merchandise on the voyage. For the moment, he was in the employ of a businessman. Soon, he dreamed, he would be established in New Brunswick again as a businessman trader himself.

12

The Streets of Saint John

The Saint John of Arnold's day emerges from the pages of the *Royal Gazette and New Brunswick Advertiser* preserved in the archives of the New Brunswick Museum and the Saint John Free Library. It was a broadsheet newspaper typical of its day, filled with official news and advertisements. In the absence of photographs and graphics, it consisted mainly of pages and pages of dense type. Yet it was crucial to people who craved news from home and abroad. As refugees from America's middle and upper classes, most of the Loyalist residents of Saint John were literate. The newspaper was their information lifeline. It portrayed a new community filled with political rivalries and unrest, emerging businesses and legal disputes.

Saint John as a community existed on trade, tottered on the brink of civil unrest, and was sustained by slavery. Its eighteenth-century citizens displayed all the business competition, discord, civic boosterism, private jealousies, and fear of mortality that characterize evolving societies. In many ways, it was a poor man's version of pre-revolutionary New England society, transplanted north to the rocky shores of New Brunswick.

The first newspaper in town was the *Saint John Gazette*, established in 1783 when the influx of dispossessed Loyalists began. Most of its early issues have been lost to history but it became the voice of Saint John's more radical democratic leaders. Without endorsing a break with the Crown, the *Gazette* reflected many of the egalitarian influences that had fuelled the American Revolution. Its readers felt they had not resisted the excesses of the revolutionaries and endured the trauma of losing their property and status south of the border merely to come under the autocratic control of yet another unworthy, insensitive ruling class.

The rival *Royal Gazette and New Brunswick Advertiser* was, as its name implies, the voice of the Establishment. It published first in the autumn of 1785 with an announcement that Christopher Sower had been appointed King's Printer. He called for "letters, essays etc. calculated to promote loyalty to our most Gracious Sovereign, love to our happy constitution and peace and harmony amongst ourselves, or tending to the improvement or cultivation of arts, sciences, manufacturers or commerce, the promotion of fisheries, agriculture etc. or affording rational and useful amusement will be thankfully received and impartially inserted." Anything "contrary to good order and morals" or supporting a "party position" would not be accepted, no matter how well written. Disrespect for the government or New Brunswick citizens "shall [n]ever be permitted to stain the pages of the '[*Royal Gazette and*] *New Brunswick Advertiser.*'"[1]

If nothing else, the *Royal Gazette* was clear about its mandate, which was to put the best face on New Brunswick life in its volatile early years. This was not always an easy task. Saint John at the time had a lot of rough edges.

The City of Saint John and the province that later grew around it were a haven for American Loyalists who had bet on the wrong side in the American Revolution and lost, or who had been uncompromisingly true to the British Crown on principle from the beginning. Many of them were from prominent families, and most had lost everything in the colonies that in some cases they had helped to found. Used to the perks that accrued to big fish in a small colonial pond, they arrived on the rocky shores of the Bay of Fundy as refugees, 35,000 strong and carrying with them most of what little they still owned. The Loyalists "were the first mass movement of political refugees in modern history."[2] The majority arrived in Nova Scotia but a few thousand were sent on the 1783 "spring fleet" to the natural harbour on the south shore of what would become New Brunswick, then a part of Nova Scotia. Thirty-two ships carrying almost 2,400 refugees left New York on 26 April for the mouth of the St John River with a promise of land and an allotment of tents, blankets, clothes, and utensils.[3] Two months later, another 3,600 headed north to the new colony-in-the-making.

By 1785 the barren shore had enough residents and rude houses to be incorporated as a city, the first civic incorporation in what eventually became Canada. At the time, there were five hundred male "freemen" who could vote, along with their families and servants or slaves. Thirty-four were merchants. There was a sprinkling of lawyers, who, as we shall see, dominate the history books. Most of the residents were anonymous working-class people who built the city.[4] The community boasted as many as three thousand residents that year.

They had already survived two desperate winters. "The crowded settlement at early Saint John, the shortage of fresh water to drink and of cord wood for fires, the makeshift sanitation facilities, the inclement weather, the primitive nature of shelter, the limited supply of fresh food and ... the often low morale which was the lot of most settlers probably led to an increased rate of sickness and death, at least during the first year of exile."[5]

Historians tend to describe the founders of New Brunswick as a depressed, beaten lot – an influx of losers. They

landed at Saint John angry, dispirited and vulnerable. They came not as heroic founders of a new nationality but as sufferers and exiles. They saw themselves as victims – the inexpressibly unfortunate casualties of three decades of British ineptitude culminating in the ruinous terms of peace ... Obsessed with their self-image as victims, the Loyalists arrived at Saint John certain that the British nation owed them a great deal. They came expecting and demanding a great deal. They came expecting and demanding the most tender solicitude. They were to be bitterly disappointed.[6]

The Saint John of Arnold's day was filled with crime, inequity, poverty, class divisions, marital strife, political intrigue, and opportunity for mischief. It was a minefield, in other words, for a political bumbler like Arnold. It was a tough town where justice could be rough, in keeping with the standards of the day in frontier outposts. In the downtown, a public flogging post and the regular auctioning of black slaves set the tone. In June 1786, two men and a black woman were convicted of "petit" larceny "and sentenced to receive 39 lashes each on their bare backs at the public whipping post."[7] A few months later, James Coap and George Heany made the mistake of breaking into the home of Surveyor General George Sproule. They were captured, convicted of burglary, and sentenced to death. John Culbertson, meanwhile, was convicted of grand larceny, but although his theft was on a larger scale, his victim was presumably not a local luminary. Instead of being sentenced to death, he "was burnt in the hand," the *Royal Gazette* reported.[8]

Slavery had been introduced to the colony by the more affluent refugees who brought their slaves and servants with them. It is unclear whether slave ships brought new supplies of human cargo, but there is abundant evidence that slaves were bought and sold in the city. It wasn't until 1796, eleven years later, that Emanuel Allen, the last slave sold in Canada, was auctioned off in Montreal.

On 12 September 1786, businessman James Hayt advertised for sale "a Black Boy, 14 years of age in full vigor of health, very active, has a pleasing countenance and every ability to render himself useful and agreeable in a family. The title for him is indisputable." On 21 August 1787, a female slave was offered for sale: "A wench about 23 years, is well acquainted with all kinds of household business and particular is an excellent cook. To be disposed of for no fault but want to employ."[9] The newspapers of the day were sprinkled with similar ads, or notices that a runaway slave was being hunted. In early 1786, distraught slave owner James Moore, who lived upriver from Saint John, offered five dollars for the return of a runaway, "about five feet six inches, stout and well-set, has very black thick lips."[10]

Not all the blacks in the town were slaves, but the free blacks certainly were not equal to the local whites. Upon their arrival in August 1783, four companies of free blacks who had served in Loyalist regiments during the Revolution were forced to live apart from the main white settlement. In 1785 Saint John conferred the status of municipal "freemen" on its tradesmen, barring black traders and artisans. This meant they could not vote and had few rights. And, of course, they had to watch their fellow blacks being bought and sold as property.[11]

The trade in human beings was one feature of life in Saint John, but there were other, more mundane features as well. Houses were built, bought, and sold. The first houses were made of logs or imported lumber but by 1786 lumber was available from local sawmills. In the better part of town, the houses boasted European furniture. Stores handled the food and dry goods imported from the Caribbean and Europe. After 1 May 1787 mail could be picked up at the new post office at King and Germain streets.

The men gathered at taverns like Mallard's House and McPherson's to drink, gossip, and talk politics. McPherson's Exchange Coffee House was typical of the watering holes of the day. In its twenty-five square feet, it had a coffee room and a bar. On the second floor where the owner lived, there was a parlour, a bedroom, and an assembly room where locals could hold meetings. A kitchen was built behind the coffee room on the first floor. The upstairs third floor featured eight bedrooms for paying customers.[12]

The gossip that aired in coffee-room and bar revolved, as gossip does, around politics, personalities, and sometimes the infidelities and

marital strife that keep any small community atitter. Men ran ads in
the newspaper warning against giving credit to their wives because they
had "eloped from my bed and board." On 25 October 1785, for example, Ludwig Schomber had to go public with his private affairs. Wife
Catherine had left him and "this is to forewarn all persons from trust-
ing her on my account, as I will pay no debts of her contracting from
this date hereof."[13] This led a local wit, the anonymous author of a
gossipy newspaper riddle about local events, to write: "The subscriber
and Catherine his wife have agreed to live – Pro Bono Publico."

Even more titillating was a report of April 1785 that one Thomas
Mullen had paid a friend to convince his wife Elizabeth to join him in
Saint John (the record does not say where she was coming from). Once
there, she discovered that six months earlier, he had married a local
girl, Prudence Brown, who showed little prudence in her choice of
men. Elizabeth heard the news "to her great grief, dismay and disappointment." She wasn't immobilized, however. Thomas was charged
with bigamy.

The arrival of the ships was eagerly anticipated for several reasons.
The colony was short of food and, to his annoyance, Governor Thomas
Carleton had to authorize imports from the newly independent United
Colonies to the south. Just as important for the colonial élite, who
could not live by imported bread alone, the ships carried newspapers
from Europe and the United Colonies. The news-starved colonials
devoured accounts of developments in England and in the colonies
they had one called home. How was George Washington doing, now
that he had retired to his Virginia estate? Wasn't it amazing how the
politicians who had caused the trouble in the first place still continued
to wrangle over what sort of union they should create, what powers
the states would have, whether there should be a central government,
and if so, where it should be located?

Much of this news was reprinted in the Saint John newspapers and
while many used it to mock what they had fled, it is not difficult to
imagine that many others yearned quietly for news of home, of family
and friends separated because of politics and bloodshed.

The *Saint John Gazette* hinted that the local authorities, looking at
the chaos in the United Colonies, might think twice before attempting
to preserve privilege for a few at the expense of others. The *Royal
Gazette*, on the other hand, continued to trumpet the line that the
British constitution was political perfection. To that loyal newspaper,
the American experience was a lesson in the folly of radical egalitarianism. One correspondent used thousands upon thousands of words

over three consecutive issues of the *Royal Gazette* to rehash the political debates of pre-revolutionary Massachusetts, proposing arguments that the Loyalists had already lost. Between 31 January and 13 February 1786, the essay "Common Sense: A Disquisition on Government and Civil Liberty" challenged Tom Paine's thesis in the original "Common Sense" pamphlet that all men are born equal, all men are born free, government authority comes from the people, and government is a compact between the governors and the governed.

It was a wordy display filled with the type of élitist logic guaranteed to turn a moderate working-class citizen who believed he had some rights into a slogan-spouting radical. Or maybe it just led them to buy the competition newspaper. Is government derived from the people? the anonymous writer asked. Yes, but only in the sense that "there could be no government if there were no people to be governed; if there were no subjects, there could be no kings, nor parliaments if there were no constituents, nor shepherds if there were no sheep."[14] Case closed.

But the newspaper also reminded the élite class, as well as local businessmen with an inclination to get rich quick at the expense of a captive clientele, that they were outnumbered. On 20 December 1785, just two weeks after Arnold arrived with dreams of becoming a rich merchant, the *Royal Gazette* published a letter from "A Stranger" that might well have caught Arnold's eye. It was a warning to the Yankee traders not to revert to their old tricks; an ominous complaint that, in a city short of food, merchants were hoarding goods and hiking prices while fishing boats were not being properly used to catch more fish and to employ more of the city's poor. "It is indeed a great pity that the market which is so abundantly supplied ... should not be carefully attended to and strictly regulated," he wrote. "I venture these hints from the purest motives of benevolence and good will and in the pleading hope that some of these ingenious writers who have lately employed their pens in electioneering controversy will now turn their attention to the public discussion of these (now) more important matters."[15]

If Arnold took note of that, he would also have noticed several other things about his new city. It was desperately poor, as reflected in the many advertisements and notices from people declaring bankruptcy, forsaking their debts, forcing businessmen to take them to court to try to collect. Part of the problem was a lack of jobs and local commerce. Part of it was a lack of currency.

The army garrison at Fort Howe on the hill overlooking the new community should have been one of the few stable elements in the city's economy, the soldiers providing business for the merchants, the businessmen and the prostitutes in the growing port city. Yet during these years, the government faced a persistent cash shortage, which required regular appeals from Governor Carleton to his superiors to send cash to pay the troops. On 26 July 1788, for example, he requested four thousand pounds sterling, complaining about "the scarcity of circulating money in this province."[16]

One sign of this scarcity was the number of commercial deals that landed in the courts for lack of payment. The courts were so overwhelmed and rudimentary that a common way of settling such commercial disputes was for a judge to appoint a three-member panel of local merchants to hear the evidence and then to decide who owed what to whom. Since these panels often met in the local tavern, deliberations must sometimes have been rowdy.

Within months of his arrival, Arnold experienced the frustration of the system.

Like many communities at the time, Saint John lived in constant fear of fire. On 18 January 1784, fire had destroyed eleven of the first homes built in the city and over the next two years, funds were collected to buy fire engines and dig wells. In a city of wooden houses, the fires destroyed democratically, affecting upper and lower class alike. The "fire engines" were little more than large wooden barrels of water, pulled by horses. Arnold, with a contribution of ten pounds, was the single largest donor towards a fund that eventually reached £291.[17]

If fire was democratic in its destruction, the politics of the city were not. Arnold arrived in a deeply divided city. The dividing line was class.

There were two Saint Johns in 1785 when Arnold arrived. The first was the Saint John of the upper class, comprising lawyers, successful businessmen, and those who had received government appointments. They may have had little money and been just one or two bad debts away from the courts themselves but they lived in relative luxury in houses around the Upper Cove, near where the Loyalist ships had first landed two years before.

The upper class included people like Ward Chipman, a thirty-one-year-old lawyer from a prominent Massachusetts legal and religious family who married the daughter of founding Saint John businessman William Hazen. In his early years in Saint John, Chipman was in a perpetual state of poverty but eventually became more affluent and powerful as a member of the provincial legislature and a prominent member of the Provincial Council. In 1823 his career peaked as the chief administrator of the province.[18] In private, he was an avid gardener, a family man, and a victim of gout, as so many men were in his day. New Brunswick historian W.S. MacNutt wrote of him: "It was probably difficult to detect behind the amiable personality of the young man who was blessed with a capacity for warbling in convivial company, a sharp, calculating intelligence and a driving imperious will."[19]

In 1785 Chipman wrote the charter for the incorporation of Saint John as Canada's first city, based on the charter of New York City from which he had fled. Today, the most prominent hill in downtown Saint John bears his name.

Edward Winslow was another. His was an ego to behold and beware of, a prominent Massachusetts Loyalist and military leader who arrived in the new colony expecting to be a leading social, political, and financial figure. He lobbied British officials for land grants for former Loyalist fighters. Once many of the soldiers had settled along the St John River, Winslow became a leading advocate of the separation of the growing colony from the control of Nova Scotia and the Halifax élite. He wanted the creation of a New Brunswick élite, of which he would be a prominent member.[20]

The idea for a separate colony appears to have struck Winslow as early as mid-1783 when he was acting as secretary to the Halifax commanding officer who had been sent to the mouth of the St John River to scout out land grants for the soldier-settlers. He wrote to his friend Ward Chipman that he was considering a plan for the new land that would present "the grandest field for speculation that ever offered."[21]

He campaigned publicly and privately for the idea of a separate colony and can properly be credited with being one of the reasons London decided in 1784 to carve out a new colony north of the Fundy. Like Chipman, Winslow had hoped for a prominent appointment in the government of the new colony but he too was disappointed. Neither had close contacts with the governor, Thomas Carleton – brother of Quebec governor Guy Carleton who had fought Arnold on the Plains of Abraham and Lake Champlain a decade before – and both ended up with minor low-paying positions. Winslow, usually strapped for cash and unable to pay his debts, lobbied relentlessly for appointments from the British and colonial governments that would give him the status he knew he deserved. In 1806, at the age of sixty-one, Winslow's campaigning paid off and he became that rarest of legal birds, a non-lawyer appointed to the Supreme Court of New Brunswick. Lawyers objected but Winslow kept his position until his death in

Fredericton nine years later, considering it a reward for his twenty years of "public service."[22]

In Arnold's day, Winslow's house typified upper-class pretensions. Although chronically poor, he built what he called "Felicity Hall" at Portland Point, near the base of the rock on which Fort Howe was built. There he hosted gay parties for the local élite and the military officers from the fort.

Although they were not friends or allies, Arnold's evident wealth put him in Winslow's class. Over the years, he moved into increasingly grand houses outfitted with furniture from England, and this made him stand out in the community. Historian Esther Wright wrote angrily in 1955 that Arnold was not typical of his neighbours. He lived with fine possessions, she said. "Most Loyalists were fortunate if they had one chest, one square table, four chairs, one trammel, one pot and a pair of tongs, one porridge pot, one pewter platter, four pewter plates, one pewter casson that Martha Lyon had been allowed to carry with her from her old home in Fairfield, Connecticut."[23] Other historians have noted that while some Loyalists wrote letters on tree bark due to a paper shortage, the élite lived well. "Men with capital, like Ward Chipman and Benedict Arnold, built elegant houses in Saint John and decorated them with English wallpaper and mahogany furniture," wrote one. "Elaborate balls and suppers were laid on by the Governor and others during the meetings of the House of Assembly to relieve the tedium of politics."[24]

So Arnold, by all accounts, lived like a member of the local élite. Yet there also is evidence that he was not really a member in good standing or a confidante of his ruling classmates. There was an Old Boy's club among the small provincial élite that Arnold never cracked, perhaps did not want to crack. Judges like Joshua Upham and Isaac Allen, lawyers like Chipman and Jonathan Bliss,[25] businessmen like Edward Winslow and Munson Hayt, were on boards together, organized trusts together to found schools and universities, and mingled together in the colony's political intrigues.

An illustration of this élite collusion and interconnection lies in the events surrounding Governor Carleton's decision to choose St Anne's, more than seventy miles upriver from Saint John, as the capital. On 26 August 1785, Colonel Allen and businessman Munson Hayt were among those appointed by Carleton to settle the area that became the capital city. "The duties of the trustees," wrote Fredericton historian Isabel Hill, "were to direct the surveyors, receive the applications for grants and arrange for those who had already settled, provided their improvement did not interfere with roads or squares."[26] Early the next year, Allen, Winslow and Hayt were trustees of a project to form a college in Fredericton. They auctioned land where the University of New Brunswick now stands. A few years later, when Arnold and Hayt were locked in the vicious legal battle that cemented the general's New Brunswick reputation as a greedy, disagreeable, and despised outsider, Allen was judge in the court that heard the case. Conflict-of-interest rules did not apply.

While other members of the élite intrigued and networked, Arnold concentrated on his business, travelled the world, and shunned politics. He was not a community figure. Thus, in 1786, when Arnold was establishing his commercial status and making his social contacts among the élite, the missionary New England Company came to the colony, intent on converting local Indians to both Christianity and a more-settled way of life. The provincial government welcomed the arrival of this distinguished and well-known English charity and appointed a committee of prominent local Loyalist leaders to the provincial board of directors – Allen, George Ludlow, Jonathon Odell, George Leonard, Jon Bliss, Ward Chipman, John Coffin, and Ed Winslow.[27] Arnold was not among them and probably didn't care.

Still, his outsider status clearly did not help when he went before the courts of New Brunswick in later years to try to collect debts and keep his commercial enterprise afloat. Often the judge, the opposing lawyer, and the debtor he was pursuing floated in the same élite soup that Arnold either shunned or was excluded from in that class-ridden society.

Arnold was, after all, a pure Yankee trader. He moved to New Brunswick to make money, not to acquire political power or privilege. His agenda was different from that of the Loyalist leaders who hoped to create a model society in the new colony, built on the principles of loyalty to the Crown and deference to the wealthy and powerful that they believed the thirteen colonies had embodied, in their heyday. "Like all newcomers, they wanted wealth and opportunity," wrote historian Ann Condon. "But unlike most immigrants, they also wanted to reshape society to reflect the values for which they had suffered expulsion from America and to assuage their nostalgia for their old homeland."[28]

Another local historian said the élite saw it as a chance to create a society where common people would be their grateful and obedient subjects. "Creation of the Loyalist province represented their chance to prove to the world – and to prove to themselves – that a British colony ordered on firm, hierarchical principles would flourish and become the envy of its republican neighbors ... [if not] it would mean they had fought the Revolution in vain."[29]

Like all vain and proud men, Arnold craved respect, but he seemed not to seek political position and a piece of this pre-revolutionary dream. He craved wealth for his own comfort and that of his growing family.

The other Saint John was the area known at Lower Cove, where the wharves were located. It may have been just a few hundred yards down the coast as the crow flies from Upper Cove, but it was hundreds of miles when it came to class attitudes. The two communities were opposites. In those days, the city was also known as Parrtown: "On a map, these two 'little bays' appear rather close but the Parrtown terrain is so difficult that for some time, the easiest way to pass from one to the other was to travel along the shoreline at low tide. Thus, from the very commencement of Saint John life, the population clusters at the upper and lower coves had the makings of distinct centres within a single settlement."[30] The traditional gentry clustered in Upper Cove while the self-made men and dissidents were due south.

Lower Cove was where the workers and entrepreneurs were, where the radicals were. They were seamen, storekeepers, and labourers, living in rudimentary homes and existing, many of them, hand-to-mouth. During the city's first decade, when economic depression was the norm, as many as one-third of the inhabitants of Lower Cove fled, or died from disease, poverty, or hopelessness. One of the things they thrived on was resentment of the upper classes with their properties in Upper Cove, lavish lifestyles, government appointments, and pretensions to superiority.

The radicals of Lower Cove had their legal champion, one of the more controversial figures on the streets of early Saint John – Elias Hardy.

Hardy was one of the colony's most influential and complex public men in the early days – a defender of the lower classes but not one of them; a leader of the radicals who was happy to work with and for the élite when he became Saint John's city clerk in the 1790s. Hardy was a bundle of contradictions, not unlike the Yankee turncoat he so enjoyed in fighting in court.

Hardy was a late comer to North America, a native of England who had moved to Virginia in 1775 as a thirty-two-year-old lawyer. He became a notary public and a supporter of the Crown Loyalists at a time when it was neither fashionable nor safe. He began life in America as a supporter of the critics who complained about "taxation without representation" but he quickly switched sides when a break with Britain, rather than fairer treatment, became the issue. His switch in loyalties led to at least one close brush with an angry American mob, armed with the most potent tool of early American revolutionary discourse – tar and feathers.[31]

As the Revolution raged against the British, Hardy moved to New York to hang out his shingle as a lawyer, eventually making a living handling the claims of New York Loyalists with legal grievances against the Colonies or the Crown. He was bitter about the British decision to capitulate, adding his name to a petition in 1782 complaining about the surrender and demanding that Loyalists be given refuge elsewhere. It was signed "on behalf of the loyal inhabitants and refugees within the British lines at New York"[32]

It was not long after that Hardy first surfaced as a spokesman for the less-powerful Loyalists. In July 1783, fifty-five prominent Loyalists leaders from New York petitioned British military leader Sir Guy Carleton for a gift of five thousand acres each in Nova Scotia to compensate for their losses in the Thirteen Colonies. For them it was a matter of common sense: "The settling of such a number of Loyalists of the most respectable characters who have constantly had great influence in His Majesty's Dominions – will be highly advantageous in diffusing and supporting a spirit of attachment to the British constitution, as well as to His Majesty's royal Person and Family," they wrote. Ward Chipman was one of the fifty-five "eminents."

The Loyalists of humbler position who were excluded from the request caught wind of the petition and chose four representatives to fight it. More than 600 protested. Hardy, having publicly denounced the secret petition of the Fifty-Five,[33] was one of the four. In the end, once controversy surfaced, the large land grants were denied.

By late 1783 word had arrived from London that the British government would compensate Loyalists for their losses. Hardy decided to try to become a middleman, handling Loyalist claims and earning tidy fees. Historian D.G. Bell describes him as a "me-firster" with a knack for turning Loyalist grievances into a platform for personal profit.

He arrived in Saint John in November to begin working for clients, probably not planning to stay. But he began to hear Loyalist grievances and in early 1784 was named an "agent" to carry these grievances to colonial governors in Halifax and to London if necessary. Chief among the grievances was that the best land in the newly settled area north of the Bay of Fundy was being assigned to the local élite. In February 1784 he left Saint John for Halifax to lobby on behalf of the dissidents and, within a few months, had won the agreement of the governor that the complaints should be investigated. In the spring he returned to Saint John with Nova Scotia chief justice Bryan Finucane in tow to look into the grievances.

This political coup won him working-class friends but did not endear him to Saint John's self-styled leading citizens, one of whom, in a private letter to Edward Winslow, vented his spleen about the upstart troublemaker: "The time, I hope, is not far distant when I expect to see everything undone and Mr Hardy thrown neck and heels, with his party, into the river."[34]

For all the antagonism levelled at him by the Establishment, Hardy decided to settle and practise law in the growing New Brunswick colony. He arrived not as a powerless radical but as a barrister with solid upper-class connections. He had status as a "freeman" – that is, a propertical citizen with the franchise – a lawyer, and a member of the first Masonic Lodge formed in Saint John in September 1784. He became a member of the first New Brunswick legislature and eventually the respectable, if controversial, second Common Clerk of Saint John. But in Arnold's day, he was a well-connected lawyer who represented the legal and political interests of the opponents of the élite. He became Arnold's most formidable legal opponent.[35]

The irony is that Arnold had some ties to this community as well. His warehouses and wharves were there, and for his first year in New Brunswick, he lived in Lower Cove, near his business. Beyond that, his Lower Cove neighbours were the kind of men Arnold inspired to acts of almost superhuman endurance and bravery when he was a military commander. Not now. His style of life, capital, wealth, and history as a revolutionary leader who had helped end their comfortable lives in New England ensured that he was viewed with suspicion in the Lower Cove. Anti-Arnold historians have assumed he would put on airs around working people and treat them with contempt. Nothing in the record suggests that he did. He had built a reputation as a commander who worked as hard as his men, asking them to do no more than he did. More likely those in Lower Cove judged him by the friends he kept and his increasingly conspicious consumption.

The first issue of the *Royal Gazette* after Arnold's arrival announced his presence and then carried a letter from "a native American Loyalist" about the state of political affairs in the city:

It must be confessed that too many unthinking individuals have suffered themselves of late to be carried down the mad current of party rage and violence. They are to be pitied and at the same time, their leaders are forever to be execrated and despised. The violence and injustice of party never perhaps appeared in a more disgusting and reprehensible point of light than in the course of the late election in this city ... Many grievous wounds and bruises were received and heads broken by brick bats and returned upon the mob by the brave defenders of Mallard's house, when attacked in the evening of the tenth of November.[36]

If Arnold read this letter, he might well have wondered whether he had jumped from the frying pan into the fire. How divided was this society, his new home? He had arrived in the middle of one of the most tumultuous episodes in the history of New Brunswick – the 1785 election and its aftermath, when the atmosphere of the city was "so grave that many likened it to the mood of the old colonies on the eve of the Revolution."[37]

Governor Thomas Carleton, who was not an instinctive democrat, felt he could delay elections no longer. There were calls for a popularly elected assembly, like the political bodies the Loyalists had grown accustomed to in the more-democratic thirteen colonies. On 15 October 1785 he announced that a House of Assembly would be elected, to meet for the first time in Saint John early in the new year. The port city was the acting capital until the government centre moved upriver to Saint Anne's, later called Fredericton, in late 1786. In Saint John, the largest centre, voters would go to the polls on 7 November to elect six of the twenty-six members of the legislature. The voting list would be limited to adult males who had resided in the colony for three months or more. By election day, twelve candidates had been nominated for the six positions – a slate of "Upper Covers" led by those already appointed to government positions, such as Attorney-General Bliss and Solicitor-General Chipman, opposed by a slate of "Lower Covers" led by Tertullus Dickinson, the brother-in-law of Elias Hardy, who was also a candidate but not locally. Hardy chose to contest a rural seat outside of Saint John.

Electioneering was strenuous and sometimes violent, often sometimes thanks to liquor.[37] In an unexpected twist that occupied many columns of newspaper space, the Lower Covers used Hardy's arguments to insist that since the days of Oliver Cromwell, salaried government officials like Bliss and Chipman had not been allowed to sit in Parliament. The *Saint John Gazette* carried letters arguing the point while the *Royal Gazette* made certain the other side of the argument was aired. "A letter has been received from Cork which mentions that the Attorney-General has been *ever* of late years in the House of

Commons," argued one letter writer in the 20 December issue of the *Royal Gazette.*

On 7 November polling started across the city by voice vote and on 9 November trouble erupted. A riot developed when as many as one hundred Lower Covers left their tavern on the low ground to attack the Upper Covers, who had gathered at Mallard's Tavern on the hillside, to vote. Troops were called out from Fort Howe, the Riot Act was read, some arrests were made, and voting was suspended, to be resumed a week later. By early December the results were in – Lower Covers, six; Upper Covers, nought. Bliss, Chipman, and the other members of the élite had been defeated by a vote of roughly 650 to 500. The upper class, and those who aspired to the status, were scandalized.

In his dimly lit room, articling law student Jonathon Sewell, Jr., sat down on 5 December 1785 to write to his father, Jonathon Sr., about the political turmoil. Ward Chipman, in whose law office the aspiring lawyer worked, had just been defeated in the election but his young disciple was certain a recount would show the election had been stolen by the drunken ruffians from the Lower Cove. It was just like London, he wrote his father, where the Whigs were playing class politics and using questionable electoral practices to deny the Tories their rightful place in government. "There was every reason to suppose that the majority which was attained was acquired by the most shameful and corrupt practices *à la mode de Westminster.*"[39]

The young Sewell, presumably privy to the private conversations of Chipman, Bliss, and their cronies, knew something that the radicals did not. The fix was in. The election would be challenged. Class justice, which did not include a strong political opposition, would prevail. Or else.

From 23 to 28 December, Sheriff William Oliver reviewed the qualifications of each Lower Cove elector, discovering two hundred who did not meet the residency qualification. The report filed with the governor indicated fraud. The Upper Cove slate was declared elected. The decision caused a political explosion on the Lower Cove, and the resulting unrest continued to bubble long after Arnold arrived.

Lower Cove voters protested their disqualification. The defeated candidates complained that some of their voters, sensitive to the language of revolution, had been branded "rebels" by the authorities. The colonial air was thick with talk of action and reaction, oppression and self-defence. Although Saint John was the centre of the unrest, the election elsewhere had not been entirely free of controversy.

In all ridings except Northumberland County, which elected Elias Hardy, voters had returned a government supporter. Yet there were close votes and questionable calls. Everywhere, the political élite showed itself willing to cut whatever corners were necessary to gain power in the colony it hoped to turn into a "society of gentlemen," where they naturally would govern. In Westmoreland County, a New Brunswick constituency that elected two members of the Legislative Assembly (MLA), two candidates, one of them anti-government, ended in a tie for first. The second pro-government candidate, Charles Dixon, ended up two votes behind and presumably out of office. The élite dipped into Acadie's troubled history to correct that. As the *Royal Gazette* reported on 24 January 1786, thirty years after the Acadian expulsion: "A number of Frenchmen voted at the election who had refused to take their oath of abjuration." They were disqualified, Dixon was declared the winner, and Westmoreland sent two government supporters to the assembly.

When needed, violence was not out of the question to make a political point. In February, the government newspaper carried an item about an anti-government activist circulating in York County, trying to get signatures on a petition alleging election fraud. He was beaten and thrown into a fire "from which, however, he was snatched by a bystander without receiving any further injury than that of having his clothes scorched."

Discontent even extended to Campobello Island off New Brunswick's south coast. There, trader and merchant Gilliam Butler, later a thorn in Arnold's side, complained privately that the newly elected government was "offensive" to him, a defeated candidate. As historian MacNutt recounted the story: "Butler, who a few months later was convicted and imprisoned for attempting to smuggle American whale oil through the Port of Saint John, wrote to Chipman that the government of Scots was offensive, that his candidature on behalf of the 'American' interests had been unsuccessful because of illegal practices and that the county town should be located on Campobello rather than at Beaver Harbour, where there were fewer people."[40]

The worst was yet to come. The very authority of the new Legislative Assembly was about to be challenged. It would respond with a legislative oppression that is unsurpassed in Canadian parliamentary history.

During the winter of 1786, three hundred twenty-seven Saint John electors from Lower Cove signed and sent a petition protesting the election result. "We most positively affirm these proceedings to be unjust, injurious to the freedom of election, manifest violations of the rights of our people and subversive of the first principles of the British Constitution and in the last instance, producing an extraordinary situation viz. the representatives of the people in opposition to the people."

It was a call for new election.

"We by no means think we are represented in the present House of Assembly. We can on no account conceive ourselves bound by any law as made by them so unconstitutionally composed."

Then, on 22 February 1786, *Saint John Gazette* publishers William Lewis and John Ryan published the most inflammatory article in their two-year history of gentle dissent. It was from an anonymous correspondent called "Americans" from Southy Bay and it left little unsaid about the class divisions and preferential treatment for the élite in the colony: "We, dear brethren, have sacrificed our property, have fought the battles of our sovereign and have left the place of our nativity and the beloved spots sacred to infantile sports, in quest of a Habitation where we could with hearty and jovial festivity celebrate our attachment to the Parent Country and its laws but like you, have been miserably disappointed ..."

After complaining about the unfair distribution of land, the correspondents added the inflammatory call to arms: "Dear Brethren, is that the use your country means to make of their distinguished bounty? Is the enslaving of us an object they want. No! My heart recoils at the idea! They cannot form it. We have fought, we have bled and we have conquered together ... My distressed countrymen, let us oppose every last violation of our privileges, for the preservation of which we sacrificed our all. Submit not to petit tyrants."[41]

Establishment figures reacted in three ways to these threats to their power. Many of the rioters from the Mallard's Tavern incident were charged and convicted of disturbing the peace. "Half a dozen of their leaders were arraigned before the magistrates and turned over to the Supreme Court which, in the spring, fined them heavily as well as sentencing them to extended terms in prison."[42] Meanwhile, newspaper publishers Lewis and Ryan were charged with seditious libel.[43] By charging the publishers rather than trying to find the writer of the "Americans" letter, authorities were sending a clear message that they would go after those they knew they could find and harm.

The most powerful and controversial response, though, was a decision by the assembly in late February 1786 to debate and subsequently approve "An Act Against Tumults and Disorders." It was, according to historian Bell, "the most repressive piece of legislation ever enacted in New Brunswick."[41] It also succeeded in stamping out the opposition, weak as it was. The text was published in the 21 March 1786 issue of the *Royal Gazette* under the headline "Against tumults and disorders upon the Pretence of preparing or presenting public petitions or other addresses to the Governor or General Assembly."

In essence, the law made it illegal to gather a petition with more than twenty signatures protesting actions of church or state unless it was approved in advance by three local justices of the peace or a grand jury. The penalty was a fine of one hundred pounds sterling and three months in jail. Since the assembly was so heavily dominated by government supporters, the ancient British parliamentary right of petitioning was almost the only effective way the poor and the unrepresented had to make their grievances known. The legislation, approved in early March 1786 by a vote of ten to four, effectively closed off access to the government. The effect of the law was "to stifle dissent."[45]

This Draconian legislation was first used on 7 March when the four Lower Covers who presented the petition were arrested for sedition and convicted in the May session of the Supreme Court.

The result of such oppression was what the ruling class hoped for and expected. Most leaders of the dissenters were either silenced or jailed; some decided to leave the colony. In the spring of 1786, printer William Lewis returned to the United States where his mild brand of democratic agitation was more mainstream and acceptable. In the next five years, a combination of economic depression and political oppression would convince many of Saint John's Loyalist pioneers to move on. Between 1786 and 1792, Saint John's population fell by one-third to two thousand souls.

The tale of Elias Hardy shows how the opposition was stifled or brought to heel. He managed to get himself elected as the only real anti-government legislator in the 1785 elections. He was one of four who voted against the "Tumults and Disorders" law. Hardy was vilified by the Saint John élite for his campaign against their land grab and his challenge to what they saw as a hierarchical right to govern. Yet after a few years as an assembly gadfly, Hardy made his peace with the powers-that-were. In 1790 he became the second Common Clerk of Saint John, a job he had been denied five years earlier. By 1795, he was no longer a player in New Brunswick politics.

Although none of his speeches or writings survived the past two centuries, it is as if Elias Hardy saw early on that New Brunswick would be a province run by the upper class, where the rich would build their houses on the hilltops offering a view of their fiefdoms – streets like Mount Pleasant Avenue and Rockland Road where capitalists such as the Irvings and their ilk lived in splendour in the 1960s and 1970s – while the working class and the poor would live at the foot of the hill on Waterloo Row, in harbourside slums or on streets with cruel and ironic modern-day names such as Paradise Road.

Benedict Arnold arrived in New Brunswick on Friday, 2 December, under a cloud, both literal and figurative. Political intrigues he thought he had left behind in America and then London followed him to the new land like the albatross in Samuel Taylor Coleridge's "The Rime of the Ancient Mariner," written a decade later.

He had travelled from London in the brigantine *Lord Middleton*, loaded with goods he hoped would be a primer for his merchant business. He stopped in Halifax to visit friends and then hired a pilot to navigate the reportedly treacherous approach to Saint John harbour. Arnold, an experienced and skilful mariner, was unable to do it himself because he was lying below deck, suffering from an attack of gout. The captain arrived at the mouth of the harbour on a windy day and decided it was too risky to try a docking. Instead, he sailed east into a gale-force wind that drove the *Lord Middleton* ashore into a cove. The passengers had to be evacuated, Arnold on a stretcher.

Instantly, there were allegations and rumours of foul play as Saint John officials suggested the Halifax pilot had deliberately made the landing difficult to diminish the reputation of a rival port. In private correspondence, Arnold appeared to agree it was more than pilot incompetence or bad luck.

Then things got worse. While he convalesced in Saint John, locals decided to help themselves to some of his merchandise, which had been left on board the beached ship and later piled on the shore. He lost thirteen firkins of butter (wooden tubs equal to a quarter barrel), as well as flour, beef, and pork. There is no record that the thieves were ever caught, despite Arnold's offer of a reward.

Still, he had arrived in his new home, ready to start again. Neither illness nor local thieves would hold this Yankee trader back. In Saint John, as 1785 became 1786, Arnold stood poised to try to turn his unsavoury reputation as a traitor into a community standing as an admired, successful trader.

13

Born-Again Trader

Once he climbed out of his Saint John sick bed in December 1785, Benedict Arnold hit the ground running. He had six thousand pounds to spend (the equivalent of more than $200,000 in contemporary funds), money from his deal with the British, and he went about spending it in a way he thought would secure him a fortune, or at least a comfortable living, in British North America.

He rented a house in Lower Cove and looked everywhere for opportunities to establish himself as a New World businessman. He eventually employed scores of New Brunswick Loyalists who would otherwise have been unemployed and living in abject poverty. The evidence suggests that as a new arrival with money to spend and dreams that would translate into jobs for locals, he was given the benefit of the doubt and high marks for trying. He was viewed as a potential community leader who believed that hard work and decisive action, rather than fate, would change your luck and create opportunity.

One of Arnold's first acts was to advertise to try to find the thieves who stole butter, beef, flour, and pork from the shore the night he arrived. He had no luck and moved on. Next came the search for space to set up a store in the community, with a site nearby to build a wharf where imports could be unloaded. He soon bought a house in the Lower Cove, which, when advertised for sale in the *Royal Gazette* eight months later as he prepared to move to Upper Cove, was described as having "five rooms, four of which have fire places – a good cellar and a log kitchen adjoining." In Saint John's depressed economy, the house was still for sale almost a year later. He also leased a store and wharf space nearby: "The store is three storeys high, 20 by 40 feet, the lot fronts on Prince William Street and is very centrical and convenient for the reception and delivery of goods, as vessels lay perfectly safe along side the wharf and waggons have easy access to the store in the street."[1] Meanwhile, Arnold contracted with a shipbuilder at a yard forty miles upriver to build a ship of white oak, for delivery next summer. To kick-start his trading business, he leased ships and began to advertise for goods that could be traded.

What Arnold had in mind was typical of traders of his day, in the age of sail. Since he was barred from trading into the emerging United States, his pattern would be to buy lumber, ships' masts, and other commodities in New Brunswick, take them to the West Indies to be traded for sugar, cotton, rum, and other commodities that could be sold in New Brunswick and Nova Scotia, or in England. Sometimes, the trading would be a north-south affair between New Brunswick and the southern islands. Sometimes it would be triangular, with a trip to England to bring back luxury items in demand by a colonial population starved for the tools and pretensions of civilization.

His business plan was a bit more complicated than that of a simple trader. He also hoped to speculate in land, both in Saint John and upriver. He set up trading stations in Fredericton and on Campobello Island. He bought a thousand-acre farm that he planned to lease out. He set up a store to retail goods and also acted as a wholesaler, selling to other merchants who would peddle the goods around New Brunswick or even into the US. Arnold acted in partnership with other local businessmen, employed local labourers, and brought his teenaged sons from New Haven so that they could go into the business.

It was an ambitious plan that worked in some ways but was thwarted in other ways by the poverty of the economy in which he tried to prosper, and by the tendency of many of his customers not to pay their bills.

Within weeks of arriving in Saint John, Arnold made his first deal to set up a trading business. He contracted with local shipowner James Butler to take a load of lumber to the West Indies. It was a business deal that became entangled in a court case, a bad omen for Arnold. As outlined in New Brunswick Supreme Court dispositions, it was a case of whatever could go wrong for Arnold did.

On 12 December 1785, just ten days after arriving, he made a deal with Butler to lease his 120-ton brig *Peggy* for the voyage. Butler was to be paid extra to be captain. Arnold assumed that since he was paying the piper, he would call the tune. He did not know Butler. Trouble began almost immediately. Butler took *Peggy* to Campobello Island in January and loaded 41,000 board feet of lumber. Arnold wanted the ship to catch a good wind on 1 February and set sail. Butler refused, arguing that repairs were needed. Arnold insisted the repairs could be made at sea; Butler insisted they could not. Butler won. The next favourable wind, bearing *Peggy* into the Bay of Fundy and then south, did not come until 13 February. Two weeks were lost and Arnold, who was on board but not in charge, was paying.

Six weeks later, on 25 March, the ship arrived at Barbados. "I did not think that Captain Butler exerted himself to make this voyage as short as it might have been by carrying proper sail and I frequently requested him to carry more sail, which he always refused and was angry," Arnold complained in court documents filed in the summer of 1786 when he sued Butler for damages.[2] Trouble was just starting.

The ship anchored off Barbados for several days and the two men argued about whether it should be docked right away. It wasn't completely unloaded until well into April – twenty-five days to do a week's work because of Butler's negligence, Arnold complained.

Then it was off to Dominica for sugar, cotton, and rum for the return trip. There were more arguments about the loading, which was not finished until 17 May. The trip back took more than three weeks and soon after docking at Saint John on 8 June, Arnold sent his lawyers to court, demanding compensation. During the delays on the high seas, the price of sugar and rum had fallen and he lost money. Arnold said he had expected the ship to return by 12 April "at the latest" so he did not feel he should have to pay an extra two months of charter fees.[3]

Jonathon Bliss represented Arnold, asking for five hundred pounds in damages. Butler counter-sued with Ward Chipman as his lawyer, demanding £780 for six months of chartering along with the cost of employing a crew and more than a score of men to load and unload the ship in Barbados and Dominica.[4] Arnold won but was awarded less than he had demanded.

Meanwhile, his business tentacles were spreading. On 23 December 1785, Arnold had spent £160 to purchase a half-interest in the sloop *Nancy* from Saint John businessman Fristram Hillman. She was soon put to work, plying the waters between Saint John and London.

In the minutes of Saint John Common Council, which met during those days at Mallard's Tavern, Arnold first appeared on 15 April 1786 when he asked for a grant of land along the harbour. Council decided to lease him the land and, later, three water lots. He chose a business site for a warehouse and a wharf in Lower Cove at the corner of Charlotte and Broad streets, and on 29 June he petitioned Common Council for permission to build a 160-foot wharf. Permission was granted on 1 July 1786.[5]

An advertisement in the 1 May 1786 issue of the *Royal Gazette* announced that Arnold had purchased a lumber and ship yard where "lumber of all kinds, ship and other timber" could be delivered and would be purchased "at the current prices." One month later, on 1 June, the citizens of Saint John got to see the very visible fruits of Arnold's growing business interests – the arrival in the harbour of the *Lord Sheffield,* built for Arnold by Nehemiah Beckwith of Maugerville. It was a remarkable day for a number of reasons. The *Lord Sheffield* was the first ship built for the high seas in New Brunswick. It signalled a new stature for the colony, which was destined to prosper as a ship-building and trading centre decades hence. It was a boost for Saint John as a port city because it defied the conventional wisdom that large ships could not come down the river into the harbour because of what locals called the "bug bear" falls – rough water just north of the mouth of the river that made southward passage difficult at some times of the day because of rocks and even more difficult at certain times of the day because the high Fundy tides flowed upriver, creating the famous "reversing falls." Amazingly for the locals who watched the three-mast ship come down the river, it sailed through the falls by picking the exact time when rising tidal waters covered the rocks but did not make the current so strong that the ship was stopped.

The *Royal Gazette* marked the occasion with an enthusiastic report in its 6 June issue:

On Thursday last, through the falls near this city and is safely moored in this harbor, an entire new and most noble ship belonging to Brig. Gen. Arnold. She is upwards of 300 tons burthen, built at Spry's Grant on this river, about 40 miles from this city. Her timbers are altogether white oak and is allowed to be as well constructed a vessel as any ever built in America. We are told the General has named her the *Lord Sheffield* in honour of the nobleman of that name who has proved himself a strenuous supporter of the Navigation Act of his country.

She is to be fitted for sea immediately and the command given to Capt. Alex Cameron. This ship, large as she is, met no manner of difficulty in getting through our (bug bear) falls – the General's laudable efforts to promote the interest of this infant colony have during his short residence been very productive to its commercial advantage and as such deserves the praises of every well-wisher to its prosperity.

After a few delays, the *Lord Sheffield* was plying the oceans, as both a cargo and passenger vessel. On 4 September it set sail for Jamaica, stopping at Campobello on the way. Arnold advertised for passengers. The next day the *Gazette* enthused that "she made a beautiful appearance (being entirely new) as she sailed out of the harbor."

As usual, however, controversy accompanied Arnold's ship, tainting the record of his most triumphant summer in New Brunswick. Arnold had commissioned Nehemiah Beckwith to build the ship but later he found flaws in the product and demanded that Beckwith make changes to the vessel before Arnold would take delivery. Beckwith missed his agreed-upon delivery date and had to pay a penalty. He complained that Arnold's demands were the cause of the late delivery. Arnold thought otherwise and withheld some of the payment. Some reports have Beckwith going bankrupt and spending the next few years smearing Arnold's name around the colony.[6]

Still, for all the controversy and commercial complications, 1786 and 1787 were good years for Arnold. He won lucrative contracts to supply government troops stationed in the colony. He established a business partnership with former Connecticut Loyalist Munson Hayt to operate an import, retail, and wholesale business. He built a reputation as an importer of fine goods. Typical of his business was an advertisement in 1787 after a new shipment of goods arrived. From their store on King Street, Hayt and Arnold were offering for sale an assortment of West Indian and European items, from shoes and sailing bags to cloth, clothes, rice, axes, and utensils. The list of goods occupied four full newspaper columns.[7] In addition to off-street sales at his King Street store, Arnold organized a network of agents to sell his wares throughout the colony. One agent was Peter Cook Waterbury, who purchased goods wholesale from the Saint John warehouse for sale in the countryside of the western area of the province. Titus Knapp was a middleman in Westmoreland County to the east.

Remarkably, Arnold's trading business also extended into the United States, although he was *persona non grata* there and most Americans would have been outraged at the knowledge that they were trading with the traitor. To get goods to and from the New England, Arnold used middlemen such as Thomas Hanford, who owned the schooner *George* and was a willing accomplice. A December 1787 agreement between Arnold and Hanford, allegedly unearthed by nineteenth-century politician and New Brunswick Father of Confederation Sir Leonard Tilley and now housed at the Saint John Free Library, illustrates how Arnold contrived to penetrate the American market, despite the risks.

On 27 December 1787, Hanford agreed to take his schooner from Saint John to North Carolina, then to Jamaica and back to Saint John.

The terms were that Arnold would pay Hanford three pounds sterling per month as he took his ship from Saint John to North Carolina to pick up a cargo, then to Jamaica to sell and buy a new cargo, then to North Carolina and back to Jamaica. Once that had been done, he would begin to receive six pounds sterling per month. In addition, he would receive two and a half percent of the value of the goods he bartered in North Carolina, no commission in Jamaica, then five percent of sales on the second trip to North Carolina and two and a half percent on goods bought. There was to be no added commission in Jamaica.

Clearly, the two businessmen understood that there was a far greater risk to the captain should it be discovered in the United States that he was working for or with the treasonous Benedict Arnold. The extra commission recognized the extra risk.

During these glory years, Arnold established a presence and an interest in Fredericton, the new capital of New Brunswick, although there is no evidence – merely speculation by Frederictonians – that he actually lived there. Although the historical record is a bit vague, it is clear that Arnold established a warehouse there, acquired a wharf, and may have owned a house in which he stayed when in the community on business. He had friends and commercial interests in Fredericton. The land he owned stretches along the St John River where Waterloo Row now boasts some of the priciest real estate in the city. There is a house, "Rose Hall," that various local amateur historians believe was Arnold's. In fact he owned the land and had a structure on it, probably a warehouse, but the house now standing on the site was built long after Arnold's tenure and was named by a later owner who dreamed of the southern us plantation he had occupied before the civil war.[8] Fredericton historian Isabel Hill has described his holdings: "Land leased to General Benedict Arnold extended on Waterloo Row from almost the upper side of (former premier Louis) Robichaud's house down to the first or second house beyond Grey St. The land in Fredericton was the choice of his agent who assumed that Gen. Arnold would reside in the capital of the province. General Arnold was charged 25 shillings per acre per annum. The price was high. As he preferred his headquarters to be in Saint John, the lease was not renewed when the three years expired."[9] He also bought some lots already occupied by houses.

Arnold was establishing himself in New Brunswick, creating a trading network, acquiring land, and speculating that the New Brunswick economy would take off and reward him. He purchased a hundred-acre farm on the Nashwaak River, which he leased to a former New Haven neighbour, Daniel Lyman. This American Legion follower and Yale

University graduate had followed Arnold during his 1781 incursions into Connecticut and Virginia.[10]

While his commercial interests were taking shape, Arnold's family life was less settled. At some point in 1786 or 1787, he asked his sister Hannah to bring Benedict VI, Richard, and Henry, his sons by his first wife, to Saint John. Eighteen-year-old Richard became a partner in his father's import and retail business. In London, Arnold's second wife Peggy lived with their children Edward (born 19 March 1780 in Philadelphia), James Robertson (born 29 August 1781 in New York City), and Sophia (born July 1785 in London).

Meanwhile, on 14 April 1786, possibly in Saint John, a baby boy was born. He was called John Sage in Benedict Arnold's will. The circumstances of his birth and parentage remain obscure but this baby became the ancestor of the hundreds of modern-day Canadians who can claim a genetic connection to the famous general.

Bachelor life was not Arnold's preference. In 1787, after a trading trip that took him from Saint John to the Caribbean and then to London to pick up goods and passengers, Arnold returned to Saint John with his wife Peggy and the three young children in tow. "On Wednesday last arrived here the ship *Peggy*, Capt. Wallace, in six weeks and four days from England, laden with merchandise," reported the *Royal Gazette* on 24 July 1787. "In her came passengers Brig. Gen. Arnold and Jonathon Sewell Esq. with their ladies and families."

Peggy's four years in New Brunswick were filled with social events, the work of raising three small children, and giving birth to the only one of their children to be born in Canada – George, named after King George III, who had received and befriended the Arnolds in London.

Benedict and Peggy were devoted to each other and to their children, a point illustrated both in their writings and in contemporary reports. Arnold's letters to friends often contain references to his children's progress and accomplishments. His drive for success in business was fuelled in large part by his desire that the family be cared for after his death. Peggy's arrival marked "the first time since the dark days of the Revolution that the entire family had lived together and they were a happy, affectionate group, devoted to each other."[11] From surviving contemporary accounts, it seems like an apt description of a devoted family man.

They moved into a house on the corner of King and Canterbury streets in what is now downtown Saint John. A grand structure for its day, it was built by businessman John Porteous in 1785, then sold in 1787 to the Arnolds, who lived there for four years. "The tall wooden house had "a gambrel roof, pitched toward King Street and three dormer windows projected through it." From King Street, steps led up to an enclosed porch and the house entrance. Inside, "the interior was well-finished. The rooms were large and had several fireplaces."[12]

The Arnolds sold the house to Attorney-General Jonathon Bliss in 1792. He owned it until 1810 when he was made provincial chief justice and moved to Fredericton. In 1812 it was sold to Charles McPherson, whose coffee-house and tavern was just one block away, and who lived there until his death in 1823. Meanwhile, the lower floor was converted into retail space and it became the first cut-price store in the city, on the city's first "cheap corner." Over the next decades, it became a coffee-house, a meeting hall for the Masons and others, and a post office. The original building burned down in the mid-1860s. A second building on the site burned down before the brick structure that stands there now – the Vassie Building – was built.[13]

In its day, Arnold's house was filled with the finery of a grand London dwelling, conveyed to the New World on Arnold's ships. He also made some furniture himself. Compared to most of the Saint John dwellings it, and its inhabitants, must have seemed upper class indeed. A newspaper account of the day described the Arnold furnishings thus: "Excellent feather beds, mahogany four-post bedsteads and furniture, a set of elegant cabriole chairs covered with blue damask, sopha and curtains to correspond, card tea and other tables, looking glasses, a secretary desk and book case, fire screens, girandoles, lustres, an easy and sedan chair … with a great variety of other furniture.

LIKEWISE … an elegant desert set of wedge wood gilt ware, two tea table sets of Nankeen China, a variety of glass ware, a terrestrial globe, a handsome beam, scales and 500 lb. weights, with a great number of other articles, a double wheel jack, a great quantity of kitchen furniture, etc etc … ALSO a lady's elegant saddle and bridle."[14]

Legend has it that Arnold himself designed and made some of the cabriole chairs, several of which still exist in Saint John. One, an armchair painted white, trimmed with gold, and upholstered in light blue velour, is in the warehouse of the New Brunswick Museum.

By 1787 the Arnolds had the trappings of affluence and influence – good location, fancy house, extensive commercial dealings, influential friends, and public praise. The family was together again, even if Arnold himself spent months at a time at sea or visiting contacts in New Brunswick's interior.

It appeared that Benedict Arnold had arrived.

14

Arnold vs the Lawyers

During the first eighteen months after he landed on the barren shore of the Bay of Fundy, Arnold achieved much, using his energy, cash, and decisiveness to carve out an impressive commercial niche in the New World. He was the colony's most successful businessman. He had a network of trading and commercial contacts. He had gathered his family around him in surroundings that clearly announced the Arnold family as members of the small economic élite in a poor, struggling British frontier colony.

Yet in many ways it was a façade. Arnold was spending the money he had been given for his defection during the Revolution and his subsequent service in the British army. He was not earning sufficient income to sustain the style of life to which he had become accustomed. The problem was neither lack of effort nor lack of business sense. It was, rather, the result of Saint John's poverty and Arnold's perpetual inability to collect debts from customers and other businessmen.

The New Brunswick successes that Benedict Arnold had achieved by mid-1787 were fragile, built as they were on the economic and political quicksand of a poor society with its share of hungry lawyers. As a businessman, he often found himself forced to sell on credit if he wanted to do business at all. To his distress, he found that neither the word nor the credit of many of his customers was good. It led him to court scores of times during his five years there, trying to collect debts. But court judgments in his favour did not always produce the money and sometimes, when his customers counter-sued, only the lawyers came out winners.

One of Arnold's earliest legal cases in Saint John involved Theodore Jones, a merchant who bought bulk goods at Arnold's Saint John store and used them as barter to obtain lumber in Massachusetts. He then sold the lumber to settlers planning to build houses in New Brunswick. On 22 June 1786, Jones took three barrels of sugar and four bags of coffee (445 pounds), with payment due once he sold his lumber for cash. Later, he repeated the purchase from Arnold.

Eleven months later, Jones had not paid up and Arnold had lawyer Ward Chipman take him to court for damages. The court appointed Saint John businessmen James Hayt, Rich Seaman, and Nehemiah Rogers to hear the facts. On 13 August 1787, they met at McPherson's coffee-house, weighed the evidence and decided in Arnold's favour, awarding him more than forty-one pounds sterling. It turned out to be a phantom victory. Jones skipped town and Arnold never saw a shilling of it.[1]

Such was the case in Arnold's dealings with Jabez Cables, a Saint John baker. In the grand scheme of things the amount of money involved was small but the case offers a detailed and vivid glimpse of the complicated and frustrating financial world in which Arnold was trying to rebuild his fortune.

The business relationship Arnold forged with Cables is an indication of how diversified an enterprise he was trying to build and how, as a businessman, he involved himself in the details. Like a twentieth-century Irving,[2] Arnold was trying to create a vertically integrated trading empire. He owned the lumber yards, the ships, the warehouse for middlemen, and retail stores for off-the-street customers. To extend that further, he contracted with Cables for a supply of baked goods, some to be used on board Arnold's ships and some to be sold commercially. Arnold would sell him the flour and buy back the bakery products. He made the initial deal with Cables in January 1786 and, during January and February, delivered 216 barrels of flour totalling 540 hundredweight for which he charged the going rate. He stored the flour, along with some other provisions, at the Partelow's store and gave Cables the keys so he could have access while Arnold was at sea. The agreement was that Cables would use damaged flour to bake ship's bread and good flour to bake for the commercial market. When Arnold returned, he discovered that Cables had short-changed him by more than fifteen hundred weight of flour and some cash. Cables's books were a mess. As Arnold later told his lawyer, Jonathan Bliss: "As I found Cables accounts were not correct, I was very particular in keeping mine so and on the settlement with him (not understanding accounts well himself), he got Capt. Camp to examine all my books and accounts ... who assured him they were perfectly right, with which he appeared satisfied."[3]

Arnold went to England in 1787 to buy more merchandise, as well as to fetch his young family. When he returned, he found that Cables's business was in trouble. "I viewed the debt as lost and his inability to pay prevented my making a demand of the balances." The two broke off their business relationship. Almost four years later, just as he was preparing to leave the colony for good, Arnold was arrested by the sheriff who said that he owed Cables forty-nine pounds sterling. Cables claimed that he had been employed to look after the store that housed the flour and provisions and had not been paid. Arnold insisted he had never employed Cables to run the store. In the end, Arnold won the court case but it represented another business loss, more money to the lawyers, and more vexation. And he never did receive the money. In August 1792, Bliss wrote to Arnold in London that they had won yet another judgment against the elusive baker. "Cable will never pay this or the costs," Bliss reported. "The Rogue has gone to the States."[4]

It was part of a pattern. The law, the facts, and justice were often on Arnold's side, but that did not guarantee a favourable outcome. And through his New Brunswick years, the courts were the weapon of choice in commercial dealings. When Arnold sent Bliss to court in July 1786 to try to win damages from the shipowner and captain James Butler, it was the first of many times he would stand before a judge to plead his case and to create work for Saint John's small and struggling community of lawyers. The minute books of the New Brunswick Supreme Court show that during his almost six years of dealings in New Brunswick, the general was in court fifty times, and most of those suits brought a counter-suit. Years after he left the province, a number of court cases continued to be brought in his name and in one cele-brated case, the New Brunswick courts heard a case against Arnold that had its roots in pre-revolutionary New York.

From the court records comes a portrait of Arnold as a mini-industry for the colony's lawyers, a litigious whirlwind. He sued customers and suppliers, obscure merchant middlemen, and members of the New Brunswick élite. Like most other aspects of Arnold's life story, this is a controversial series of episodes susceptible to varying interpretations. For most American writers, it is but one more blot on his character and record.

Clare Brandt, the New York-based author of a critical, almost disdain-ful 1994 biography of Arnold, is just the latest in a series of American biographers to conclude that there was something distasteful, pathetic almost, in Arnold's string of lawsuits. "He had become involved in a number of petty lawsuits," she wrote, "... his old flamboyance and pugnacity reduced to spasms of litigation."[5] Before that view can be properly assessed, it is important to give the relevant events some context, to understand the role the courts played in colonial New Brunswick and the use that Arnold made of them.

Like most of the structures of civil society, the court system in New Brunswick was in its infancy in Arnold's day. It handled all manner of cases – criminal, civil, and commercial. When money was in dispute from a commercial transaction, the courts often appointed local businessmen to hear the details and make a judgment, which would then be reported to, and enforced by, the courts. In a poor and transient society like New Brunswick's, much of the courts' time was taken up with cases involving non-payment of debt. Judgments were often impossible to enforce, leaving debtors' prison as the final remedy. In May 1786, the lawyer Ward Chipman wrote to a friend about another client who was in jail for defaulting on a small debt. "Really, everybody is so poor. There is no such thing as money to be had ... [A court case] is the only way to obtain payment."[5] As a relatively well off businessman with a slew of cash-starved customers and middlemen, Arnold often had just two stark choices: go to court or write off the debt as a loss.

In such circumstances, how was he to conduct his affairs? Two glimpses into Arnold's personality in these years shed some light on his choices. He was portrayed by a contemporary as a proper businessman who believed others should fulfill their obligations to him, a man with a narrow focus on the world of business and not the worlds of politics and social affairs, a generous but prideful man given to vengeance when he thought he had been deliberately wronged.

The first glimpse comes from Stephen Sewell, an aspiring lawyer who was involved in one of Arnold's cases at the time. He almost certainly was referring to his famous client when he wrote to his brother Jack in September 1790:

I think he is rather more bashful than modest but he is modest, true to his own interest but I think not farther than is perfectly right and proper. He is generous and I think capable of friendship but in most other instances, he is as waivering as a weather cock. His sentiments seem to change with the day but he has resolution when business calls, to do his duty – too dogmatical – and I think aims at no universal knowledge but of a pretty good capacity of not sufficient application. He is governed a great many instances by this world in his notions of propriety which very often degenerates into pride and folly. He is extremely fond of being proper in his dress for he has very good taste ... Often disgusted at women, which may proceed from his bashfulness but he is of a cold nature. He is by no means credulous, much the reverse, and in separating probability from improbability, his understanding is very good. He aims to have everything about him like a gentleman.[7]

The historian Willard Randall portrays Arnold as a compassionate man who defended his interests in court but also recognized the plight of some of his customers in the struggling colony: "When tenants reneged on notes, Arnold could not bring himself to dispossess men with families."[8]

Many of the lawsuits truly were for petty amounts and many were launched in the name of the business partnership Arnold established with his son Richard and Munson Hayt. There was a February 1788 suit against Henry Betner for £2.13.6, a case against Ephraim Bitts for £12.1.9, and another against Francis Eaton for £13.5.3. In each case Arnold was seeking payment of small debts.

Other cases were more significant. The was, for example, a May 1788 claim against Christopher Hatch for four hundred pounds sterling. There were continuing legal battles between Arnold and Alexander Cameron, the captain of the *Lord Sheffield,* which sailed so triumphantly out of Saint John harbour in 1786. By 1789 Arnold was in court claiming that Cameron owed him for food and liquor supplied to the ship for its crew and never accounted for by the captain. He claimed six hundred pounds for money owing, injury, and damages. There were suits against traders such as Hatch, who took goods from Arnold for resale and never paid him back. In 1788 Arnold sued him for two hundred pounds. There were small suits such as the 1789 claim of forty-one pounds against Robert Pears, based on an earlier, unpaid credit purchase worth £20.7. In November 1789 the case was submitted to two Saint John businessmen – James Hayt, auctioneer, and Thomas Jennings, blacksmith. They found in Arnold's favour, but Pears could not be found to pay the bill.

It was like that for Arnold. He won many of his cases because the court heard clear evidence of men using credit or borrowing money and then refusing or failing to make good on the debt. However, he rarely received compensation despite the court award because the debtor left the province, went underground, or faced the prospect of prison. At times, these lawsuits were complicated matters of obligations and debts passed from one businessman to another. In 1790, for example, Charles McPherson swore an affidavit to the effect that he owed Arnold thirty pounds. But the obligation was connected to a claim Arnold had against James Holmes and since Holmes had left the province, McPherson was free of the debt. He was a downtown businessman who appears to have been one of the early eccentric characters of Saint John. In 1785 he was convicted of selling liquor without a licence and fined five pounds by the city's common council. He threw himself on the mercy of the newly installed councillors. "Charles McPherson, having solicited for a remitting of the said fine and sent a letter to the corporation apologizing for his standing out continuously against the forces of the laws concerning them and confessing his error," said the minutes of a 1785 Saint John Common Council meeting, "it is ordered the said letter be filed and that the said fine be remitted accordingly."[9] McPherson eventually became a respected citizen, running the coffee-house down the street from Arnold's house, getting a licence to sell liquor there, and getting a job from the city as a salt measurer on the east side of the harbour.[10] It was a petty bureaucratic job of the day, assessing the quantity of salt passing through the port. In the days before refrigeration, salt was a key preservative for meat.

Still, as Arnold found out, a bureaucratic position and income did not mean McPherson would pay his debts.

In some cases, Arnold's court actions were echoes from his past, lingering controversies carried from the bloodied soil of the thirteen colonies to the new colony. A suit in August 1786 by Jesse Lawrence was a good example.

Lawrence had been a Loyalist who took refuge in New York in 1781, as did thousands of others, General Arnold among them. The two Loyalist fighters met in the refugee city. Presumably, they lost touch when Arnold went to England and Lawrence joined the sealift to Nova Scotia and New Brunswick. Five years later, when the two men found themselves living in the same small community, Lawrence purchased some goods from Arnold and failed to pay. Arnold took him to court, winning a judgment from a panel of city merchants. In response, Lawrence decided to use the courts to settle an old score. He used a court deposition in New Brunswick in 1786 to revive a grievance from half a decade before when the two men lived in the American colonies. On 7 October 1781 at New York, he alleged "a certain discourse was had and moved between the said Jesse Lawrence and the said Benedict Arnold."[11] It was argued that there had been a negotiation during which Lawrence agreed to perform some dangerous work for Arnold

– carrying letters from New York to Philadelphia, through enemy lines. He claimed Arnold had not paid him the full fee agreed upon and sued for fifty pounds. Presumably, they settled out of court, since there is no record of a resolution.

Daniel Lyman also became a courtroom echo from Arnold's American past. Once a Loyalist colleague who served under the general, Lyman later became a delinquent debtor who managed to avoid paying his obligations to Arnold for years. It was a case that dragged on well into the 1790s, after Arnold was back in London. Lyman had been a pre-revolutionary neighbour of Arnold's in New Haven who stuck with the British, even when his neighbour was off winning accolades for his revolutionary exploits. He graduated from Yale University in 1770 and rose to the rank of major with the Prince of Wales Regiment during the war. Once Arnold changed sides, the two were reunited and Lyman joined Arnold's American Legion, taking part in the sacking and burning of New London, Connecticut, on 4 September 1781.[12] In New Brunswick, it was natural for Arnold to seek out familiar faces when he looked for business partners. When he purchased potential farmland on the Nashwaak River northeast of Saint John, Arnold leased it to his old neighbour, Lyman. His tenant, it seems, did little to generate revenue on the farm but Lyman did get himself elected to the first Legislative Assembly of New Brunswick, giving him immunity from the consequences of debt judgments by the court. He also managed to run up debts, forcing him to mortgage 250 acres of land that he owned along the river.

Arnold's partner, Munson Hayt, held the mortgage and it was acquired by Arnold in payment of a debt owed. Then began a legal battle to recover the debt, a battle that lasted for close to a decade. Over the years, Lyman used various creative excuses to avoid paying, including an eighteenth-century version of "The cheque is in the mail." Sometimes, he was inventive. He would be able to pay it if he could have a little more time. He expected his wife to receive an inheritance and he would pay then. He was a member of the legislature and could not be sued. "You know how difficult it is to negotiate in this country, especially when one of the parties lives in York County and the other in Saint John," Jonathan Bliss wrote to Arnold in September 1792, "... and how difficult it is to obtain payment of a debtor who is a member of the Legislature."[13]

Several times, Bliss thought he had a deal and wrote to Arnold accordingly. One of those times was in late 1793 when Arnold was in London, sounding thoroughly disgusted with his former New Haven comrade and the financial deceit. "I am glad that you have settled respecting Lyman's farm," he wrote Bliss on 4 November 1793. "He is now here and I am told wandering about the country to avoid paying debts that he has contracted since his arrival. I fear that I shall never recover anything more from him and beg you will be so good as to take the proper steps to secure this by placing a tenant on it who will make such improvements as to prevent its being escheated, which my good friends at Fredericton will be disposed to do if in their power." Alas, a settlement was not to be had and the news from home was not encouraging. "Lyman's farm remains as when I wrote last," Bliss replied on 22 January 1794. "There is no tenant upon it. Labor is now so extremely high in this country that it would not be advisable to save the land from escheat, as tis called, by having men to clear and improve the quality of land required by the grant, if this could be done at any rate. You had better lose the land as it is, and your whole debt, than incur so heavy a charge." Bliss promised to keep trying but had little hope. Enlisting in the King's New Brunswick Regiment "holds out more present advantages to the inhabitants than the cultivation of land and I have no great prospect for a tenant." Two months later he reported: "I have been advertising Lyman's farm these two months to be let on very easy terms. No tenant has yet offered."

Almost two years later, Lyman wrote to say that he was broke and one thousand pounds in debt, could not pay the full amount, had been deceived by Munson Hayt in the original transaction, and would pay one hundred pounds for clear title to the farm. Arnold rejected the offer. In a blistering letter of 6 December 1795, he complained to Bliss that Lyman had not acted "candidly" in his dealings over the land. Arnold said he would accept the hundred pounds only if Lyman then agreed to pay another £150 within three or four years with interest. "I neither want his farm or to distress him but shall be glad to have the debt paid or secured."

So it went. By January 1797 Lyman was offering £164.12. "He does not think it right that he should pay interest on charges after the assignment or action commenced," Bliss reported. "I cannot conceive on what reason this opinion of his is founded. He may expect that you should be generous because his other creditors have been so, not recollecting that when they compounded with him, his circumstances were very different from what they are now." This seems to have finally triggered a negotiation and settlement. By August Bliss had received £259.20.1 from Lyman, from which he deducted just over eleven pounds in legal fees. In late November Arnold wrote to Bliss acknowledging his receipt of money on the Lyman account. By then, Lyman had obtained a government job as Commissary of Prisoners and presumably had some income.

As if Arnold did not have enough enemies among New Brunswick's élite, he showed them no special consideration when they owed him money. He took them to court, sometimes pursuing them relentlessly for what he thought was owed him. Neither social status nor friendship deterred Arnold from his single-minded debt collecting. He sued several sitting members of the legislature. In 1788 he sued the sheriff of York County, John Murray. In a fit of hard-headed (and at least one of his disgusted friends considered it hard-hearted) commercial righteousness, he tenaciously pursued a debt owed him by Edward Winslow, a founder of the colony and high flyer who had fallen on hard times.

As noted earlier, Winslow arrived in New Brunswick destined in his own mind for greatness. He had been a Loyalist hero during the Revolution, a negotiator on behalf of army veterans looking for land grants after the war, and, briefly, the military secretary to the troop commander at Halifax. He graduated from Boston's Harvard University in 1765 and acted as muster master general of Loyalist forces in America at the end of the Revolution. He has been described as a man with "a volatile temperament and gay exuberances.[14] He also had pretensions of class position and wealth, unmatched by his ability to make money in the wilderness. At one point, he found himself sixty-three pounds in debt to Arnold and gave him a promissory note to cover it. By May 1789 Arnold had given up trying to collect the money and went to court. By July he was accusing Winslow of "fraudulently and craftily" trying to get out of paying the debt. The court ordered the sum paid and in what must have been a humiliating experience for Winslow, the sheriff had to track him down at King's Clear, near Fredericton, to deliver the court papers. By early 1790, Arnold had won the case and received the original amount of the promissory note. He was not satisfied and demanded that Winslow also pay interest on the money. The demand angered one of Arnold's friends and best connections in Saint John, lawyer Ward Chipman. He was also a friend and lawyer to Winslow and on 26 March 1790 Chipman wrote about his anger in a letter to Winslow:

I enclose to you as a curiosity Arnold's note to me after settling your demand with him. It is more pitiful than I thought even his conduct would be. In the first place, he is not entitled to interest beyond the time of his judgment which was the first week in February and if he was, after such an accumulated interest as he got and putting you to the costs of a suit, renders it abominable in the extreme. I was too angry to answer his note and resolutely determined not to pay the balance. I have heard nothing from him since. I suppose he will sue again, in which case I shall answer that I presume after his whole conduct to you that you will not pay anything more than you are obliged to, that he is not entitled to this balance, that you have his receipt in full but that I have written to you for instructions respecting it.[15]

If Chipman was angry about Arnold's take-no-prisoners stance on Winslow's debt, he must have been livid a few years later when he tasted some of the same from his old friend Benedict. When the Arnolds moved from Saint John to London in 1791, Chipman purchased some of their furniture for forty pounds. Being constantly short of cash, he was slow in paying the bill. Finally, in March 1794 Chipman paid up by giving the money to Jonathan Bliss, who represented Arnold's lingering interests in the colony. Again, Arnold was not satisfied and he instructed Bliss to collect interest as well. It was not until March 1797 that Chipman agreed to pay the interest. This nasty exchange happened even as Arnold and Chipman continued to correspond as friends. Benedict Arnold was not one to concede ground generously, whether in war or in commerce.

Still, Chipman got a measure of revenge. He represented Saint John Common Council as it refused in 1796 to relieve Arnold of taxation on harbour lands he no longer needed that generated no revenue. Bliss asked Chipman to propose that, rather than charge Arnold for taxes in arrears, the city should simply take the land back. "But I have no hopes that the Common Council will listen to anything favorable to you," he wrote to Arnold in mid-1796.[16] Bliss was correct. Council insisted that Arnold pay back taxes, with a penalty.

This barrage of court actions and legal disputes paled in significance to Arnold's legal battle with Munson Hayt, a business partner turned enemy. Even though Arnold ended up winning the case, its aftermath led to the historical assumption that the American traitor-turned-Loyalist was chased out of New Brunswick and the Loyalist City in an uprising of popular anger against him.

The advertisement in the 27 October 1789 issue of the *Royal Gazette* was brief and to the point: "The co-partnership of Arnold, Hayt and Arnold and Monson Hayt & Co. being dissolved by mutual consent, all persons indebted to the said firms are requested to settle their accounts with Monson Hayt."[17] Arnold, Hayt and Arnold ... for a time, it must have seemed Benedict Arnold's perfect vehicle for building the comfortable and respectable life he craved. As a seaman and trader,

Arnold could bring to the shores of New Brunswick the goods that the growing colony wanted and needed. Hayt brought his own strengths to the partnership. As a man with good connections throughout the Loyalist community, ties to the colonial élite, a presence in Frederic-ton, connections to the government, and an acquaintance with Arnold that went back half a decade to the American Legion and the last days of the revolutionary war, Hayt seemed like a good partner to work the goods distribution side of the business. As a crowning touch for the concerned father, Arnold brought his second son, eighteen-year-old Richard, into the business as a partner and gave his younger son Henry a job helping to guard the goods from thieves.

From the start, though, it was a troubled business association. As noted earlier, the colony's demand for goods was not matched by the population's ability to pay. Much of the business was done on credit and many customers failed to pay on time, if they paid at all. To make matters worse for Arnold, Hayt turned out to be a man with connec-tions and dreams but few means. He borrowed relentlessly from Arnold and the business and when the partnership ended in 1789 after just two years, Hayt was more than two thousand pounds in debt to Arnold, more than most people in the colony earned in two or three years.

The business received a severe setback on 11 July 1788 when its harbour warehouse burned to the ground, taking a neighbouring house with it and sparing the rest of the city only because the winds were not blowing in from the harbour. Richard and Henry were asleep in the warehouse at the time; Henry was burned and almost lost his life. Arnold was in England on a trading trip. By what he said was happy financial coincidence, the year before Arnold had received a suggestion from his London agent, Mr Goodrick, that he invest in insurance to protect his growing business. Insurance was an eighteenth-century financial invention, created to gamble on the likelihood that cargoes would make it across the sea to their destination. In later years, it was expanded to cover the value of real property on land as well. In the days of wooden cities when local fires had a nasty habit of spread-ing extensively, increasing numbers of businessmen found it a good investment to gamble the cost of annual premiums against the risk of losing their property to fire.

As one of the few traders who went regularly to London, where the insurance industry was centred, Arnold was probably the first New Brunswick businessman to insure his business. He had moved quickly after receiving Goodrick's letter of 26 May 1787 recommending the move. Effective 24 July 1787, he insured his harbourfront storehouse and its contents for five thousand pounds and his King Street retail outlet for one thousand pounds.[18]

A year later the disastrous fire struck but at least Arnold had insurance. Nevertheless, the loss of his goods must have left Arnold strapped for cash and the business became more aggressive in trying to collect outstanding debts through the courts. On 18 January 1790, for example, Arnold convinced Supreme Court justice Joseph Upham to publish a notice indicating that Joseph Ward of Fredericton owed him money and was hiding, or had escaped the province, to avoid paying up. Within three months if he did not appear, his assets would be sold and divided among his creditors.[19] Arnold was relentless.

Within the partnership, Hayt's debt to Arnold grew and the general presumably began pressuring his partner to repay some of the money he owed. It may well be that the financial dealings between the two partners led Hayt to become "obsessed with a hatred of Arnold." It led to their ultimate break. "Arnold was not long to seek recourse in the courts for his money."[20]

May 1790 was a crucial month. On 7 May, in the wake of the fire, Arnold filed an insurance claim for five thousand pounds. Meanwhile, Hayt was due to repay three loans – for £505.1.3, £152.1.6, and £398.7.10 – all incurred in October 1789, by 1 May 1790. He reneged, and as a consequence, Arnold's lawyer, Jonathan Bliss, said Hayt owed Arnold fifteen hundred pounds, including interest and damages. "Nonetheless, the said Munson not regarding his said several promises and undertakings so made but continuing and fraudulently intending craftily to deceive and defraud the said Benedict Arnold ... hath not yet paid him the said several sums of money."[21]

By then, Arnold was in no mood to compromise. He was demanding two thousand pounds from his old partner, which was a fortune in that era. When Hayt failed to enter a plea within twenty days, he was found guilty and ordered to pay by 15 July. As was the custom, however, Hayt counter-sued, claiming that Arnold had "robbed" him of goods worth four hundred pounds – presumably goods that Hayt claimed he had owned in the burned warehouse. The fight was made worse by a confrontation between the two men in Saint John. On the day that Arnold filed his insurance claim he and Hayt met, and during the heated exchange that followed, Hayt said to Arnold's face what he had been saying behind his back: "I will convince the world that you are the greatest rascal that ever was, that you burnt your own store and I will prove it," he said, according to court documents, "with a loud voice ... in the presence and hearing of His Majesty's faithful subjects." When

Arnold protested that his character was being blackened, Hayt replied: "It is not in my power to blacken your character, for it is as black as it can be, but one thing I will let the world know that you burnt your own store." As if that wasn't enough, Hayt accused Arnold of theft: "You and your family have taken goods from me to the amount of three hundred pounds and your family have robbed me. You and your family have robbed me of near four hundred pounds and I will prove it."[22]

For someone as proud as Arnold, these must have been stinging accusations, coming from a man whose main role in the partnership had been to bleed the business dry. It also had commercial implications as the rumours started by Hayt spread. The insurance company delayed payment of Arnold's claim while waiting to see whether Hayt's accusation was true. In Saint John, customers began to avoid Arnold's business. Ward Chipman told the court that the public charges and rumours tainted Arnold's reputation and brought him "into much disgrace with the king's liege subjects that they should not trade or deal with him and to cause him to be punished for willfully setting fire to his store." Many people "withdrew themselves from his acquaintance and he is greatly damaged and injured in transacting his business and in his trading with divers people with who he used to trade ... many subjects have on this account wholly refused to have any dealings or connection with him. And he hath been compelled to undergo great bodily pain and labor and great anxiety of mind to make known his innocence ..."[23]

Arnold's only recourse, if his all-important reputation was to be salvaged, was to sue Hayt for slander. It resulted in a dramatic trial, "the most sensational lawsuit in early New Brunswick history."[24] Arnold hired Ward Chipman and Jonathan Bliss to represent him – two of the most prominent lawyers in the city. Hayt hired Elias Hardy, long an adversary of Arnold's in court cases and politics. The trial began on 7 September 1790, in Saint John. Arnold, as a well-to-do merchant and former American revolutionary hero turned traitor in a city of down-at-the-mouth Loyalists, was not popular. Elias Hardy was a prominent lawyer with a reputation for taking no flack from the upper class. Edward Winslow's descendant, Fredericton lawyer J.J. Fraser Winslow, called it "the first slander trial in New Brunswick."[25]

The deck was stacked against Arnold. In the courtroom, he faced antagonists from both the lower and upper classes. Three of the twelve jurors had signed the petition against the result of the 1786 election, which included victories by Arnold's lawyers, Bliss and Chipman. Several of the jurors, including the tavern keeper Charles MacPherson, had been on the losing end of lawsuits filed by Arnold for bad debts.

Moreover, nine of the twelve jurors – Adam Hennigan, Edward Ervin, David Lovitt, Stephen Humbert, William Clark, James Saverner, Thomas Muller, John Whiteman, and MacPherson – had already served as jurors during the same court circuit in an arbitration case involving Arnold and Hayt. The jury rejected Arnold's claim, presented by Chipman, that he owed nothing and awarded Hayt fifty pounds.[26] Such a jury could hardly be described as sympathetic, or even neutral, towards Arnold.

On the bench hearing the case were judges Isaac Allen and Joshua Upham. It will be remembered that Hayt and Allen worked together on a board of trustees to help establish a college in Fredericton. Allen, a former military commander of the New Jersey Volunteers with no legal training, had been appointed to the bench over some protests. Upham, who also moved in Hayt's circles, likewise had no legal background. Hayt himself was an officer of the court, serving as a magistrate in York County, surrounding Fredericton.[27]

The facts, as presented to the court by Chipman in Arnold's defence, were straightforward. Arnold, he said, had purchased the insurance a year before the fire. There was no evidence that he had set the fire. Arnold, during his years in Saint John, had been "reported of good character" who through the years "has kept and fulfilled his faithful contracts and promises as a merchant."

According to the transcript of his address to the jury, as recorded in his own files, Chipman challenged directly Hayt's claim that Arnold had no reputation worth protecting. "What is a proof of good character? His promotion? His rank? Are these nothing? What crimes has he ever been guilty of to contaminate his character? Has he been accused or convicted of any crime? Is he dishonest? Has anything unfair in his dealings been proved?" His description of Hayt was less than flattering. "He was a captain in the late war," Chipman reminded the jury. "He has been a magistrate since. He is a man of soft, insinuating manners."

He appealed to their logic. If nothing else, Arnold was a family man and a man with considerable investment in Saint John. Would he want to see all that harmed? "Had the plaintiff in this instance been guilty, he must have been an infernal spirit indeed. The tide was out, one other house was actually burnt. Had the wind sprang up at southeast, at which point it blows fresh, the whole city might have been in danger. His son too he must have risqued sacrificing. His most inveterate enemies will not accuse him of a (lack) of paternal tenderness." Would Arnold do all this just for the insurance? "Hell itself would not produce so great a monster."[28]

So what did happen on the night of 11 July 1788? According to articling lawyer Stephen Sewell who worked with Arnold and Chipman preparing the case, he and the general went up the Saint John River in early August in search of two Black Loyalists who had worked for Arnold at the warehouse in 1788. They found them and the two, interviewed independently, told essentially the same version of events. On the night in question, one of them had gone into the top floor of the store with Henry, looking for some oak wood to make a boat. He had carried a candle and it had accidentally started the fire, which then trapped and burned Henry. Sewell told his brother Jonathan in a letter that he had no doubt the two were telling the truth: "There was such an appearance of veracity and fear withal of what might be the consequences, their story so direct which they told without leading questions, the declaration that they had not seen any of the General's family, that no one ever said a word to them respecting the fire, their strong appearance of truth, candor and simplicity which is always visible particularly in Black men, altogether is sufficient presumptive evidence against anything that Hoyt can allege that the store was burnt otherwise than by accident."[29]

This evidence was presented to the jury as Chipman called twenty-nine witnesses, including Arnold's two sons. But it was as if Chipman knew the jury was hostile to Arnold, no matter what the evidence. He suggested that Hardy was relying on the prejudice and "partiality" of the jury. He implored the twelve men to stick with the facts and find Hayt guilty of slander for publishing a known and hurtful lie. And he pleaded for a large settlement to reinforce the point, arguing that a small judgment would be as damaging as a judgment against Arnold. Chipman, in his final address, said: "The jury will, I trust, shew they have feeling. The jury, I trust, will convince the plaintiff that slander so gross and so groundless shall not with impunity be persisted in so maliciously and obstinately. And that no general prejudices on the one hand or partiality on the other will influence a jury to forget the obligation of their oaths or neglect to do justice to an injured fellow subject who has in the fullest confidence of their uprightness and his own innocence appealed to them to vindicate and address his wrong."[30] There is historical record of Hardy's address to the jury. Presumably he appealed to their prejudice against Arnold's personal status and class position.

Chipman was not merely a hired legal gun in this case. According to Sewell, he was upset by the case and considered it "one of the most hellish plots that ever was laid for the destruction of a man." What, then, must he have thought of Isaac Allen's final instruction to the jury. As young Sewell saw it, the charge to the jury was "very lame ... In fact, he stopped twice or thrice for the space of a half minute, apparently at a loss for thought ..."[31]

The jury quickly brought in a contradictory judgment. They found that Arnold had been slandered, effectively agreeing that he had not burned his own store. They also recommended a minimal settlement, implying that Arnold's damaged reputation was worth little. The judges brought in an award of twenty shillings, an insult to Arnold.

Two centuries later, in the mid-1990s, experienced New Brunswick lawyer Eric Teed assessed the judgment as a politically inspired loss for Arnold, driven in good part by the enemies he had made through his revolutionary past or his recent business dealings, which more often than not ended in court, with a new enemy for Arnold. "One can only conclude that had Arnold not been so engrossed in court proceedings during the past two years, had he not just been found liable in debt by substantially the same jury as heard his own case, there might well have been a different result," Teed has written. "But such is the stuff upon which our legal system founded, on the sandy base of human emotion stands."[32]

The judgment was a sharp rebuke to Arnold and likely influenced his decision a year later to leave the colony, some of whose residents clearly held a hostile view of him. However, the judgment had one positive result. Soon after he was cleared of torching his own warehouse, the insurance company made good on his claim. At best, it was a bittersweet victory for the proud general.

Arnold was not a total outcast in New Brunswick society, despite his legions of court opponents. He had friends, among them the Chipmans, Sewells, and Blisses. When he was not travelling and trading, the Arnolds were an integral part of social round of dinner parties, gatherings, and balls with which the small upper class of Saint John entertained themselves. He may also have been in touch with a cousin in the neighbourhood.

The Reverend Oliver Arnold had just turned thirty when Benedict arrived. They shared great-great-grandfather William Arnold, who had emigrated to Rhode Island 149 years earlier. Oliver Arnold had attended Yale University in Benedict's home town of New Haven, graduating in 1776 as his famous cousin was leading the retreat from Canada and the decisive Lake Champlain defence to save the thirteen colonies from British invasion. Still, Oliver did not share his cousin's revolutionary zeal and he was part of the first wave of refugees to land in New Brunswick from New York on the first fleet in 1783. He was soon appointed secretary to the refugee and land agents dealing with the influx of immigrants. In the early days of Saint John, when tents were the dwellings of choice and necessity, Oliver Arnold was known as the "town clerk."[33] It was a position of prominence and in the first land lottery, he obtained two well-positioned lots – one a few hundred yards inland near where his cousin Benedict eventually came to live and one on the waterfront. Yet Oliver appears never to have lived on either of his lots, choosing to move east to Sussex to take charge of a recently built Indian school.

In 1791 Oliver Arnold was ordained and then appointed Sussex missionary for the Society for the Propagation of the Gospel. He soon established and ran a school for Indian children, the act for which he is best remembered. While there is no record that Benedict and Oliver were in touch, it is difficult to believe that they were strangers to one another in such a small community. According to a biographical sketch of Oliver Arnold prepared for the New Brunswick Museum files, the Connecticut Loyalist and missionary left his mark on the province: "The Arnold family which is to be found in New Brunswick today are descendants of the Rev. Oliver Arnold, the first rector of the Parish of Sussex, Kings County."

Once the judgment in the Hayt case was handed down, there is evidence that Arnold returned to his commercial life as a trader and to his normal life as a resident of the port city. There also are hints that the judgment may have led to some local social unrest, with the Arnolds as the target. The evidence is flimsy and the veracity of the story suspect. Nonetheless, it has become part of the historical record, at least as portrayed in books about Arnold written during the past half century. For modern American biographers and their Canadian disciples, the legal humiliation of the American turncoat has taken on mythical proportions as a vindication of the view that "Arnold's Canadian neighbours liked him little better than so many Americans would have done."[35] In version after version of the court case, it is written as fact that the judgment led to an outpouring of popular anger against the general. This demonstration – during which a mob swarmed his house and he was burned in effigy – is said to have led directly to Arnold's departure from the colony. It has also served to convince

American biographers that his crime against George Washington and the fledgling American state made Arnold an outcast everywhere, even in Loyalist New Brunswick.

In truth, there is no corroborating evidence for this dramatic story. It may never have happened. The evolution of the story of "The Night Arnold Was Burned in Effigy" gives a fascinating glimpse of how history can be a joke that the present plays on the past, how the prejudices of an age (in this case, mid-nineteenth-century America) can become written in stone; how they can gain the credibility of accepted truth, simply through retelling. It also is a vivid illustration of how Canadians' view of their own past has at times been moulded by American sensibilities and prejudices. And it is an illustration of a frustrating truth for a researcher: it is extremely difficult to prove that something *did not* happen in the past. Lack of evidence could simply mean that it has been overlooked, that the research was not thorough enough, or that details of the incident were not recorded.

The most that can therefore be said is that the story of the September 1790 Arnold Riot, accepted as fact by serious American and Canadian historians, is questionable – very questionable. Its occurrence has never been proven. The evidence accounts to flimsy hearsay and unattributed American storytelling. Nonetheless, it has become firmly entrenched as part of the Benedict Arnold story in Canada.

It is a colourful tale of the night a Saint John mob told the Arnolds, through angry voice and threatening flame, exactly what they thought of this traitor's character and high living ways ... or did they?

In March 1963 the Fredericton-based *Atlantic Advocate* provided one of the few major local portraits of Benedict Arnold's years in New Brunswick. As New Brunswick writer Jean Sereisky tried to describe why Arnold decided to abandon the colony in 1791, she delved into what she imagined to be his embittered memory: "Arnold remembered vividly the effigy-burning incident before his home when the Riot Act had to be read and troops called out to disperse the noisy mob."[35] It is a powerful scene, recreated in scores of books and articles. Six months later, the Toronto *Globe and Mail* carried a tourist-page story about Saint John headlined: "Gen. Arnold Wasn't Popular." It described the downtown street where he had lived and the popular discontent against him. "And in that same King St, now thronged with modern traffic, an angry mob once gathered before his home and burned an effigy of him – an effigy labelled 'traitor.'"[36] A similar version appeared in the *Saint John Telegraph Journal* in the early 1970s and again in 1993 when the hometown newspaper reported that the riot had been connected to the trial: "When the outcome of the trial became known in Saint John and while Benedict and his wife were still in Fredericton, a mob gathered outside the Arnold residence on King Street and broke into the house, surging through it and doing some damage before the authorities could call out the troops and bring events under control."[37] The gravity of the incident escalated as time, and the telling, progressed.

This was not just a journalistic flight of fancy aimed at selling subscriptions, as it turns out. The journalists had numerous sources for their stories. For decades, authors and biographers who have created the modern image of Arnold have solemnly recorded this popular uprising against an unpopular figure. In 1994 American Clare Brandt connected the incident to the trial judgment and embellished the story somewhat, now including Arnold's children in the drama. "The citizens of Saint John expressed their feelings by burning Arnold in effigy in the middle of the night in front of his King Street house with Peggy and the children looking on."[38] She dated the incident 1790. Four years before Brandt published, University of Vermont historian Willard Sterne Randall tied the incident to the political turmoil of the day, as well as to the trial. He dated it 1791 and did not include the children. "The day after the verdict became known in Saint John, while the Arnolds were still in Fredericton, a mob loyal to Hayt's radical lawyer Elias Hardy surged around and into and through the Arnold house on King Street, burning an effigy of Arnold with a one-word sign fastened to its chest: "Traitor." They sacked the house before a justice of the peace could read them the Riot Act and summon red coats from Fort Howe."[39] In 1954 author Willard Wallace noted the "classic touch of irony" in the fact that Loyalists were calling the betrayer of the American Revolution a traitor. "They might have done more had not the Riot Act been read to them and troops been called out."[40]

To the reader of these various accounts of that traumatic night in Old Saint John, several factors stand out. There are the inconsistencies in the stories. Was it 1790 or 1791? Was Arnold driven from the province as a result of that night, or did he hang on for a year? Did the mob merely demonstrate their disgust on the street or did they actually break into his house during a rampage? Were the Arnolds in Fredericton, or was Peggy at home with the children watching? One version even had Peggy fainting and Arnold carrying her upstairs away from the mob. Why would they be in Fredericton, since the trial was in Saint

John? Details, details. Added to these inconsistencies is the curious fact that the incident has become a staple of Arnold biographies only in the past half century. American Oscar Sherwin's 1931 *Benedict Arnold: Patriot and Traitor,* for example, made no mention of the incident, despite Sherwin's best efforts to prove that Arnold suffered through the rest of his life for his sins against the Revolution. Likewise, Charles Burr Todd, a descendent of Aaron Burr, wrote a 1903 exposé, "The Real Benedict Arnold," that made no mention of the King Street riot. Only in writings after 1931 was the riot portrayed as the pinnacle of disgust with which the citizens of Saint John looked upon Arnold.

What is the origin of this latter-day revelation? What is the source of the critical new-found knowledge? There are no contemporary newspaper accounts to corroborate the story. There are no records on file from the 54th Regiment, then stationed at Fort Howe, to indicate they had been called out in 1790 or 1791 to quell a riot. There is no mention of the incident in the minutes of the Saint John Common Council for those years, although the mayor of the city would have been involved in calling out the troops. And there is no mention of such a major incident for such a small colony in the private dispatches that Gov. Thomas Carleton sent to London during those years, at least in the copy of the dispatches on file at the National Archives of Canada. Randall, in a meticulously sourced book, does not cite an authority for his tale about the riot. Brandt, for her part, concedes the lack of objective evidence for her assertion but suggests it is true anyway, based on circumstantial evidence. "There is no first-hand documentation of this incident but a letter written later by Arnold seems to confirm the legend that persists in Saint John to this day."[41] The letter she cites was written 26 February 1792 from Arnold, then in London, to Jonathan Bliss in Saint John. "We had a very rough and disagreeable voyage home but our reception has been very pleasant and our friends have [been] more than well attentive to us since our arrival," he wrote in part. "The little property that we have saved from the hands of *a Lawless Ruffian Mob* and *more unprincipled judges* in New Brunswick is perfectly safe here as well as *Our Persons from Insult ...*"[42]

Clearly, Arnold was glad to escape and felt misused by the people of New Brunswick, both common and exalted. It is a stretch, however, to see a mob scene and an effigy burning in that description. The source of the anecdote must surely lie elsewhere. One common citation in many of the renditions of the tale was a 1928 description of Arnold by J. Clarence Webster, an icon of New Brunswick historical records. Webster was a New Brunswick native who moved to Massachusetts in the late nineteenth century to practise medicine and to make his fortune. He moved home for his retirement years, flush with money and fired by a desire to collect authentic historical artefacts of Canada and New Brunswick. In the 1920s he became a member of the Historic Sites and Monuments Board of Canada. From his home in Shediac, Webster set about with gusto to pursue his self-appointed task of history collecting, acquiring documents, amassing one of the best collections of prints depicting the 1759 battle on the Plains of Abraham, and becoming one of the key New Brunswick contacts for those interested in the history of the province. The Webster Collection at the New Brunswick Museum is a priceless portfolio of prints, photos, and historic documents. The file is replete, as well, with letters from American museum curators and historians inquiring about this or that moment in New Brunswick history. It may have been these inquiries and his growing reputation that enticed the physician and amateur historian to write, in 1928, *An Historical Guide to New Brunswick*. From Decker through Brandt, this became a source for American authors writing about Benedict Arnold.

The guide, published by the New Brunswick Tourist Association as a lure for American tourists, noted Arnold's years as a city merchant and described the 1788 fire, as well as reporting the "rumour" at the time that the business was overinsured. This unflattering portrayal of Arnold concludes with this description: "Arnold's overbearing manners and his reputation for crookedness made him very unpopular and on one occasion, they made an effigy of him, labelled 'Traitor,' and burned it in front of his house." It should be noted that Webster did not draw the conclusion that fuelled the speculations of so many who followed – that the effigy incident was tied to the trial, even though the two incidents follow each other chronologically in the 1928 narrative.

But what was the source of this new information, published in 1928 but missed by a century of biographers before that? The answer appears to lie in one of the Benedict Arnold files at the New Brunswick Museum in Saint John. Dated November 1861, it is a story in the American *Harper's New Monthly Magazine*, then in its thirteenth year, published in New York City. The relevant issue came out in the early days of the American Civil War, during which an entire section of the country had decided to forsake the "American Dream." *Harper's*, staunchly favouring the North over the defiant South, chose this time to write about "eminent traitors" to the American cause during the Revolution. Benedict Arnold was the primary example.

The article, a faded clipping, would have been in the museum file when Webster did his research on Arnold for his pamphlet. This is what he would have read, ostensibly authoritative but factually flawed and without attributed sources:

After the war, Arnold made his abode at St John's, in the British province of New Brunswick, where many refugee loyalists who fled from the United States had settled. He engaged in a profitable shipping business, made money, lived in a style of ostentatious profusion and thus purchased entrance into the society of the so-called upper classes. His known fraudulent dealings and haughty deportment made him very unpopular with the people and on one occasion, they showed their resentment and contempt by suspending his effigy in public, labelled TRAITOR, in such a position as to be easily seen from his house. It was then committed to the flames with loud huzzas. This was in 1792. He went to St John's in 1786. Every year, his unpopularity increased and in 1794, he closed his business, sailed first for the West Indies and then for England and there made his permanent abode.[43]

Never mind that the *Harper's* writer got the name of the city wrong, or that Arnold arrived a year earlier than the article reported and departed a full three years before *Harper's* thought he did. What is remarkable is the similarity between the *Harper's* version and Webster's tale, particularly the descriptions of the effigy incident. It seems that one of the seminal incidents that defines Benedict Arnold as a New Brunswick outcast is based on an historical source as questionable as an unattributed American magazine article written at the start of a civil war in which betrayal of the American revolutionary ideal was a major issue. To his credit, W.S. MacNutt, the dean of New Brunswick historians, did not repeat the King Street riot story when he briefly described Arnold's sorry years in New Brunswick. Instead, he added a twist of his own about the hostility of common Saint John citizens towards Arnold. Citing Pennsylvania author Charles Sellers, who wrote a 1930 critical biography of the traitor, MacNutt wrote in his 1963 text *New Brunswick: A History* that the hostility was evident the night in July 1788 when the harbourside warehouse burned. "During the conflagration, there were voices in the crowd calling upon Arnold to tell them if the fire resembled that of New London – a reminder of one of his bold but ill-judged actions during the war."[44]

There are two problems with this story, which was unattributed in Sellers's book. First, some of the Loyalists in Saint John, including Munson Hayt, were part of the torching squads in New London,

Connecticut, and they had acted in defiance of Arnold's orders to attack only military installations. New London would not likely have been a big issue to Loyalists who had often suffered dispossession and torture at the hands of zealous revolutionaries. Second, Arnold was in London when the fire broke out in Saint John. He could not have been there to hear the taunting, contemptuous voices in the night, even if they were being raised.

It is far from the only questionable piece of evidence the Americans cite to "prove" Arnold's sorry state as a New Brunswick social leper. Another story about his Canadian years, much beloved by American biographers, came from a yellowed and frayed clipping in the Arnold collection at the New Brunswick Museum in Saint John. The file includes extracts from "Eastport and Passamaquoddy, a Collection of Historical and Biographical Sketches," compiled in 1888 by William Henry Kilby. There is no date and no other verification of this recollection. It includes a sketch of Capt. John Shackford of Newburyport, who came to Moose Island (Eastport, Maine) in 1783 to settle and to establish a fishing business and later a passenger service between Eastport and Boston. Shackford, a veteran of the march through Maine against Quebec under Arnold's leadership, was captured in the assault and then released; afterwards he served as a soldier under Washington. Then came a tale about his later encounter in New Brunswick with Arnold: "After the Revolution, Benedict Arnold became a merchant and ship owner in St John, N.B. and Capt. Shackford loaded a ship for him at Campobello under Arnold's personal direction." In referring to the circumstances, he says: "I did not make myself known to him but frequently as I sat upon the ship's deck, watched the movements of my old commander who had carried us through everything and for whose skill and courage I retained my former admiration despite his treason. But when I thought of what he had been and the despised man he then was, tears would come and I could not help it."[45]

It may have been absolutely authentic but the image of brave Captain Shackford weeping quietly because of the high tragedy that had befallen his beloved but greedy and flawed leader seems too perfect a fit for the American image of Arnold. It was also first published in the late nineteenth century when being anti-Arnold was in vogue. But it was too good an image to pass up for the writer of the most thorough and balanced modern-day biography of Arnold, Willard Sterne Randall of the University of Vermont. Randall quotes the memoir in his 1990 biography and attributes it to a 1893 Boston publication, *Campobello*, by Kate Gannett Wells, who had picked it up from the 1888 sketches.[46] She also picked up and published a tale about Arnold's inviting another Eastport revolutionary veteran to dine with him. "Before I would dine with that traitor, I would run my sword through his body," she quoted this patriot as saying.[47] It was without attribution and allegedly recreated a conversation that had taken place more than one hundred years before. That yarn has not been picked up by many biographers, even if it does fit their image.

Whatever the circumstances of Arnold's relations with his fellow New Brunswickers, Benedict, Peggy, and their young family pulled up stakes in September 1791 and left New Brunswick, bound for London. Finances and unfulfilled business dreams likely figured in the decision as much as politics and local resentment. Arnold, after all, was accustomed to personal abuse. He left his sons Richard and Henry in Saint John, along with his devoted sister Hannah. As was the case when he had come to New Brunswick six years earlier, gout – an inflammation of the joints often felt most intensely in the toes – plagued the now-fifty-year-old Arnold on the voyage across the Atlantic. The family settled on Hollis Street in London, from where Arnold wrote that he had suffered from a "severe fit of the gout" during a voyage that had been "very rough and disagreeable." Still, he was happy to be back in London and out of the clutches of the poverty and petty politics of Saint John. "I cannot help viewing your great city as a ship wreck from which I have escaped," he wrote to Jonathan Bliss.[48]

He returned to a different Europe, a Europe abuzz with the fall-out from the French Revolution, launched two years earlier and inspired, in part, by the American version. Lafayette, never one of Arnold's favourites, was a hero in revolutionary France. But by then, the first flush of power for the masses was being replaced by anarchy, oppression, and terror. In London, early popular support for the French Revolution was turning to unease at the possibility of a new war against an ancient enemy: "By 1792, with refugees arriving by the boatload, seditious meetings burgeoning in rich profusion and revolutionary posters headed 'A House to Let' posted on the walls of Newgate Jail, it [the city] was soon screaming as loudly for war against France as it had screamed for peace with the American colonists."[49]

At the same time, there was a distinct mood of embarrassment about the battle against the American colonies. Whigs hostile to those who had pursued the war were now setting the political tone. As one who had used treachery to side with the British cause, Arnold was a political outsider. Meanwhile, his supporter King George III was falling in and out of fits of madness, visibly in worse shape than when Arnold and Peggy had first been received at court in the early 1780s.

Two incidents illustrate Arnold's political isolation. During a June 1792 debate in the House of Lords, the radical Whig Lord Lauderdale criticized the Duke of Richmond by invoking the example of Arnold's treason, accusing both Richmond and Arnold of "political apostasy," or reneging on their beliefs.[50] Arnold considered this to be an attack on his character, demanded an apology, and, when the apology proved inadequate in his view, challenged Lauderdale to a duel. They met on 6 July 1792. Arnold fired first and missed. Lauderdale refused to fire and apologized. The London newspapers erroneously declared that Arnold had been killed. The second incident happened the following spring, at an inn in Falmouth, a port on England's south coast. There, Bishop Maurice de Talleyrand, on the run from the Reign of Terror in France and being expelled as a "political undesirable" from refuge in Britain, spent a night *en route* to Philadelphia. His ship had been damaged in a storm and put into the harbour for repairs. Arnold was also staying at the inn and the two met. Talleyrand later wrote that Arnold would at first not reveal his name but told the Frenchman he could not give him letters of introduction for America. "I am perhaps the only American who cannot give you letters for his own country. All the relations I had there are now broken. I must never return."[51] Simon Schama, an historian of the French Revolution, provides a slightly different version of the meeting: he imagined two "fallen heroes" talking about "the ingratitude and misunderstanding of the ignorant world."[52] Since the encounter was recorded later by Talleyrand and not Arnold, it is not possible to know the general's thoughts. Still, that the now-isolated but once-leading figure of the French Revolution considered America his best bet as a safe haven might well have led Arnold to contemplate the sad fact that he really had no safe haven where he would be welcomed as a hero.

London in the early 1790s was in the throes of change. From the muddy and rutted streets of Saint John, the Arnolds moved to a modern metropolis where most of the streets were paved with cobblestones and where each evening, a lamplighter came with a ladder and oil can to light the boulevards, which were increasingly crowded with traffic. On the streets, among the aristocracy and merchant classes, fashions were changing as powdered wigs began to go out of style and older, more elaborate coat styles were being replaced by simpler lines. "The most revolutionary change of all," however, "was the substitution of trousers for knee-breeches."[53] Musically, the great Viennese composer Franz Joseph Haydn – teacher of both Wolfgang Amadeus Mozart and Ludwig van Beethoven – was the toast of London. He was living there when the Arnolds arrived in 1791 and wrote a series of "London Symphonies" which packed London concert halls.[54] Undoubtedly, Arnold would have been aware of the music, fashions, and the life of the city. But for the aging businessman-warrior, it was a less-hospitable place than it had been a decade before when he had arrived as a celebrated defector to the British cause. Now, he was simply another failed businessman from the colonies looking for a better life. He had some friends, but also enemies. Costs were high, his family was large, and he looked desperately for a way to re-establish his commercial network and financial security.

15

After New Brunswick

To read Benedict Arnold's London letters to his friends in Saint John is to see several sides of the man.

There was the fretful and proud father. He worried about the sons he had left behind. "I have not heard from or of my son Richard since he left the States bound to the West Indies and I am very apprehensive for his safety," he wrote to Bliss in February 1792.[1] Over the years, he exchanged proud parental gossip with his friends. "I have the pleasure to say that my little family are all well and improved very much since our arrival here," he wrote in August 1795. "Edward is nearly as tall as myself and bids fair to be very tall. They are both excellent scholars and have lately carried most of the prizes in the academy where there are near one hundred boys. They all speak French as well as English and the master of the school assures me that George (who is a master of his grammar) will make a figure. He has great ambition." He lived to see his sons sent to good English schools and his eldest son, Benedict, become a rising star in the British army. Then, in February 1796, he received word that Benedict had died in Jamaica of fever. "His death ... is a heavy stroke on me as his conduct of late years had been irreproachable and I had flattered myself with seeing him rise to eminence in his profession," Arnold wrote to Bliss on 20 February 1796.

There was the side of Arnold that was generous to the friends he had left behind, whether Bliss, Chipman, or Judge Upham. He sent them warm clothing for the winter and recommended remedies for colds and the gout. "I have taken the liberty to send you (enclosed in a small parcel to Mr Chipman) a Flury Hosiery Cap and a pair of under-hose which I beg you to accept, the latter very proper to keep your feet warm at church," he wrote to Bliss in a letter of 15 October 1792. "Should you choose to find a substitute, Mrs Bliss will find them very comfortable in cold weather." Yet for all his familiar chat and professions of missing his friends, Arnold was clearly thrilled to be away from Saint John and back in London. "Our situation here is very pleasant and more so when contrasted with that at St John," Arnold wrote to Bliss on 10 April 1792. As late as 17 May 1796, he still was casting stones at the New Brunswick élite that had shunned him. He said he had heard that Saint John had been under threat of attack by the French and yet had not been protected by government officials in Fredericton. He was not surprised by their stupidity. "I believe the province would be better off without them ... I am truly rejoiced to hear that you have escaped the threatened danger, not that I have any regard for Sodom and Gomorrah, but for the few Righteous that are therein whom I believe to be my friends." To Ward Chipman he sent flannel hose, socks, and a pair of gloves in 1792. "Should you be again attacked with the gout, you will find them serviceable. I most sincerely wish it may be the case. I certainly would not, had I the power to transfer the disease to some of my *good friends* at St John."[2]

For their part, Arnold's New Brunswick friends seemed envious of his move. Bliss wrote on 22 January 1796 that England was "the best of all possible countries for the residence of a man, in the best of all conditions, that of a British subject. I lived too long in that country to hope to be content in this wretched corner of His Majesty's dominions."[3] On 30 August 1792 Ward Chipman wrote to Arnold that he hoped the general and his family were "in full enjoyment of the luxuries and comforts of the finest country on earth."[4] All the while, Arnold continued to have money troubles and continued to pressure his Saint John lawyer friends to sell his properties, collect his debts, and extract as much for him as they could.

There was, for example, a ship's frame at Digby, Nova Scotia, that he wanted sold. It sat deteriorating for several years while Arnold sent ever more frantic letters wondering why it had not been sold. By October 1794 the frame had been sold at terms "more advantageous than I had expected." There was a wharf at Lower Cove, Saint John, which he decided should be kept in repair so that it could later be sold. It was not to be. In January 1792 a storm swept over the harbour and "very much injured [the] wharf at Lower Cove. We did not think it advisable to lay out any money in repairing it," Bliss reported. In January 1794 Bliss wrote that the wharf was being battered by waves and storms and dismantled by thieves. "The wharf at the Lower Cove is going to ruin and not worth repairing. I could probably sell the old stone foundation of the barns store for a trifle if you think it best but tis not in my power to prevent dilapidations there... in other words, the rogues carry off the stones."[5] Arnold had been robbed on the weekend he arrived in New Brunswick, and he continued to be worked over by thieves even after his departure for London.

Arnold had other properties in New Brunswick that he hoped would produce revenue but rarely did. A few were sold but most merely cost him in taxes. He had set out to be a land speculator in a community on the rise. He ended up losing substantial sums on most of the property investment he made. He owned some land on Germain Street, for example, now in downtown Saint John. Then, it was open land and before he left, Arnold made a deal with a local entrepreneur named Stimact to plant potatoes for sale to a hungry population. In January 1794 Jonathon Bliss reported the bad news:

Truly, it turned out bad enough. There were not ten bushels of potatoes to divide between you and him and these so bad that your share, which I divided to be sold, yielded only 9p a bushel, on credit to a poor woman who has not yet paid for them. I don't think Stimact a good husbandman but the season was so uncommonly wet that the field was under water a great part of the summer. The last year, I did better. I prevailed on a black man to plant part of the ground with potatoes as the rent of one half, I finding all the seed. I could not get the whole planted on any terms. Your share of the produce was 45 bushels, for which I have credited you 45 shillings, the price current. I find it impossible to prevent vagabonds from pulling down the fences and I fear that the lots will be henceforth quite open and uncultivated.

Arnold was a soldier and a trader, not an owner of sharecropping land. His insistence on the pursuit of small debts in Saint John was an indication of his dire financial straits in high-priced London. Much of his wealth had been invested in New Brunswick and little of it was paying off. On 4 November 1793 he wrote to Bliss about a series of small debts outstanding – Ebenezer Brown owed £14.10, Michaill McNally owed £12.15, Isaac Atwood owed £22, Jasper Belding owed £14, Edward Steele owed £8, and so on. The total was more than £139, not a large sum for an entrepreneur like Arnold. Yet it seemed very important to him. "Last, I wish to be informed if there is any probability of their being recovered," he wrote.

In most cases, the answer was no. New Brunswick was as poor as when he had left it. Debtors were as devious as they had ever been.

"I am much obliged to you for the care you have been so good as to take of my affairs at St John and in saving the debts you mention," he wrote to Bliss on 3 January 1795. "I wish I could realize all the little property I have at and near St John." There was not a chance of that. Saint John and New Brunswick would continue to consume his wealth thanks to poor investments.

Poverty and boredom led Arnold, at age fifty-two, with a bad leg and chronic gout, to head to the West Indies on a trading voyage. He had applied for a military posting and been rejected. There was little else he could do. He lived an exciting life during his West Indies trip. He made a fortune. He lost a fortune. He was captured by the French as a British spy and then threatened with delivery to the Americans, who the French knew would like to get their hands on him and would pay top dollar to do so. Arnold escaped from the French in a daring escapade. This later-life experience seemed to cause Arnold, the life-long warrior, to reconsider the glories of conflict. In January 1795 from St Pierre, Martinique, he wrote to Bliss almost wistfully: "You are doubtless free from the dangers of war, which is a great happiness at this time, when it is carried on with a brutality unknown to former times and very little to the honor or humanity or the cause of freedom. My situation has often been dangerous and critical, my affairs some-times have prospered and sometimes not. I have made and lost a great deal of money here but I hope to return to England in April a gainer upon the whole."

It was not to be, yet Arnold in his poverty maintained his new-found view of the horrors of war. It even made New Brunswick look attractive. "In this age of revolutions and the consequent horrors and devasta-tions of war, you are certainly fortunate to be placed in a snug corner, in a great measure out of reach of them, a happiness which thousands of the great ones of the earth sigh for in vain," he wrote Bliss in August 1795 after he had returned to England. "If we are disposed to philos-ophize, there is great consolation to be drawn from our situations, which are comfortable but not sufficiently elevated to be objects of envy and distinction. We therefore ought to be content, which is the greatest happiness to be expected in this world."

For Benedict Arnold, of course, this contentment was not a perma-nent state of being. He worried about his family, his legacy, the future of his family. His trade results were mixed. In Grenada, he made money on investments but then lost property worth three thousand pounds in a bad deal. He returned to London even more impover-ished than he had been, "which makes it necessary for me to collect as many of my old debts as possible," as he told Chipman by letter on

4 May 1795.[6] Money troubles led him to complain to Chipman in a letter the following March about an attempt by the local government in Carleton County, New Brunswick, to charge him rent for a piece of land he had leased for a shipyard but had never developed. He had expected the government to take the land back, but instead, they sent a bill. "I never supposed they would in conscience or common honesty make a demand for the rent after I had given it up and left the country." Arnold implied he was not being treated as fairly as others, including Chipman. "I well remember that you and others who had lands from them at more than their value were permitted to give them up." He asked for Chipman's help.

Arnold also joked with Chipman about the lawyer's investment in a seemingly successful farming operation in the colony. It could help the province and the legal profession, said Arnold. "I am glad to learn that farming is succeeding with you. It is the only thing that can support trade or make the province worth preserving and ought to meet with every encouragement and as farmers grow rich, they will be better able to pay for law and more inclined to promote suits." It is one of the rare written examples of dry Arnold wit. And if he allowed himself a small smile over his lawyer joke, it was likely one of the few times during his last years in London that he was amused.

His money troubles continued, his health declined, he started to drink heavily. "For more than three months, I have had a severe fit of the gout and it is only within a few days since the beginning of February that I have escaped from the confinement of my room," he wrote to Bliss on 17 May 1797. "I am now, thank God, able to move about and attend to business. I believe the fit was owing to my having lately indulged too freely in drinking cider, which I had for many years before given up, but having had very little gout for six or seven years past, I had flattered myself that it would never return. This fit will, however, make me cautious for the future."[7]

With Arnold's abiding interest in securing assets to leave for his wife and children, his commercial losses must have tormented him. "You know the solicitude of their beloved and lamented father to render them independent," Peggy wrote to Bliss on Christmas Day, 1801, from London. One of his few successful efforts to leave a financial legacy came in the 1790s when he made a bid from London for some land in what would become Ontario. He eventually acquired 13,400 acres, which became a base for three of his sons.

Predictably, acquisition of the land became a politically charged series of intrigues that involved Arnold and one of the icons of early Canadian history – John Graves Simcoe, the first governor of Upper

Canada, a soldier who had served under Arnold during the Revolution and a Loyalist with a grudge against his old commander. It also became another incident that Canadian writers use to cast Arnold in a bad historical light. Simcoe's coolness, sometimes outright hostility, have been treated as proof positive that Arnold was an outcast in British North America. As usual, the truth was somewhat more complicated than the story that has been told. It begins with the founding of Upper Canada in the wilderness north of the Great Lakes in the years following the American Revolution.

In 1791 the colony of Upper Canada had been created out of the open spaces west of the French colony of Lower Canada. In the preceding years it had been populated by two groups: Loyalists fleeing from the thirteen colonies who were awarded the title United Empire Loyalists for their stance; and decommissioned British military men. Both were eligible for land grants from the British government, though the ex-soldiers received the most favourable treatment. Originally, Arnold had been designated a United Empire Loyalist, but he asked to be struck from the list because military claimants were eligible for more land.

On 4 July 1796 one of the first petitions for land read at the second meeting of the executive council of Upper Canada was from Gen. Benedict Arnold and two of his sons – Lieutenant Richard Arnold and Ensign Edward Arnold. They said they were on the half-pay list as reduced officers and they asked for the grant of a township. Since the land grants were being used as a tool to lure settlers, the rule was that the applicant had to agree to live in the colony to receive it. The executive council land committee, led by Simcoe, decided curtly that it would make no exception for the famous Arnolds. "When these officers appear and incline to settle in this province, the land they are entitled to will be granted them."[8] In an aside, Simcoe wrote to London that he and other settlers were opposed to any favours for "a character extremely obnoxious to the *original* loyalists of America." It was enough of a comment, with its emphasis on "original," to convince *Mail and Empire* newspaper reporter Fred Williams, who dug the story out in 1933, that Arnold was a reprehensible character. It was meant "to manifest the contempt which Simcoe and all true Britishers must have felt at that time for the double traitor and that is why the province of Upper Canada was not the refuge of the man who had been driven out of the United States and then forced away from Saint John, New Brunswick by public opinion." Later, he added: "Upper Canada can be congratulated that Simcoe blocked Arnold's settlement in this province, though it seems rather hard that his sons should have suffered for their father's sins but that is the law set forth from the beginning of time."[9]

There are two problems with the story of Arnold's being denied a foothold in Upper Canada. First, Arnold had never planned to live in Upper Canada. He was old and settled in London, totally uninterested in another frontier beginning. He was trying to secure land for his sons. Second, at his next attempt, on 12 June 1798, he did win a large land grant on orders from London to the executive council of Upper Canada. The duke of Portland, Lieutenant General Hunter, instructed that the land be granted as a "mark of Royal favor."[10] A five-thousand-acre block was located south of what became Lake Simcoe, northeast of Toronto, and the remainder lay in eastern Upper Canada, in bush land south-east of the present-day community of Renfrew, Ontario. The owner was required to live on the land for at least six months a year in each of the first three years. The land grant lured Arnold's sons Richard, Henry, and John to Upper Canada, where they carved out farms.

The third factor to consider is that John Graves Simcoe and Arnold were not strangers. Simcoe's decision to justify the lack of special treatment for Arnold by calling him an affront to the original Loyalists must be evaluated in light of earlier contacts between the two men. Their paths had crossed many times. They shared many of the same characteristics, these two men – they were good soldiers, proud military officers, brave and inventive on the battlefield. Simcoe proved to be much better in the political corners, however, and far better at administering the peace that emerges after a war than Arnold.

Simcoe was born in England in 1752, making him eleven years Arnold's junior. He came from military stock, the son of a naval officer who died of disease on the British army campaign at Quebec in 1759. Young Simcoe joined the army and was sent to America in the early days of the Revolution, arriving in Boston two days after the Battle of Bunker Hill, which had galvanized Arnold into joining the rebel side. Simcoe served the British in many of the major battles of the Revolution, receiving three wounds along the way. Not only was he blessed, like Arnold, in defying battlefield death but he also had a reputation for serving in pain. After his wounds, "he always came back as soon as he could sit on a horse to lead his men again."[11]

He bought a commission and began his real climb to military fame in October 1777 when he obtained command of a free-wheeling mobile light infantry unit – the Queen's Rangers. Simcoe used American

Loyalists and revolutionary deserters to build a corps that acquired a reputation for skill and tenacity. "The war [was] for him a great personal success," wrote the historian S.R. Mealing. "He had risen in army rank from lieutenant to lieutenant-colonel. In action, he had been one of the two or three most consistently successful of British regimental commanders."[12] In 1780 British North American commander-in-chief Sir Henry Clinton wrote of him: "Lieutenant-Colonel Simcoe has been at the head of a battalion since October, 1777 and since that time, has been the perpetual advance of the army. The history of the corps under his command is a series of gallant, skillful and successful enterprises against the enemy without a single reverse. The Queen's Rangers have killed or taken twice their own numbers ..."[13]

When, in September 1780, he learned of Arnold's defection to the British side, Simcoe was no doubt familiar with the tales of the famous American general, but his interest in the story would have been more personal and painful. More than three years before, John André had lived with Simcoe after being sent to America. Willard Randall called Simcoe a match for André, "another rebel hater."[14] Now André was dead and many blamed Arnold.

Simcoe's first meeting with Arnold may well have occurred a few months later when Clinton assigned him and his Queen's Rangers to serve under the newly minted British general in his first major campaign for the King – a daring plan to go into Virginia to capture American supplies and to establish a British base. It is said that Simcoe's troops headed for Virginia "with black and white feathers attached to their horses' bridles, a sign of mourning for Simcoe's closest friend, John André."[15] If that is true, it is hard to imagine that Simcoe did not harbour resentment against Arnold, who had caused André's death and was now so very welcome in the upper echelons of the British army, which Simcoe had entered only through hard work and the purchase of a commission. Yet Simcoe's military journal about the southern campaign under Arnold shows no resentment. It is a matter-of-fact recounting of a campaign that began on 11 December 1780. Simcoe records an order from Arnold on 20 December that the countryside not be devastated. The troops arrived in Chesapeake on 30 December and pushed up the James River in the early days of 1781. The journal is filled with tales of good military decisions by Arnold, which ended in the capture and fortification of Portsmouth as the British base. "Gen. Arnold had constructed a great many boats, excellently adapted for the transportation of soldiers and capable of carrying 80 men besides the rowers," Simcoe wrote in his journal, which was later published in

London. "By these means, he had it in his power to reinforce any of the points within 10 minutes ... The garrison was in great spirits, full of confidence in the daring courage of Gen. Arnold."[16]

The suggestion has been made, however, that Simcoe was sent on the campaign to keep an eye on Arnold as much as to help him. It is a passing American reference but it is the type of unsubstantiated reporting that has helped cement Arnold's modern-day reputation. It appears in an 1844 republication of Simcoe's journal, this time as the first American edition. The publisher, Bartlett and Welford of New York City, included an "appendix" by an unnamed journalist who, in turn, included an "extract from Dunlop's History of New York, Vol. II," which contained the following account:

It appears strange that Sir Henry Clinton should entrust a traitor with the lives and liberty of armies as he did but I have been assured by a gentleman of the most unblemished character, now far advanced in years, that when Arnold departed New York in the command of the army, with which he committed depredations in the Chesapeake, a "dormant commission" was given to Cols Dundas and Simcoe jointly by Sir Henry Clinton, authorizing them, if they suspected Arnold of sinister intent, to supersede him and put him in arrest. This proves that Clinton did not trust him and we may reasonably suppose that such a watch was set upon his conduct on other occasions. The gentleman who communicated this fact to me was in his youth a confidential clerk in Sir Henry Clinton's office and copied and delivered the "dormant commission" as directed. This explains a passage in Clinton's letter to his government in which he says 'this detachment is under the command of General Arnold with whom I have thought it right to send Colonels Dundas and Simcoe as being officers of experience and much in my confidence.'[17]

Whether this is a little-known slice of historical truth or another piece of American anti-Arnold fiction, Simcoe the military man found nothing about Arnold to complain about in the version of his military journal that was published several years after the war. The source of the story would indeed have been "far advanced in years." The incident had happened sixty-four years before and at the time, the witness was already advanced enough to be a confidential secretary to the commander-in-chief of British forces in the midst of a war – surely not a post given to a teenager. At the very least, it shows a remarkably solid memory for someone in his eighties or nineties. In any event, a very nasty feud broke out between the two men after the war. The issue was the booty from the Virginia expedition. On 8 September 1782 a group

of veterans from that expedition wrote to London complaining that
Arnold had gone back to England and through high-level lobbying
won for himself his one-eighth share of the £16,546 booty from the
expedition. Less-exalted members of the expedition living in New York
had not received their proper share. Simcoe was one of those who
signed the letter.

Arnold responded in a blind fury. As recorded earlier, Arnold felt
he had worked hard in London to win compensation for the other
officers in the expedition. His efforts, he thundered in a letter on the
issue, had been "grossly misrepresented and my conduct unjustly
calumniated." The letter from Dundas and Simcoe, which did "little
credit to their good sense or good nature, passed very severe censure
on my conduct and at the very time when I was making every exertion
for their interest." He complained that it was poor thanks for all he
had done on their behalf, drawing "the ill will and abuse of many
gentlemen in the navy" for his efforts to win compensation for the
others from the Chesapeake expedition. He said he had received his
share early because of special consideration by the King but had
insisted the others receive their share too. "If the gentlemen thought
my conduct blamable [sic], why not in a candid manner say so to me
and give me an opportunity of explaining my conduct before they
proceed to pass censure. But for my exertions and perseverance to
obtain their money, they would never have received a shilling of it and
this is their grateful return."[18]

Once Simcoe left New York after the war, he returned to England
and the life of an aristocrat. In 1790 he was elected to the British House
of Commons and shortly after was promised the lieutenant-governorship
of the new Loyalist colony of Upper Canada. The commission was
issued on 12 September 1791. He had hoped for better but took what
he was given and for almost five years governed the new colony with
enthusiasm and foresight, establishing the machinery of government,
encouraging settlement, and using former members of the Queen's
Rangers for road-building projects. It was inspired leadership.[19]

It is hard to imagine that, as he considered the absentee land request
from the Arnolds in 1796, Simcoe did not remember his old battles
with the general, the death of André, the Chesapeake booty. He did
not discriminate against Benedict and his sons. He simply enforced
the rules and made no exception. Then, within days, he left to return
to England in July 1796 to convalesce from an illness. He never
returned to Upper Canada and resigned his position in early 1798,

before King George III ordered a land grant to the Arnolds. Simcoe lived his last years hoping for a new appointment and was rewarded in 1806 with the title commander-in-chief and an appointment to India. He died within weeks of the appointment. His legacy in Upper Canada was the beginning of a structure of government, the rule of the conservative élite, and a form of rule of law that was to mark the colony as it developed through the nineteenth century. He was "the most persistently energetic governor sent to British North America after the American Revolution."[20] But on the Arnold file, he had reason to be less than objective.

On 18 August 1801 New Brunswick's *Royal Gazette* carried a short notice on page three: "Died in England, Brigadier General Benedict Arnold, late of this city."[21]

That was it. No obituary, no mention of his remarkable past, his accomplishments and heroics, his flaws, his dealings in the city, his notoriety. His death rated just the telling, without embellishment. It was fitting. Arnold, in his last years in London, received few kudos. He associated with some members of the élite, was consulted by the King, and carried on business. He also slid deeper into debt and ill-health. By the summer of 1801 he was dying and in despair, having lost thousands of pounds in a recent business investment gone bad. A privateering ship that he owned captured a £25,000 prize and then lost it, along with his investment in the venture. The British government promised, and then retracted for budget reasons, compensation for past expenses incurred and never covered.[22] Arnold's despair was compounded by dropsy, swollen legs, and breathing difficulties. In 1888 his descendant Isaac Arnold wrote a book about Benedict's life, which included the following description of his death, taken from a letter written on 1 July 1801 by Peggy to his sons Richard and Henry in British North America: "Your dear father whose long-declining state of health you have been acquainted with, is no more. In him, his family have lost an affectionate husband, father and friend and to his exertions to make a provision for them may be attributed the loss of his life."

She noted that he had been troubled by various speculative investments that had not worked out. "For many months before his death, he never lay two hours of a night in his bed and he had every dreadful nervous symptom, attended with great difficulty of breathing that can possibly be imagined ... On the 8th of June, he became much worse and suffered greatly for several days and on Sunday, the 14th at half past six o'clock in the morning, expired without a groan. For some days previous to his death, he had but short intervals of reason when the distressed situation of his family preyed greatly upon his mind and he was constantly imploring blessing upon them."[23]

Peggy is said to have written: "For his own sake, the change is a most happy one, as the disappointment of all his (pecuniary) expectations, with the numerous vexations and mortifications he has endured, had so broken his spirits and destroyed his nerves that he has been for a long time past incapable of the smallest enjoyment."[24] Without attribution and with little credibility, several American biographers have described a deathbed scene in which Arnold asked Peggy to get out his Continental Army uniform and lay it on his bed, vowing that he never should have renounced it. As a man not known for second-guessing himself, the story does not emit the scent of truth but rather the tarnish of propaganda masquerading as history. There is no mention of the incident in Peggy's subsequent letters to friends and family. If there is doubt about his final words, there is no doubt that Arnold died heavily in debt, leaving Peggy to fend off creditors and lawsuits. On Christmas Day, 1801, she wrote a pitiful letter to Jonathan Bliss in Saint John, who had lost his wife two years before. She sounded frightened, depressed, and thoroughly lonely for Benedict:

A most sincere blow it has indeed proved such as I have scarcely been able to support. The absence of my two eldest sons and the pressure of harassing and unsuccessful business has rendered the loss I have sustained doubly painful and the constant anxiety of mind I have endured for the last twelve months, added to almost total loss of rest, have broken my spirits and injured my constitution and but for my children, I have not a wish to live. But for their sakes, I must still struggle on, for greatly do they want that protection which our diminished income renders more necessary to them.[25]

Benedict had left her the property with instructions that money be given to his children and his sister Hannah in Upper Canada. "At the time this will was made, fair prospects presented themselves which however were never realized and it is yet impossible to say what will be saved from the wreck." As it turns out, not much was saved. In the summer of 1802 Peggy wrote to Bliss again, admitting that she had been immobilized by the mess that was left by Arnold's death. "It has almost proved too much for me and brought on a train of nervous complaints that for some months past have almost incapacitated me from transacting any business and but for the kind exertions of my friends, I should have sunk under the pressures of misfortune." She said she had a list of Arnold's assets. "The property, after paying the debts and some legacies and annuities, is left solely at my disposal among the children. But I am fearful that little or nothing will be left for them."[26]

Peggy moved to cheaper accommodation, fought in court against creditors, and pursued those in debt to Arnold in an attempt to collect the money. A 1931 biography of Arnold had Peggy selling her furniture, wine, and other possessions to pay off debts. Then, she bought furniture from one of her former servants "who is now a more independent woman than her mistress."[27] She wrote to her stepsons in Canada: "My conduct has been dictated by regard to you, respect to your dear father's memory and an earnest desire to act with uprightness, feeling and tenderness. Although I had much to be thankful for during your father's lifetime, I had much to struggle with."[28] She told them that her attitude towards them would be dictated by their father's hopes for them.

Peggy died in 1804, at the age of forty-four, from an internal tumour, proud that she had paid off the family debt.

Arnold's children, about whom he worried so much, were settling into their various lives when Benedict died. Most were drawn to the military life that had provided their father with his finest hours. Benedict Arnold had three families – three children by his first wife, Margaret, in New Haven, five children in the United States, Canada, and England by Peggy, and a ninth mystery child.

Benedict VI, his eldest son, the victim of an infected wound in Jamaica, had been dead almost six years when his father died. Richard, thirty-one, was a landowner in eastern Upper Canada. He became a successful farmer and, three years after his father's death, married a local fifteen-year-old who presented him with nine children over twenty years. Richard became a magistrate and farmer in Augusta Township.[29] Henry was twenty-eight when his father died. He was already married to a New York woman, Hannah Ten Eyck. He too lived as a farmer in eastern Upper Canada, in the Grenville County area. They had eleven children, only one of whom survived – a daughter who moved to the United States to marry. Henry himself moved to New York City, where he died in 1826.

Edward, Arnold's first child with Peggy Shippen, was twenty-one when his father died. Like his father, he was a military man, a lieutenant in the 6th Bengal Cavalry. He died serving in India in 1813. James, twenty, already in the Royal Engineers when his father died, was destined for an illustrious career, heading the Royal Engineers in British

North America at one time and being knighted by the king in recognition of his achievements. He died in 1854. Arnold's daughter Sophia was just fifteen when her father died. She married an army officer serving in India and died at age forty-two in England, having given birth to four children. George, thirteen when his father died and the only Arnold born in Canada, rose to the rank of lieutenant colonel in the Bengal Cavalry. He died in 1828 in India at the age of forty-one, just months after his sister Sophia died. One of his two children was named for his sister. William, born in London and the youngest of Benedict's children, saw his father die just days before his seventh birthday. He went on to become a captain in the Royal Lancers and a justice of the peace in Buckinghamshire, England.

For Canadians, John Sage Arnold, the ninth presumed child of Benedict, is the most significant Arnold offspring because he is the ancestor of most of the Arnold descendants who have helped build Canada during the past two centuries. His origins are shrouded in mystery and controversy.

In a tiny, dishevelled pioneer graveyard in eastern Ontario south of Smiths Falls, a stark white headstone marks the final resting place of John Arnold, who died on 22 October 1831, aged forty-five years, six months, and eight days. The simple unadorned marker in the Leheigh Cemetery does not clarify the details of John Arnold's life. It merely adds to the mystery. Who was this John Arnold, other than an established and prosperous farmer who headed one of the founding families of the area? Where was he born? Who was his father?

Historians have offered the following answers. John Arnold, born John Sage, was an illegitimate son of Benedict's, born in Saint John to a local woman. There are many references in biographies of Benedict Arnold. "He produced an illegitimate son, John Sage, who was born about 1786 to an unknown woman whom he probably found in Saint John," according to the *Encyclopedia of the American Revolution*.[30] "He fathered a half-breed Indian son," wrote biographer Cornel Lengyel in 1960.[31] Clare Brandt wrote that in 1786 Arnold went to sea "turning his back ... on his pregnant mistress."[32] It is a view that the Arnold descendants accept. In 1984 John R. Arnold of Peterborough, who traces his lineage through John Sage, compiled a family history that took the conventional view that conception occurred in the winter of 1785–86 when Benedict was at sea after recently establishing himself in New Brunswick. Peggy was in London with the younger children.

"It was during this winter of separation from his wife that Benedict formed a liaison that resulted in the birth of an illegitimate son called John Sage."[33]

All of this speculation is based on one historical fact. On 30 August 1800, when Benedict Arnold wrote his last will and testament in London, he provided for John Sage as if he were a son. Without ever calling him a son, Arnold ensured that the teenager, living in Canada with Richard and Henry Arnold, would be cared for until he came of age. At least one historical reference suggests that John actually lived in London for a time. When Arnold's will was read in the summer of 1801, it left instructions that on Peggy's death, his land and estate should be divided equally among his children. An equal share was to be given to a fourteen-year-old teenager who seems not to have been mentioned in family correspondence:

I give, devise and bequeath to John Sage, now in Canada living with my sons there (being about 14 years of age) twelve hundred acres of land ... I also do hereby give and bequeath to the said John Sage twenty pounds per annum to be paid to my sons Richard and Henry for his use for Board, Cloathing and Education until he shall be of the age of twenty one years, to be paid out of the estate I may die possessed of. I also give and bequeath to the said John Sage fifty pounds to be paid to him when he shall attain the age of twenty one years.[34]

From this portion of the will has come the conventional wisdom that John Sage was Arnold's bastard son. However, there are several problems with that interpretation, the main one being timing. Benedict Arnold arrived in Saint John on 2 December 1785. According to his tombstone, John Sage Arnold was born on 14 April 1786. On the day of his arrival, John's mother would have been mid-way through her pregnancy. It may be that she was from London and came on the ship with Arnold, but the assumption is that she was from Saint John. It may be that the tombstone dates are incorrect, although there are two pieces of corroborating evidence. In his 1800 will, Arnold said John would have been fourteen years old, making 1786 his year of birth. Moreover, in the Montague Township census of 10 March 1803, John Arnold was identified as sixteen years of age. According to the tombstone date, the census would have been taken a month before his seventeenth birthday. Or it may be that John actually was the result of a 1785 liaison in London before Arnold left for New Brunswick, since one land grant document identifies John Sage as a London resident. If so, it could have been that Arnold sent him to Upper Canada to live with his sons from the first marriage, rather than leave him as a ward of Peggy's, to whom presumably he was unfaithful.

There is another intriguing line of unsubstantiated speculation lying in a thick file in the Ontario archives in Toronto. It is the theory that Benedict Arnold was not John Sage's father but his grandfather. The speculation lies in a sheaf of correspondence, started 1 March 1960, between Indianapolis researcher James Speers and chief Ontario archivist Dr George Spragge.[35] Speers was planning a book about Arnold and was trying to find information about his family in Canada. He was a man obsessed and at one point, he confessed to Spragge that he was frustrated by his inability to pin down the facts: "I'm as lacking as a frog is of feathers. In the beginning, my interest was casual but getting into the thing, I've reached the point where I awaken at night and lie there turning this or that incident over in my mind in search of an explanation that is sensible."[36]

In the end, he left behind nothing but a theory – that John Sage's real father was Benedict Jr, Arnold's eldest son, who would have been seventeen when John Sage was conceived and presumably living in New Haven with his aunt Hannah and his brothers Henry and Richard. Speers based his theory on the fact that John Sage first surfaced in records in June 1798 when Benedict petitioned for lands in Upper Canada. By then, Benedict Jr was dead and Benedict Sr wanted to care for his young descendant. He did so by including him in the will, by making sure his two eldest sons looked after him, and by giving him twelve hundred acres of his own land. That is where Speers's speculation begins and ends. Nothing in surviving Arnold records casts light on the mystery of John Sage.

His later life in Upper Canada, though, is not mysterious. It can be reconstructed from the public record. The 1803 census identified him as a sixteen-year-old resident, along with Henry, Richard, and Richard's wife Hannah. A land grant document dated 13 August 1804 legitimizing the previous year's grant of twelve hundred acres in Elmsley Township identified him as "John Arnold of the City of London, gentleman, son of the late General Benedict Arnold." In 1812 John married Vermont native Sarah Brunson and the two raised a brood of seven children on their Kitley Township homestead. From that homestead, the Arnolds and their descendants fanned out across the country, helping to build small towns, homesteading on the Canadian Prairies, fighting in Canada's wars, and becoming colourful and binding threads in the Canadian tapestry, like the descendants of so many immigrants.

John's brothers left less of a mark on their adopted country. Henry
and his wife, Hannah Ten Eyck, moved to eastern Upper Canada to
become farmers. Henry was clearly a well-respected community figure.
He became a justice of the peace and, by 1810, was designated a magistrate in Elizabethtown. Still, neither he nor his family stayed in Canada. His one surviving child, a daughter married a New York City man,
and her parents seem to have moved to New York as well. Henry died
there in December, 1826.[37] Richard, the eldest, also moved to eastern
Upper Canada to farm land that had been granted by the Crown. He
married Margaret Weatherhead of nearby Augusta and farmed there
until 1840 or 1841. By the time of his death, Richard was reportedly
living with a daughter in western Upper Canada near Sarnia, but his
grave has not been found. He too became a notable local figure,
amassed a large tract of land, and in 1810 was named a magistrate in
Augusta. Some of their nine children remained in Upper Canada, many
becoming prominent local citizens. George Weatherhead was a city politician in Brockville, Ontario, in the 1840s and president of the board
of Police. His daughter Margaret married John McEwan, who for thirty
years was the sheriff of Essex County in southwest Upper Canada.
Descendants still live in Ontario and throughout Canada.

There is one other small unsolved historical mystery from these years.
What happened to Benedict's sister, Hannah? Through the years,
Hannah had stuck with her brother, raising his three young boys after
their mother, Margaret, died in 1775 in New Haven. She suffered abuse
from neighbours and former friends after her famous brother's 1780
defection, then joined him in Saint John in 1787 with two of his sons.
She was his confidante in letters during the Revolution and did what
she could to manage his New Haven trading business while he was off
fighting. Some American writers have made her a heroic counterpoint
to her brother. An influential 1861 article in *Harper's New Monthly Magazine* described her as his "sweet sister Hannah" who essentially sacrificed her life for her brother. She remained "the fast friend of her
erring brother in his abasement ... and was never married, owing probably to the wickedness of her brother in early life."[38] There had been
tales of Arnold chasing away his sister's suitors when they were growing
up in New Haven. Where did this "saintly" sister end her days?

Family legend, picked up in numerous biographies, suggests that
Hannah moved to Upper Canada with her nephews and lived with
Henry on the farm in Montague Township, dying on 31 August 1803.
The grave has never been found. Perhaps it's because Hannah Arnold,

Benedict's sister, never lived there, or at the very least may not have died there. That is the theory of Alice Hughes of Easton's Corner, Ontario, a feisty local amateur historian. In late 1994 the seventy-five-year-old was brandishing old census records to make her point. On 10 March 1803 heads were counted in Montague Township and four Arnolds were recorded – Richard, Henry, John, and Hannah. It was not, however, Aunt Hannah as most of the biographers have assumed. It was Henry's wife, Hannah Ten Eyck, who was thirty-one years old at the time. If Aunt Hannah lived there, she was not counted and if the assumed date of death is correct, she would presumably still have been at the farm. "I doubt that Hannah the sister ever lived there," said Alice. "I think it was Hannah the daughter-in-law."[39] She probably has a point.

John Arnold's descendants became a mainstay of the farming area that lies between Smiths Falls and Brockville. They were businessmen, supporters of the Liberal party of Wilfrid Laurier and William Lyon Mackenzie King, and members of the Methodist church, which became part of the United Church of Canada in 1925. Typical was Henry Arnold, who for more than seventy years farmed the two hundred acres left to him by his father. When he died in 1901, one hundred years after his grandfather Benedict, the *Brockville Recorder* said that "one of the connecting links between the long gone past and the present is removed and one of the best and truest men in the community is taken."[40] It noted that he had cleared the land from the bush. "He was the grandson of Benedict Arnold, the famous American general, and had many stirring reminiscences to tell in his younger days of the times of his celebrated grandfather."

Other brothers and cousins farmed in the area, played politics, built churches and businesses, and helped build the towns that dot this rustic area of eastern Ontario. One, Isaac Henry Arnold, was born on 1 July 1867, the day Canada was created. Another, Henry Hazelton, moved from the farm to Athens, Ontario, where he operated a general store and served for years as secretary of the Athens High School board. When he died in 1945 at age ninety, H.H. Arnold was hailed as one of Athens' "most prominent citizens."[41] H.H. Arnold's general store in Athens was immortalized in 1986 as part of the town's inventive mural program in which local buildings became the canvas for paintings depicting the history of the community. The ninety-six-by-twenty-five-foot mural "Main Street," painted on the side of Stedman's Store, depicts the townspeople gathered on 12 July 1910 to watch the

annual Orange Day parade. In the foreground, with clerks and customers captured from old photographs, is the H.H. Arnold store.

These were the pioneering Arnolds who helped build rural Ontario.
Another branch of the family decided that their future rested in vast
tracts of farmland known at the turn of the century as the North-West
Territories. Richard Morton Arnold was born and raised in the Arnold
enclave of eastern Ontario but found that the family farm was too small
when his sons were ready to join the business. He moved to Addison,
Ontario, and set up a business that included moving lumber and
horses west to a small dot on the map in the south-east corner of the
territories – Glen Ewen, in what became, in 1905, the new Province of
Saskatchewan. He saw an opportunity there and purchased 480 acres
of nearby land in 1900. Four years later, at the age of sixty, R.M. Arnold
moved west from Ontario to follow his investment. He travelled in a
freight car with his "settlers' effects" while his wife, Arletta, and a ten-
year-old grandson travelled in a passenger car, canaries in tow.

The move from established Ontario to the wilds of frontier
Saskatchewan was a shock for Arletta. Later, she recalled those early
years. As described in a history of the town, "she gathered wolf willow
sticks in her apron for kindling" and "told of writing to relatives in
Ontario asking for flower seeds, since she missed her garden very
much. They sent her dandelion seeds."[42] In 1917 the couple moved
to nearby Glen Ewen to run a feed-and-seed business. Other Arnolds
moved west, attracted by tales from their relatives. The Oxbow area
had first been settled in 1882 by immigrants from Europe and Ontario.
It was just miles above the forty-ninth parallel, which had been drawn
in 1874 as the border between Canada and the United States. North
West Mounted Police arrived in the area in 1875. By the turn of the
century, farms and towns were populated by settlers from Russia with
names like Barnblatt, and by settlers from Ontario with names like
John E. Arnold, who started with a hardware store and brickyard near
Smiths Falls, Ontario, then moved west to operate a brickyard in
Winnipeg, going from there to a North Dakota farm and finally, in
1902, purchasing farmland near Oxbow, Saskatchewan, at age sixty-one.

Charlie Arnold, a store clerk in the family firm in Athens, arrived in
Glen Ewen in March 1910 with his wife Edith Purcell. He had been a
travelling salesman, working the western territories, and had been persuaded by his uncle, Richard Morton Arnold, to buy land and settle
down. The land he purchased extended north from the American
border and he soon had a grain and cattle operation. Despite the small
distance, his children, Anita and Henry, rarely got to Glen Ewen. "We

used to go to town from the farm at the end of October and we
wouldn't see town again til spring," an eighty-one-year-old Anita
recalled in 1994.[43] Her brother Henry later took over the farm and,
in the mid-1920s, became a founding member and early advocate of
the farmer grain growers' cooperative, the Saskatchewan Wheat Pool.
In their early years, Henry and Anita took a sleigh to the Souris Flats
School, on the American border. The classrooms contained both Canadian and American children. Part of the family memory was an understanding that they were related to Benedict Arnold, the traitor, but
they did not make an issue of it. "When we went to school, we wouldn't
admit we were related to him," Anita laughed as she recounted the
memory of school days. "The farm was right beside the US border, you
know. We didn't want to stir things up."

Part of the family legacy was a British military coat, handed down
from father to son as having belonged to Benedict. Anita's brother
Henry owned it. He had returned to Saskatchewan to farm after serving in the merchant marine during the Second World War. When he
died, it was passed to his son Tom, who died in an automobile accident.
The coat was passed on to Tom's son Jayson, who was born in 1980.

In May 1994, students in the Grade eight class at Oxbow Prairie
Heights School were given the assignment to prepare a talk on a famous
person. Fourteen-year-old Jayson arrived that day with a speech about
his famous ancestor, and a British military coat to prove it. "I didn't say
he was a great guy," Jayson recalled later. "I did say he was a traitor ...
but I'm quite proud of him. A lot of people say 'Aren't you embarrassed? He was a traitor.' I say 'No, I'm proud. He was famous. He was
brave.'" For Jayson, it was "neat that I'm related to a famous general."[44]

Other descendants of the "famous general" have fanned out across
the country. For those who felt Ontario offered too little opportunity,
Saskatchewan was a favourite destination. They homesteaded in Gull
Lake, East End, Battleford, Lloydminster, Harris, and elsewhere. From
there, descendants have moved to Alberta, British Columbia, and points
east. They have been doctors and lawyers, teachers and nurses, armed
forces men, farmers and business people. Like all pioneering families,
the Arnolds have left footsteps across the entire Canadian landscape.

Benedict Arnold, American hero and anti-hero, Canadian businessman and peacetime misfit, a man who described his departure from
Canada as an escape from a shipwreck, made his mark on Canada
through the descendants that he left to populate and help create
a nation.

Epilogue

In 1992 the *Saint John Dictionary, Fifth Concise Edition,* was published as an irreverent look at the city. It took as its title a spoof on the American tendency to identify almost every place George Washington ever visited. The little booklet was titled "Benedict Arnold Slept Here?"

The Benedict Arnold entry was equally concise and to the point in this satirical look at the Loyalist City: "Benedict Arnold: British patriot ... no, an American traitor ... no, a Loyalist ... no, a ... who knows? Former Frederictonian?"[1]

It is as good a summation as any of Benedict Arnold's place in New Brunswick and Canadian history. He is an enigma, his name synonymous in Canada, as in the United States, with the concept of traitor. Yet he fought for British interests and left his mark in New Brunswick as one of the colony's earliest businessmen. He is little known.

Local amateur historian Eric Teed saw him as a smart businessman, a good family man, and an asset to his community. "In my view, Arnold wasn't a traitor. He was a patriot to the British side and unlike his image, I don't think he was a failure in Saint John. I think he was a successful wheeler-dealer."[2]

Historian and Loyalist specialist Ann Condon has a two-sided view of Arnold. She sees his tendency to have strong women by his side as an interesting clue about him as a man. "He was dashing and macho but he also seemed to have a vulnerable side. He was not a bastard."[3] Nor, as it turns out, does she think he was much of a Canadian historical figure. "I don't think he was very important ... Aside from being a good soldier, he doesn't seem to have had an interest other than making money. I don't ever get the sense that he made a difference here. You have to have had an office and a following to have made an impact here."

Canada's historians, with the task of telling us where we came from and who came before, appear in general to agree. School curricula do not mention Arnold. Canadian history does not, in most cases, give him a place. Arnold's several appearances on the stage of early Canadian history initially came to my attention in 1970 while working at my first newspaper job as a reporter for the *Saint John Telegraph-Journal.* One day, exploring my new city, I came upon a plaque on a building at the corner of King and Canterbury Streets in the downtown. It identified the building as the site of Benedict Arnold's house. I was intrigued. Through eleven years of Quebec schooling and five years of Canadian university, it had escaped my attention that Benedict Arnold had played a role in Canadian history, almost capturing the country and then living here for the better part of six years, leaving inevitable footprints. I set about over the next quarter century, casually at first and more seriously later, to learn a bit more about the Canadian footprints of this famous American traitor.

In January 1995, the circle was completed. I was in Saint John, researching a book on Benedict Arnold. I went back to the building that first had piqued my interest but instead of a plaque, there was simply a faded spot on the wall where a plaque had been. In the Saint John Tourist Bureau, I mentioned this and asked what had happened. "The plaque keeps getting stolen, I guess by tourists," said a helpful clerk. "We haven't replaced it."

Stolen by tourists? It must have been Americans. Canadians interested in their own country's history would not know enough to grasp its significance.

Notes

INTRODUCTION

1 Walter Stewart, *True Blue: The Loyalist Legend* (Toronto: Collins 1985), 2.

2 "Benedict Arnold," *The Canadian Encyclopedia,* 2d ed., vol. 1 (Edmonton: Hurtig Publishers, 1988), 120–1.

3 Interview with Mark Bonokoski, *Ottawa Sun,* by telephone in Ottawa, 31 May 1996.

4 Stephen Brunt, "Keenan Sideshow a burden on Ranger shoulders," *Globe and Mail* (14 June 1994).

5 Dennis Adair and Janet Rosenstock, *Thundergate Book 3: The Story of Canada* (New York: Avon Books, 1982), 278.

6 Andrew H. Malcolm, *The Canadians* (Markham, ON: Fitzhenry & White-side 1985), 134.

7 Sydney F. Wise, interview, 7 November 1994, at his Carleton University office in Ottawa.

8 Willard Sterne Randall, *Benedict Arnold, Patriot and Traitor* (New York: William Morrow, 1990), 138.

9 Michael Pearson, "When Benedict Arnold Almost Captured Canada," *Weekend Magazine* 22, no. 53 (1972): 3–7.

10 Jean E. Sereisky, "Benedict Arnold in New Brunswick," *Atlantic Advocate* 53, no. 7 (1963): 33.

CHAPTER ONE

1 Randall, *Benedict Arnold,* 23.

2 National Archives of Canada (NA), Ottawa, Chipman Papers, Lawrence Collection, Peggy Arnold to Ward Chipman, 4 June 1795.

3 In Curtis Fahey, "Benedict Arnold," *Dictionary of Canadian Biography*, vol. 5, 1801–1820 (Toronto: University of Toronto Press, 1983), 33.

4 In Kenneth Roberts, ed., *March to Quebec: Journals of the Members of Arnold's Expedition* (New York: Doubleday, Doran, 1940), 98.

5 Randall, *Benedict Arnold*, 123.

6 The account of Arnold's early years is drawn from a number of published accounts. The most comprehensive are Isaac N. Arnold, *The Life of Benedict Arnold* (Chicago: A.C. McClug, 1886); Clare Brandt, *The Man in the Mirror: A Life of Benedict Arnold* (New York: Random House, 1994); Malcolm Decker, *Benedict Arnold, Son of the Havens* (Tarrytown, NY: William Abbatt, 1932); Randall, *Benedict Arnold*; Charles Seller, *Benedict Arnold: The Proud Warrior* (New York: Minton, Balch, 1930); and Oscar Sherwin, *Benedict Arnold: Patriot and Traitor* (New York: Century Company, 1931).

7 Randall, *Benedict Arnold*, 29.

8 Some hostile biographers have implied, inaccurately, that drinking was a problem. See, for example, Decker, *Son of the Havens*, 445. Decker draws a portrait of Arnold as a greedy merchant arguing with a business colleague over profits "stalking there in [Campobello] fog with rum on his breath."

9 Randall, *Benedict Arnold*, 33.

10 Ibid., 39.

11 Robert McConnell Hatch, *Thrust for Canada: The American Attempt on Quebec, 1775–76* (Boston: Houghton Mifflin, 1979), 21.

12 Mark Boatner III, *Encyclopedia of the American Revolution* (New York: David McKay, 1976), 25.

13 John Joseph Henry, *Accounts of Arnold's Campaign against Quebec* (Albany, NY: Joel Munsell, 1877. Reprint. N.p. Arno Press, 1968), 12.

14 Roger Spiller, ed., *Dictionary of American Military Biography. Vol. 1* (Westport, CT: Greenwood Press, 1984), 40.

15 Henry, *Accounts*, 12.

16 Randall, *Benedict Arnold*, 189. Historical hindsight, however distorted, has led many writers to conclude that even during these days of valour, the seeds of Arnold's destruction and treachery were evident in his vanity, his inability to work with the politicians in Philadelphia, his worries about money, and his constant complaints that he was being undermined by domestic enemies. Perhaps, but it was not evident in the opinions of his peers at the time.

17 In Roberts, *March to Quebec*, 73.

18 Ibid., 67.

19 Letter to Charles Carroll of Annapolis, 30 April 1776, in Ellen H. Smith, *Charles Carroll of Carrollton* (Cambridge, MA: Harvard University Press, 1942), 146.

20 Letter of January 1776, in Hatch, *Thrust for Canada*, 143.

21 Letter of 6 January 1776, in Roberts, *March to Quebec*, 108.

22 James Thomas Flexner, *The Young Hamilton* (New York: Little, Brown, 1978), 307.

23 Randall, *Benedict Arnold*, 84–7.

24 Isaac Arnold, *The Life of Benedict Arnold*, 396.

25 Decker, *Benedict Arnold*, 34–8

26 Randall, *Benedict Arnold*, 41.

27 Ibid., 61.

28 Carl Van Doren, *Secret History of the American Revolution* (New York: Viking Press, 1941), 268.

29 Brandt, *Man in the Mirror*, 16.

30 Randall, *Benedict Arnold*, 57–60.

31 Allan Greer, *Peasant, Lord and Merchant: Rural Society in Three Quebec Parishes, 1740–1840* (Toronto: University of Toronto Press, 1985), 155–8.

32 Ibid., 171.

33 Ibid., 165.

34 Robin Neill, interview, 11 December 1994, Carleton University, Ottawa.

35 NA, File MG23 B27, Benedict Arnold to Samuel Jacobs. Copy of the original is owned by the Chicago Historical Society.

CHAPTER TWO

1 The sermon called "Sinners in the Hands of an Angry God," was preached on 8 July 1741. John A. Garraty, *The American Nation* (New York: Harper and Row, 1966), 54.

2 In ibid.

3 Edward Countryman, *The American Revolution* (New York: Hill and Wang, 1985), 23–4.

4 Garraty, *The American Nation*, 54.

5 Countryman, *The American Revolution*, 40–3.

6 Ibid., 48–9.

7 Bernard Bailyn, *The Ideological Origins of the American Revolution* (Cambridge, MA: Balknap Press, 1967), 99.

8 Randall, *Benedict Arnold*, 57–60.

9 Letter of 9 June 1770, quoted in ibid., 68.

10 *The Quebec Act*, reproduced in Gustave Lanctot, *Canada and the American Revolution, 1774–1783* (Toronto: Clarke, Irwin, 1967), 229–37.

11 Hatch, *Thrust for Canada*, 5–8.

12 Paul R. Reynolds, *Guy Carleton: A Biography* (Toronto: Gage, 1980), 5.

13 Ibid., 38.

14 Ibid., 42–52.

15 Ibid., 55–7.

16 In Countryman, *The American Revolution*, 70.

17 Flexner, *The Young Hamilton*, 81.

18 In Lanctot, *Canada and the American Revolution*, 23.

19 In ibid., 25.

20 Randall, *Benedict Arnold*, 147.

21 Stephen P. Halbrook, *That Every Man Be Armed: The Evolution of a Constitutional Right* (Oakland, CA: The Independent Institute, 1984), 29.

22 In ibid., 33.

23 In ibid., *That Every Man Be Armed*, 60.

24 In ibid., 62. It was the radical and elegant Henry who said, in 1775, "Give me liberty or give me death." He was a strong proponent of the American constitutional bill of rights. He died in 1799.

25 Quoted in Bailyn, *Ideological Origins*, 20.

26 Ibid., 1.

27 In Page Smith, *John Adams 1, 1735–1784* (New York: Doubleday, 1962), 238.

28 Garraty, *The American Nation*, 89–112.

29 Ibid., 98.

30 Ibid., 104.

31 Jean-Jacques Rousseau, *The Social Contract and Discourses*, translated with introduction by G.D.H. Cole ([1762] London: Dent & Sons, 1966), 3.

32 Dero Sawders, ed., *The Portable Gibbon* (Penguin Books, 1952), 12.

33 Bailyn, *The Ideological Origins*, 35–43.

34 Ibid., 66.

35 John Keane, *Tom Paine, A Political Life* (Toronto: Little, Brown, 1995), ix. Keane's is the most balanced book about Paine.

36 R.R. Fennessy, *Burke, Paine and the Rights of Man* (The Hague: Martinus Nijhoff, 1963), 18–19.

37 Smith, *John Adams* 1 (1735–1784), 239.

38 Fennessy, *Burke*, 42.

39 Ibid., 21.

40 Keane, *Tom Paine*, 133–4.

CHAPTER THREE

1 Sellers, *Benedict Arnold: The Proud Warrior*, 17.

2 Randall, *Benedict Arnold*, 50.

3 Ibid, 60.

4 Smith, *John Adams*, 163–4.

5 Randall, *Benedict Arnold*, 71–7. There is no record that Arnold actually took part in the Philadelphia debates.

6 Brandt, *The Man in the Mirror*, 17–18.

7 Randall, *Benedict Arnold*, 84.

8 Ibid., 86.

9 "Benedict Arnold's Regimental Memorandum Book," in *Bulletin of the Fort Ticonderoga Museum* 14, no. 2 (Winter 1982): 71.

10 Randall, *Benedict Arnold*, 85–7.

11 Ibid., 93–7.

12 Brandt, *The Man in the Mirror*, 25.

13 Ibid., 28.

14 In John Pell, *Ethan Allen* (Boston: Houghton Mifflin, 1929), 5.

15 Ibid., 34.

16 Ibid., 69–71.

17 Ibid., 72–3.

18 Ibid., 77.0

19 Ibid., 91.

20 Sellers, *Benedict Arnold*, 28–9.

21 Randall, *Benedict Arnold*, 103.

22 "Arnold's Regimental Memorandum Book," 72.

23 Ibid., 73.

24 Ibid., 77.

25 Randall, *Benedict Arnold*, 130.

26 "Arnold's Regimental Memorandum Book," 80.

27 Ibid., 80.

CHAPTER FOUR

1 James T. Lexner, *Washington: The Indispensable Man* (New York: New American Library, Times Mirror, 1979), 35–56.

2 Randall, *Benedict Arnold*, 136.

3 In Pell, *Ethan Allen*, 102.

4 Randall, *Benedict Arnold*, 123.

5 NA, Congressional Papers, no. 42, vols. 2–7.

6 NA, Continental Congress Papers, no. 41, vol. 10, 655.

7 Lanctôt, *Canada and the American Revolution*, 16.

8 NA, Sir Guy Carleton Papers, 1775, MG 11 0 Series vol. 11, 196–7.

9 NA, MG23, B7, "Journal of the Most Remarkable Events which happened in Canada between the months of July, 1775 and June, 1776." Copy of a diary purchased by the National Archives in 1932 from London.

10 NA, Sir Guy Carleton Papers, 1775, 197–200.

11 Lanctôt, *Canada and the American Revolution,* 46.

12 Randall, *Benedict Arnold,* 143.

13 Arthur Schlesinger, *The Almanac of American History* (New York: G.P. Putnam's Sons, 1983), 119–20.

14 Randall, *Benedict Arnold,* 123–4.

15 Richard Ketchum, ed., *The American Heritage Book of the Revolution* (New York: American Heritage Publishing, 1971), 122.

16 Justin Smith, *Arnold's March from Cambridge to Quebec* (New York: G.P. Putnam's Sons, 1903), xi.

17 Randall, *Benedict Arnold,* 149–50.

18 Richard Morris, ed., *Encyclopedia of American History* (New York: Harper and Row, 1965), 89.

19 Washington's instructions to Arnold were reprinted as appendices in Roberts, *March to Quebec,* 2–7.

    The message carried by Arnold was called "an address to the Inhabitants of Canada from His Excellency George Washington Esquire, Commander-in-Chief of the Army of the United Colonies of North America." It is interesting to note that this call to arms, this assertion of the invitability of armed conflict, was written several months before Washington learned that King George III had rejected the "Olive Branch" petition. Clearly, Washington did not expect a political settlement. The sincerity of the American proposals for peace can be questioned.

20 In ibid., 5.

21 Roberts, *March to Quebec,* 6.

22 Ibid., 2.

23 Ibid., 3–5.

CHAPTER FIVE

1 In Roberts, *March to Quebec,* 44.

2 John Currier, *The History of Newburyport, Massachusetts, 1764–1905.* A facsimile of the 1906 edition (Somersworth, NH: New Hampshire Publishing, 1977), 556–7.

3 NA, MG23 B8, cited in manuscripts acquired 10 September 1908 from Patrick Day of Quebec City, 20–1.

4 In Brandt, *The Man in the Mirror,* 47.

5 Randall, *Benedict Arnold,* 150.

6 Pierre Berton, *The Invasion of Canada, 1812–1813* (Toronto: McClelland and Stewart, 1980), 152–3.

7 John Joseph Henry, *Accounts of Arnold's Campaign against Quebec.* Reprint of an 1877 original in the "Eyewitness Accounts of the American Revolution" series (New York: Arno Press, 1968), xii.

8 Randall, *Benedict Arnold*, 151.

9 Fawn Brodie, *Thomas Jefferson: An Intimate History* (New York: W.W. Norton, 1974), 398–9.

10 In the election of 1800, Burr and Jefferson were colleagues on the Democratic-Republican ticket against the Federalists, led by President John Adams. Jefferson and Burr each got the same number of votes from the electoral college and neither would agree to be second. The messy issue was finally settled in congress. After thirty-five ballots in the House of Representatives, the tie was broken. Partly through the deal making of Alexander Hamilton, who was Adams's inspector general, Jefferson was elected president and Burr vice-president. They were sworn into office on 4 March 1801.

Burr served as Jefferson's vice-president but the battle had soured relations between the two. In 1804 Burr ran for the governorship of New York with the support of some vaguely secessionist federalists and was defeated, in part because of the opposition of Alexander Hamilton, who had become a bitter personal, professional, and political opponent. He slandered Burr in public and was challenged to a duel. On 11 July 1804 the two met in New Jersey, across the Hudson River from New York City. Hamilton was shot dead after refusing, for some reason, to fire.

Hamilton had been seen as a potential president. He was Washington's right-hand man during the Revolution, the aide who was with him the day Arnold defected. He was a creative soldier and military leader, a brilliant propagandist and political thinker, and the architect of early America's financial system. He also made an enemy of the "brilliant, compelling but most unstable" and envious Burr and died by his hand (Garraty, *The American Nation*, 186–7).

Later in 1804 Burr secretly contacted the British government to suggest that if it supported him, he would lead the western territories out of the United States. He suggested a plot to assassinate Jefferson, his former ally, and to establish the capital of this new British territory in New Orleans. For the next three years, he worked on his treasonous plan and in 1807 Burr attempted to set up his new British satellite. He led a small group of soldiers and mercenaries down the Mississippi River to capture New Orleans. He was a laughable counter-revolutionary, open in his disdain for the nation he had helped to create and quite public in his plans to tear it apart.

In February, on the way down the Mississippi, Burr was captured and taken back to Virginia where he faced charges of murder in New York and New Jersey. The then president, Jefferson, made it clear that he wanted Burr convicted and executed for treason. A judge who was hostile to the president acquitted Burr. Freed by the court, Burr went into

voluntary exile in Europe, returning later to New York where he practised law in "relative obscurity" until his death.

11 Henry, *Accounts of Arnold's Campaign*, 11.

12 Hatch, *Thrust for Canada*, 68.

13 In Roberts, *March to Quebec*, 44a.

14 Ibid., 44c.

15 Randall, *Benedict Arnold*, 163.

16 Brandt, *The Man in the Mirror*, 49.

17 NA, Sir Guy Carleton Papers, 1775, 249–51.

18 Ibid.

19 Pell, *Ethan Allen*, 116.

20 Ibid., 118.

21 In ibid., 225.

22 NA, Continental Congress Papers, no. 41, vol. 10, 665.

23 Hatch, *Thrust for Canada*, 59–60.

24 NA, Sir Guy Carleton Papers, 1775, dispatch of 25 October 1775 to Lord
Dartmouth.

25 Roberts, *March to Quebec*, 44b.

CHAPTER SIX

1 Roberts, *March to Quebec*, 68fn.

2 Currier, *The History of Newburyport*, 558.

3 Roberts, *March to Quebec*, 68–9.

4 Ibid., 69.

5 In modern-day Showhagen, a papermill town in the midst of rugged terrain, there is a radical piece of historical record. The United States is
almost devoid of references to Benedict Arnold by name. At one time,
any such references were forbidden by law. The gravestones of the four
preceeding Benedict Arnolds were destroyed two centuries ago by citizens angry at the memory of the traitor, Benedict v. Yet in Skowhagen,
on one wall of a pub in the middle of town, there is a painting celebrating the fact that Arnold had passed through. "1775: Benedict Arnold's
ill-fated revolutionary expedition passed through on their way up the
Kennebec to engage the British Army in Quebec." The painting depicts
revolutionary soldiers on the move, led by a heroic-looking Arnold.

6 Roberts, *March to Quebec*, 46.

7 Ibid.

8 Hatch, *Thrust for Canada*, 74.

9 Roberts, *March to Quebec*, 47–8. Entries for 3 and 4 October 1775.

10 Ibid., 48.

11 Ibid., 49.

12 Ibid.

13 Smith, *Arnold's March*, 127.

14 Henry, *Accounts*, 13–48.

15 Roberts, *March to Quebec*, 50–1.

16 Smith, *Arnold's March*, 129.

17 Morris, ed., *Encyclopedia of American History*, 89.

18 Roberts, *March to Quebec*, 70–1.

19 Ibid., 72–3.

20 Smith, *Arnold's March*, 473.

21 Roberts, *March to Quebec*, 73.

22 Smith, *Arnold's March*, 474–5.

23 Ibid., 136.

24 Roberts, *March to Quebec*, 75.

25 Ibid., 53.

26 Ibid., 54.

27 Ibid., 54–5.

28 Brandt, *The Man in the Mirror*, 53.

29 Roberts, *March to Quebec*, 75–6.

30 Ibid., 76.

31 Smith, *Arnold's March*, 479.

32 Roberts, *March to Quebec*, 137.

33 Details of the Enos desertion saga are taken from Randall, *Benedict Arnold*, 179–80. In a remarkable example of American historical double standard, considering the hatred heaped on Arnold for his later treachery, the authors of a textbook on the Revolution, *The American Heritage Book of the Revolution*, edited by Richard Ketchum, excused Enos's treachery and desertion by arguing that it "actually saved the whole expedition, since it diminished the mouths to be fed" (p. 124). It also took supplies and medicine that the troops in the front were counting on for survival.

34 Smith, *Arnold's March*, 480.

35 Roberts, *March to Quebec*, 77.

36 Ibid., 78.

37 Ibid., 79.

38 Smith, *Arnold's March*, 482.

39 Letter from Sartigan, 31 October 1775, in Roberts, *March to Quebec*, 80.

40 Roberts, *March to Quebec*, 258.

41 Henry, *Accounts*, 69.

42 Roberts, *March to Quebec*, 526.

43 Ibid., 205–13.

44 Ibid., 219.

45 Ibid., 261.

46 Ibid., 139.

47 Ibid., 219.

48 Henry, *Accounts*, 73.

49 Roberts, *March to Quebec*, 81.

50 Randall, *Benedict Arnold*, 187.

51 Henry, *Accounts*, 193.

52 For a modern-day traveller trying to retrace Arnold's trek through Maine by following Highway 16 (called Arnold's Trail on some American maps), several unexpected markers await. The first, in a mountainous area approaching the Height of Land, is one of the few tributes to Arnold in the US. In the area called the Cathedral Pines, there sits a plaque more than eighty years old, commemorating the invasion and naming Arnold as the leader. "This tablet is erected by Mrs Sarah Lambert Prescott, colonial chapter, Daughters of the American Revolution [DAR], Farmington, Maine, 1913." The politics involved in winning approval for the memorial to Arnold in the conservative, patriotic year of 1913, in a small-town conservative DAR chapter, must have been amazing.

Nearby, Mount Bigelow towers above its surroundings. A plaque tells the story of its name and indirectly records the desperate dreams of Arnold's troops as they struggled through the mountains, praying for an early end to the torment. The mountain, looming in the distance, figured in many of the troop diaries as they struggled through portages, floods, and overgrown swamps. Always it was there in the distance as a beacon. When the troops arrived near the base, Col Timothy Bigelow scaled the mountain, hoping to see Quebec City. All he saw were more mountains to the north and wilderness to the south. He descended, disappointed, to tell his mates that little awaited them but more of the same. It would be almost two weeks before they saw the walls of Quebec City. Today, a tourist sign near Bigelow Mountain in Maine promises "scenic mountains, next 21 miles."

Emerging out of Maine and into Quebec, there sits the town of Wilburn, which is marked by the Arnold River and graced by the Hotel Arnold, a pub distinguished by an outdoor sign on which there stands a figure looking vaguely like a soldier from an earlier century. A visitor looking for local history, colour and lore asked a waitress who this Arnold fellow was. "Benedict Arnold, I think." But why was the hotel named after an American? "I guess we have to honour our traitors, eh? What'll you have?"

CHAPTER SEVEN

1 Roberts, *March to Quebec*, 81.
2 Ibid., 82–3.
3 Ibid., 87, letter of Nov. 14 from Arnold to Montgomery.
4 Letter from Quebec, 9 November 1775, NA, file MG23 B8. Manuscripts relating to the invasion of Canada, purchased in 1908 from Patrick Day of Quebec City.
5 William B. Willcox, ed., *The American Rebellion: Sir Henry Clinton's Narrative of his campaigns, 1775–1782* (New Haven: Yale University Press, 1954), 21.
6 "Benedict Arnold," *Harper's New Monthly Magazine* 23, no. 138 (November 1861).
7 In Roberts, *March to Quebec*, 87.
8 Letter of 25 October 1775 to the earl of Dartmouth, secretary of state for the northern district in the British cabinet, NA, Sir Guy Carleton Papers, 1775, 275.
9 Roberts, *March to Quebec*, 89.
10 Ibid.
11 Ibid., 90.
12 Letter of 20 November 1775 to Montgomery, in ibid., 90–2.
13 Letter of 20 November 1775 to Washington, in ibid., 93–4.
14 Smith, *John Adams*, 202.
15 Reynolds, *Guy Carleton*, 71–2.
16 Ibid., 72.
17 Ibid., 73.
18 Details of Carleton's personality, performance and legacy are taken from Reynold's biography, *Guy Carleton*, cited above, as well as the *Canadian Encyclopedia*, edited by James Marsh. Various texts on the American invasion were also consulted, most notably Lanctot, *Canada and the American Revolution, 1774–1783*, and texts on the politics of Quebec during the last quarter of the eighteenth century, particularly Hilda Neatby, *Quebec, The Revolutionary Age, 1760–1791* (Toronto: McClelland and Stewart, 1966).
19 Neatby, *Quebec*, 150.
20 NA, Sir Guy Carleton Papers, 1775, 318–20.
21 Ibid., 325.
22 Ibid., 220.
23 Ibid., 198.
24 Ibid., 221–5.
25 Letter from Carleton to Dartmouth, 14 August 1775, in ibid.

26 NA, Sir Guy Carleton Papers, 1775, 210–5.

27 Ibid., 217–18.

28 Ibid., 342.

29 Ibid., 268–71.

30 Ibid., 336.

31 G.A. Rawlyk, ed., *Revolution Rejected, 1775–1776* (Scarborough, ON: Prentice-Hall, 1968), 66.

32 D.G. Creighton, *The Commercial Empire of the St Lawrence, 1760–1850* (Toronto: Ryerson Press, 1937), 63.

33 Lanctot, *Canada and the American Revolution*, 47.

34 NA, contained in papers purchased in 1908 from Patrick Day of Quebec, 5–8.

35 Randall, *Benedict Arnold*, 194. See also NA, "Journal of the Most Remarkable Events," 23. Allegedly, the journal was in the possession of Carleton's descendants when purchased in London in 1932.

36 Lanctot, *Canada and the American Revolution*, 52. Part of the American appeal to the French habitants was to warn them that the British government would conscript them to fight against the rebellious colonies to the south.

37 Carleton to Dartmouth, 5 November 1775, NA, Sir Guy Carleton Papers, 1775, 274.

38 This was evident in October 1780 when British North American commander-in-chief Sir Henry Clinton, seeking to condemn George Washington, called him "a murderer and a Jesuit." "Clinton's Narrative," in Van Doren, *Secret History*, 480.

39 Randall, *Benedict Arnold*, 22.

40 Hatch, *Thrust for Canada*, 127.

41 Lanctot, *Canada and the American Revolution*, xiii.

42 Any attempt to explain or describe the Quebec of the 1760s and 1770s is a political minefield. One school of nationalist Quebec writers has found a vibrant pre-1763 Quebec economy that was crushed and decapitated by the English, leaving the province in the priest-ridden, English-dominated backward state it found itself in until the Quiet Revolution of the 1960s. Another school, the "revisionists," sees pre-Conquest Quebec as a largely rural and feudal society that actually developed into a more complex structure under English rule. To explain the French habitants' reaction to the American invasion, I have leaned more to the "revisionist" school. For the understanding I have of this family quarrel among historians, I am indebted to interviews with Fernand Ouellet of the University of Toronto and Dominique Marshall of the Carleton University History department.

I also consulted Ronald Rudin's "Revisionism and the Search for a Normal Society: A Critique of Recent Quebec Historical Writing" in the *Canadian Historical Review 73* (Toronto: University of Toronto Press, 1992).

43 Greer, *Peasant, Lord and Merchant*, 98–121.

44 Neatby, *Quebec*, 56–8.

45 Lanctot, *Canada and the American Revolution*, 4.

46 NA, Sir Guy Carleton Papers, 1775, 290–4.

47 Creighton, *The Commercial Empire*, 51.

48 Greer, *Peasant, Lord and Merchant*, 47.

49 "Print Industry," in the *Canadian Encyclopedia, 2d ed.*, vol. 3, 1756.

50 Allan Greer, "The Pattern of Literacy in Quebec, 1745–1899," *Social History* 11, no. 22 (November 1978), 335.

51 Neatby, *Quebec*, 148.

52 NA, Sir Guy Carleton Papers, 1775, 285–7.

53 Lanctot, *Canada and the American Revolution*, 102.

54 Interview with Dominique Marshall, 11 November 1994, at Carleton University, Ottawa.

55 Letter of 27 October 1775, in Roberts, *March to Quebec*, 79.

56 Greer, *Peasant, Lord and Merchant*, 152–3.

57 Lanctot, *Canada and the American Revolution*, 105.

58 Rawlyk, *Revolution Rejected*, 10.

CHAPTER EIGHT

1 NA, Sir Guy Carleton Papers, 1775, 334–5.

2 Roberts, *March to Quebec*, 101.

3 Randall, *Benedict Arnold*, 213.

4 NA, Sir Guy Carleton Papers (correspondence between Gov. Carleton and Lord Germain, 1776), 11.

5 NA, Sir Guy Carleton Papers (Carleton to Germain), 17.

6 Henry, *Accounts*, 98.

7 Ibid., 106.

8 NA, "Journal of the Most Remarkable Events," 25–8.

9 Roberts, *March to Quebec*, 228.

10 NA, "Journal of the Most Remarkable Events," 25–8. Creepers were jagged attachments strapped to boots to allow walking on ice.

11 Ibid., 33.

12 Ibid., 34.

13 Randall, *Benedict Arnold*, 219.

14 Roberts, *March to Quebec*, 102.

15 Henry, *Accounts*, 107.
16 Michael Pearson, *Those Damned Rebels* (New York: G.P. Putnam, 1971).
   Excerpts reprinted in Weekend Magazine, 30 December, 1972, 3–7.
17 Ibid., 5.
18 Randall, *Benedict Arnold*, 220–1.
19 Roberts, *March to Quebec*, 149.
20 Randall, *Benedict Arnold*, 224.
21 NA, *Journal of Captain William Humphrey*, entry for 30 December 1775.
22 Roberts, *March to Quebec*, 234.
23 Ibid., 113–14.
24 Letter of 6 January 1776, in ibid., 109.
25 Roberts, *March to Quebec*, 114.
26 Ibid., 103.
27 Ibid., 115.

CHAPTER NINE

 1 Roberts, *March to Quebec*, 105.
 2 Ibid., 105–6.
 3 Ibid., 106.
 4 Letter of 5 January 1776, in ibid., 108.
 5 Letter of 11 January 1776, in ibid., 109–13.
 6 Roberts, *March to Quebec*, 118.
 7 Ibid., 122.
 8 Ibid., 120.
 9 Ibid., 121.
10 Ibid., 123.
11 Lengyel, *I, Benedict*, 68.
12 Smith, *John Adams*, 239.
13 NA, Continental Congress Papers, vol. 2, no. 41, 135.
14 Ibid., 136.
15 NA, Colonial Office, Q Series, correspondence between Governor Carleton and Lord Germain, 1776, 1.
16 Ibid., 4–6.
17 NA, "Journal of the Most Remarkable Events," 51–84.
18 In Roberts, *March to Quebec*, 235.
19 In Creighton, *The Commercial Empire*, 66.
20 In Rawlyk, *Revolution Rejected*, 95–6.
21 Ibid., 67.
22 In Hatch, *Thrust for Canada*, 144.
23 Randall, *Benedict Arnold*, 229–30.

24 In Ronald Clark, *Benjamin Franklin. A Biography* (New York: Random House, 1983), 281.

25 Ibid., 282.

26 Brandt, *The Man in the Mirror*, 85.

27 In Clark, *Benjamin Franklin*, 283–4.

28 In Hatch, *Thrust for Canada*, 182.

29 Randall, *Benedict Arnold*, 232.

30 In Hatch, *Thrust for Canada*, 210.

31 In Randall, *Benedict Arnold*, 236.

32 Hatch, *Thrust for Canada*, 172.

33 NA, *Journal of Capt William Humphrey*, MG23 B9.

34 NA, MG11 Q Series vol. 12, 8, *Sir Guy Carleton Papers, 1776, Carleton to Germain, 14 May, 1776.*

35 Ibid., 27–8, proclamation sent as part of a dispatch to London.

36 Clark, *Benjamin Franklin*, 284.

37 Hatch, *The Thrust for Canada*, 227.

38 In Randall, *Benedict Arnold*, 233.

39 Ibid., 235–7.

40 Hatch, *The Thrust for Canada*, 224.

41 In Randall, *Benedict Arnold*, 237.

42 NA, *Carleton Papers 1776*, 45–6. Letter of 21 June 1776.

43 Neatby, *Quebec*, 152–3.

44 In Stanley Ryerson, *The Founding of Canada, Beginnings to 1815* (Toronto: Progress Books, 1960), 118.

45 Lanctot, *Canada and the American Revolution*, 146.

46 Copies of the petitions are housed at NA, MG23 B8, in Congressional Congress Papers.

47 NA, *Congressional Congress Papers*, no. 35, vol. 4, 87–9.

48 Ibid., no. 41, vol. 10, 665.

49 Ibid., no. 42, vol. 4, 513.

50 Ibid., no. 42, vol. 2, 416–16.

51 Ibid., no. 42, vol. 3, 451.

52 Ibid., no. 42, vol. 4, 418.

CHAPTER TEN

1 Mitchell, *Military Leaders*, 26–7.

2 Brandt, *The Man in the Mirror*, 96.

   The most comprehensive account of the intrigues on Lake Champlain in 1776 is in Randall, *Benedict Arnold*, 248–64.

3 In Fahey, "Benedict Arnold," 33.

4 Randall, *Benedict Arnold*, 265–6.

5 Ibid., 271.

6 Ibid., 310. For Randall's account of the battle, see ibid., 301–17.

7 Ibid., 299.

8 Brandt, *The Man in the Mirror*, 110.

9 Boatner, *Encyclopedia of the American Revolution Bientennial Edition*, 26.

10 Mitchell, *Military Leaders*, 32–3.

11 Fahey, *Dictionary*, vol. 5, 33.

12 Brandt, *The Man in the Mirror*, 120.

13 Fahey, "Benedict Arnold," 33.

14 Randall, *Benedict Arnold*, 358–9.

15 Historical marker at Saratoga National Park.

16 Randall, *Benedict Arnold*, 340–9.

17 Mitchell, *Military Leaders*, 91.

18 Randall, *Benedict Arnold*, 358–64.

19 Brandt, *The Man in the Mirror*, 39.

20 Mitchell, *Military Leaders*, 93–5.

21 Randall, *Benedict Arnold*, 367–8.

A description of the scene is provided for visitors at the site of Arnold's heroics in a commentary recorded by the American National Park Service.

> Before the enemy's flanks could be rallied, General Benedict Arnold – who had been relieved of command after a quarrel with Gates – rode onto the field and led Learned's brigade against the German troops holding the British centre.

> Under tremendous pressure from all sides, the Germans joined a general withdrawal into the fortifications on Freeman's Farm. Within a hour after the opening clash, Burgoyne lost eight cannon and more than four hundred officers and men. Flushed with success, the Americans believed that victory was near. Arnold led one column in a series of savage attacks on the Balcarres Redoubt, a powerful British fieldwork on the Freeman farm. After failing repeatedly to carry this position, Arnold wheeled his horse and dashing through the crossfire of both armies, spurred northwest to the Breyman Redoubt. Arriving just as American troops began to assault the fortification, he joined in the final surge that overwhelmed the German soldiers defending the work.

22 Ibid., 375.

23 Mitchell, *Military Leaders*, 160.

24 Randall, *Benedict Arnold*, 343.

25 NA, Continental Congress Papers 1778, no. 166, 97.

26 Ibid., 111.

27 Ibid., 93.

28 Letter of 20 February 1778, ibid., 97.

29 Letter of 20 February 1778 from Hazen at Albany to General Horatio Gates, ibid., 117.

CHAPTER ELEVEN

1 Mitchell, *Military Leaders*, 149.

2 Spiller, *Dictionary*, 40.

3 Randall, *Benedict Arnold*, 411.

4 Spiller, *Dictionary*, 41.

5 Brandt, *The Man in the Mirror*, 95–8.

6 In ibid., 112.

7 Boatner, *Encyclopedia*, 27.

8 Van Dorn, *Secret History*, 150.

9 The description of the politics of Philadelphia and Arnold's tenure as governor is based on Randall, *Benedict Arnold*, 434–52; Boatner, *Encyclopedia*, 28–30; Van Dorn, *Secret History*, 168–88; and Arnold letters cited in Isaac N. Arnold, *The Life of Benedict Arnold*.

10 Lexner, *Washington*, 143.

11 Van Dorn, *Secret History*, 183–5.

12 In Isaac N. Arnold, *The Life of Benedict Arnold*, 228.

13 "He would never have done it if not for his second wife," a staff member of the New Haven Historical Society said resolutely when a visitor asked to see the few items they had related to Arnold, one of New Haven's most famous citizens. The remains of his first wife Margaret lie buried in the crypt beneath the church on New Haven's Common Green.
   In local graveyards, all references to the Arnolds buried in them have been destroyed.

14 New Brunswick Museum (NBM), *Benedict Arnold Papers*, letter from Peggy Arnold to Jonathan Bliss, 5 December 1795.

15 In Isaac N. Arnold, *The Life of Benedict Arnold*, 230.

16 In Van Dorn, *Secret History*, 192–3.

17 The account of the trial comes primarily from Lengyel, *I, Benedict Arnold*, 61–74.

18 Ibid., 64–5.

19 Ibid., 68.

20 In Van Dorn, *Secret History*, 244.

21 Ibid., 250.

22 Randall, *Benedict Arnold*, 499.

23 In ibid., 495.

24 While the story of Arnold's act of treason has been told, retold, analyzed and embellished by scores of American writers, the main sources for the description of the treasonous negotiations and the context of the times are Van Dorn, *Secret History*, and John Bakeless, *Turncoats, Traitors and Heroes* (New York: J.B. Lippincott, 1959).

25 In Lengyel, *I, Benedict Arnold*, 48. Robinson eventually moved to Canada as a Loyalist and fathered a son, John Beverley, who in the nineteenth century became a judge and an associate of Upper Canada's Family Compact so despised by Canada's 1837 rebels.

26 On this point, see Van Dorn, *Secret History*, v. Van Dorn produced his account of espionage and counter-espionage in the Revolution after poring through the records of the British secret service in the thirteen colonies. "The war had its rise in a political controversy and it remained a civil conflict in America after it became a struggle between the United States and Great Britain."

27 Ibid., vii. On the same point see also Mitchell, *Military Leaders*, 24–5.

28 Countryman, *The American Revolution*, 141.

29 Stewart, *True Blue*, 3.

30 Lengyel, *I Benedict*, 58.

31 Van Dorn, *Secret History*, 37.

32 The entire Arnold-André correspondence is published in ibid. The letter of 15 September is on p. 473.

33 In Flexner, *Washington*, 145–6.

34 In Flexner, *The Young Hamilton*, 72.

35 In Clark, *Benjamin Franklin*, 370.

36 In Brodie, *Thomas Jefferson*, 135–6.

37 In Van Dorn, *Secret History*, 477–9.

38 In ibid., 348.

39 Randall, *Benedict Arnold*, 581.

40 Brandt, *The Main in the Mirror*, 242–3.

41 Brodie, *Thomas Jefferson*, 143.

42 Randall, *Benedict Arnold*, 594–9.

CHAPTER TWELVE

1 *Royal Gazette* 1, no. 2.

2 Ann Gorman Condon, "Loyalist Arrival, Acadian Return, Imperial Reform," in *The Atlantic Region to Confederation: A History*, edited by Phillip A. Buckner and John G. Reid (Toronto: University of Toronto Press, 1994), 186.

3 Ester Clark Wright, *The Loyalists of New Brunswick* (Fredericton: n.p., 1955), 48–59.

4 Ibid., 161.

5 D.G. Bell, *Early Loyalist Saint John: The Origin of New Brunswick Politics, 1783–1786* (Fredericton: New Ireland Press, 1983), 53.

6 Ibid., 46.

7 *Royal Gazette* 1, no. 36, 13 June 1786.

8 Ibid., 1, no. 53, 10 October 1786.

9 Ibid., no. 49, 12 September 1786.

10 Ibid., no. 23, 7 March 1786.

11 Bell, *Early Loyalist Saint John*, 57.

12 Based on an advertisement in the *Saint John Gazette*, 12 October 1787, offering the coffee-house for sale.

13 *Royal Gazette* 1, no. 7, 25 October 1785.

14 Ibid. 1, no. 17, 31 January 1786.

15 Ibid. 1, no. 11, 20 December 1785.

16 NA, Thomas Carleton Papers, letterbook of Brigadier General Thomas Carleton, 1788–1801, 26 July 1788.

17 Eric Teed, *Footprints of Benedict Arnold, the late Major General, Congressional Army of the American Colonies: late Brigadier General, British Army* (Saint John: New Brunswick Historical Society Collections, 20, 1971), 68.

18 Phyllis R. Blakely and John N. Grant, *Eleven Exiles: Accounts of Loyalists of the American Revolution* (Toronto: Dundurn Press, 1982), 146–65.

19 W.S. MacNutt, *New Brunswick, A History: 1784–1867* (Toronto: MacMillan of Canada, 1963), 51.

20 Wright, *The Loyalists of New Brunswick*, 15–20.

21 Ibid., 125.

22 *Dictionary of Canadian Biography*, 5, 35.

23 Wright, *The Loyalists of New Brunswick*, 221.

24 Susan Kathleen Leyden, *Crimes and Controversies* (Saint John: Saint John Law Society, 1987), 41.

25 Ibid., 39–40. Bliss, another Massachusetts lawyer who fled north, became New Brunswick's attorney general and later chief justice but never accepted that the colony paid him what he was worth. As he appealed to the British government a few years later for more compensation, Bliss complained that New Brunswick was a "wretched country," implying that he could and should do better.

26 Isabel Louise Hill, *Fredericton, New Brunswick, British North America* (Fredericton: York-Sunbury Historical Society, 1968), 5.

27 Condon, *The Loyalist Dream*, 188–9.

28 Condon, *Loyalist Arrival*, 186.

29 Bell, *Early Loyalist Saint John*, 97.

30 Ibid., 130.

31 Ibid., 71.

32 Wright, *The Loyalists of New Brunswick*, 26.

33 Bell, *Early Loyalist Saint John*, 64–5.

34 Ibid., 82.

35 Sharon Dubeau, *New Brunswick Loyalists: A Bicentennial Tribute* (Agincourt, ON: Generation Press, 1983), 67.

36 *Royal Gazette* 1, no. 9, 6 December 1785.

37 Bell, *Early Loyalist Saint John*, 62.

38 While MacNutt makes brief mention of the election, it is most fully described by Bell and Wright.

39 NA, Sewell Correspondence, vol. 2, 458–63.

40 MacNutt, *New Brunswick*, 62.

41 Bell, *Early Loyalist Saint John*, 150–5.

42 MacNutt, *New Brunswick*, 61.

43 Bell, *Early Loyalist Saint John*, 78.

44 Ibid., 114.

45 Ibid., 115.

CHAPTER THIRTEEN

1 Advertisement in the *Royal Gazette*, 29 August 1786.

2 New Brunswick Archives, *Minute Books of the New Brunswick Supreme Court*, Arnold vs. James Butler, 7 July 1786.

3 Ibid.

4 Ibid., James Butler vs. Arnold, 17 July 1786.

5 *Canada's First City, Saint John, The Charter of 1785 and Common Council, 1785–1795* (Saint John: Lingly Printing, 1962), 95.

6 See, for example, Jean E. Sereisky, "Benedict Arnold in New Brunswick," *Atlantic Advocates* 53, no. 7 (March 1963): 37.

7 *Royal Gazette*, 4 September 1787.

8 A note in the Chipman papers housed in the National Archives of Canada contains the following record of purchases in Fredericton (St Anne's): "His first purchase of land was in St Ann's March 15, 1786, lot 41, from Edward Earle for £150. On the 18th of March, he purchased lot 1379 on the north side of Main St, lower in the second from Charlotte, from Judehaih Fairwether for £50. On the 19th of April, he bought from E. Spicer lot 1412, west end of Sheffield St facing the water, for £62.10. In the interim, he purchased at St Ann's from Peter Clements lot 35 on the western bank of the river containing one half acre for £110. On it was a storey and a half wooden building." A 1963

article in the *Atlantic Advocate* incorrectly suggested this building may be the site of the existing Rose Hall: "A warehouse that he owned at the corner of Waterloo Row and University Avenue was later renovated into a dwelling. Rose Hall was sold to Capt. Jacob Ellegood who sat as a member of the Legislative Assembly."

9 Hill, *Fredericton*, 61.

10 Randall, *Benedict Arnold*, 599.

11 Charlotte Gourlay Robinson, *The Pioneers of King Street* (Collections of the New Brunswick Historical Society, no. 14).

12 Ibid.

13 A.H. Wetmore, *Saint John's Old and Historic Buildings*. A paper delivered 15 October 1934 to the Fortnightly Club.

14 *Royal Gazette*, 6 September 1791.

CHAPTER FOURTEEN

1 New Brunswick Archives, *Minute Books of the New Brunswick Supreme Court*, Arnold vs. Jone 4 July 1787.

2 K.C. Irving was a small-town kid who created an empire from his first purchase of a service station in his hometown, Buctoche, New Brunswick. By the 1960s, he was the province's premier businessman with an integrated business empire. He owned or controlled vast tracts of forest that provided pulp for his papermills, lumber for his construction business, and paper for his five provincial daily newspapers, which blanketed the province. He also owned a fleet of oil tankers to import oil, a Saint John refinery, and service stations around the province to sell the oil and gasoline products. By the turn of the century, his sons were running the business.

3 New Brunswick Museum Arnold Collection (S29B), Jonathan Bliss to Benedict Arnold, 4 October 1791.

4 Ibid.

5 Brandt, *The Man in the Mirror*, 263.

6 In Randall, *Benedict Arnold*, 601.

7 NA, Sewell Correspondence, vol. 3, 7 September 1790.

8 Randall, *Benedict Arnold*, 601.

9 *Canada's First City, Saint John. The Charter of 1785 and Common Council 1785–1795* (Saint John: Lingly Printing, 1962), 76.

10 Ibid., 76, 99.

11 New Brunswick Archives, Glendenning Collection, Minute Books of the New Brunswick Supreme Court, 1785– Jesse Lawrence vs. Benedict Arnold 24 August 1786.

12 Randall, *Benedict Arnold*, 599.

13 Letter of 20 September 1992, NBM, *Arnold Collection*. Details of the Lyman case are drawn from Minute Books of the New Brunswick Supreme Court, as well as from letters exchanged between Arnold and Bliss.

14 MacNutt, *New Brunswick*, 28–9.

15 University of New Brunswick Harriet Irving Library, Archives and Special Collection, *Winslow Papers*, vol. 7, item 45.

16 NBM, Arnold Collection, Bliss to Arnold, 12 July 1796.

17 *Royal Gazette* 4, no. 223 (27 October 1789). In official records and correspondence, Hayt's Christian name is variously spelled "Munson" or "Monson." He was also referred to as both "Hayt" and "Hoyt."

18 Taken from Ward Chipman's address to the jury in Arnold vs. Hayt, 1790 as recorded in NA, Chipman Papers in Lawrence Collection, vol. 70, 110 (MG 23, DI). A Benedict Arnold notebook in the collection was compiled by Archdeacon William O. Raymond (1853–1923), one of three historians who combed the collected Chipman Papers to write about people Chipman had known or represented during his years as one of New Brunswick's leading early lawyers.

19 *Royal Gazette* 4, no. 232 (9 March 1790).

20 Teed, *Footprints of Benedict Arnold*, 74–5.

21 University of New Brunswick Harriet Irving Library, Archives and Special Collections, *Arnold-Hayt file*. Donated 17 October 1950 by J.J.F. Winslow, 22 June 1790 declaration filed before the court by Jonathan Bliss.

22 NBM Benedict Arnold Collection (F4 legal papers, 1783–94).

23 NA, *Lawrence Collection, Chipman Papers*, 70, notebook 110.

24 Randall, *Benedict Arnold*, 603.

25 J.J. Fraser Winslow, "The First Slander Trial in New Brunswick," *Atlantic Advocate* 49, no. 3 (November 1958).

26 Teed, *Footprints of Benedict Arnold*, 77.

27 MacNutt, *New Brunswick*, 51.

28 NA, Chipman Papers.

29 Sereisky, "Benedict Arnold in New Brunswick," *Atlantic Advocate* (March, 1963), 38.

30 NA, Chipman Papers.

31 NA, *Sewell Correspondence*, Stephen Sewell to Jonathan Sewell, 7 September 1790.

32 Teed, *Footprints*, 79.

33 Bell, *Early Loyalist Saint John*, 44. Other in information about Oliver Arnold comes from an original text in the New Brunswick Museum: Leonard Allison, *The Rev. Oliver Arnold, first rector of Sussex, N.B. with some*

account of his life, his parish and his successors and the Old Indian College (Saint John: Sun Printing, 1892).

34 Van Dorn, *Secret History*, 424.

35 Sereisky, 41.

36 "Gen. Arnold Wasn't Popular," in *Globe and Mail*, Toronto, 7 September 1963.

37 Jim Mason, "Benedict Arnold – and Saint John," *Saint John Telegraph Journal*, 9 October 1993.

38 Brandt, *The Man in the Mirror*, 263.

39 Randall, *Benedict Arnold*, 604.

40 Wallace, *Traitorous Hero*, 295.

41 Brandt, *The Man in the Mirror*, 316, Arnold's emphasis.

42 NBM, Benedict Arnold Collection, F1.

43 *Harper's New Monthly Magazine* 23, no. 38 (November 1861).

44 MacNutt, *New Brunswick*, 86.

45 Clipping in NBM, Benedict Arnold Papers, F1.

46 Randall, *Benedict Arnold*, 601.

47 Extract from Kate Gannett Wells, *Campobello* (1893), contained in NBM, *Benedict Arnold Collection*.

48 Letter to Bliss, 26 February 1792, NBM, *Arnold Collection*, F1.

49 Bernard Ash, *The Golden City* (London: J.M. Dent and Sons, 1964), 116.

50 Randall, *Benedict Arnold*, 605–6.

51 From Talleyrand's memoirs, cited in ibid., 607.

52 Simon Schama, *Citizens: A Chronicle of the French Revolution* (New York: Alfred A. Knopf, 1989), 684.

53 Ron Stuart, *London through the Ages: The Story of a City and its Citizens* (Esher, UK: James Burns, 1956), 199–200.

54 Maynard Solomon, *Beethoven* (New York: Schirmer Books, 1977), 69.

CHAPTER FIFTEEN

1 NBM, Benedict Arnold Collection, F1.

2 NA, Chipman Papers in Lawrence Collection. Undated letter from Arnold in response to 30 August 1792 letter from Chipman.

3 NBM, Benedict Arnold Collection, F2.

4 Letter of 30 August 1792, NA, Chipman Papers in Lawrence Collection.

5 NBM, Benedict Arnold Collection, F2.

6 NA, Chipman Papers in Lawrence Collection.

7 NBM, Benedict Arnold Collection, F1.

8 Cited in Fred Williams, "Simcoe Refused Lands to Arnold," *Mail and Empire*, 23 October 1933. Ontario Archives, Toronto, Frank Yeigh Papers.

9 Ibid.
10 Ontario Archives, H.R. Morgan Papers (MU3593, envelope 7), Duke of Portland to the Upper Canada executive council, 24 July 1800.
11 Introduction to John Graves Simcoe, *Simcoe's Military Journal, a History of the operations of a Partisan Carps called the Queen's Rangers* ([1784] Toronto: Baxter Publishing, 1962), vii.
12 S.R. Mealing, "John Graves Simoe," *Dictionary of Canadian Biography,* vol. 5 (Toronto: University of Toronto Press, 1983), 754.
13 Simcoe, *Journal,* v.
14 Randall, *Benedict Arnold,* 380.
15 Brandt, *The Man in the Mirror,* 240–1.
16 Simcoe, *Journal,* 90–102.
17 John Graves Simcoe, *Simcoe's Military Journal, Now First Published with a Memoir of the Author and Other Additions* (New York: Bartlett and Welford, 1844), 325.
18 NA, Chipman Papers in Lawrence Collection, "The Chesapeake Prize Money."
19 Mealing, "John Graves Simcoe," 754–9.
20 Ibid., 759.
21 *Royal Gazette* 16, no. 796, 18 August 1801.
22 Brandt, *The Man in the Mirror,* 272.
23 In Arnold, *The Life of Benedict Arnold,* 394.
24 In Fahey, "Benedict Arnold," 35.
25 NBM, Benedict Arnold Collection, F1, letter from Peggy Arnold 25 December 1801.
26 Letter of 30 June 1802, ibid.
27 Sherwin, *Benedict Arnold: Patriot and Traitor,* 367.
28 Ibid., 368.
29 Details on the lives of Arnold's children come from *The Descendants of Benedict Arnold in Canada,* a labour of love by John Richard Arnold of Peterborough, Ontario, great-great-great-grandson of Benedict, a graduate of the Royal Military College and later a community college teacher.
30 Boatner, *Encyclopedia,* 29.
31 Lengyel, *I, Benedict Arnold,* 199.
32 Brandt, *The Man in the Mirror,* 261.
33 John Richard Arnold, *The Descendants of Benedict Arnold,* 9.
34 Ibid.
35 Ontario Archives, Morgan Papers, Dr George Spragge letters.
36 Letter of 6 April 1960, ibid.
37 Details on the Upper Canadian lives of Benedict's three sons come from John Richard Arnold, *The Descendants of Benedict Arnold.*

38 "Benedict Arnold," *Harper's New Monthly Magazine* (November, 1861), 722.

39 Interview with Alice Hughes at Easton's Corner, Ontario, 11 November 1994.

40 "Death of Henry Arnold," *Brockville Recorder,* 25 April 1901.

41 "Henry H. Arnold, Retired Merchant, Passed at Athens," *Brockville Recorder,* 11 June 1945.

42 *Furrow to the Future* (Oxbox-Glen Ewen history book committee, 1984), 353.

43 Interview with Anita Winteringham at Oxbox, Saskatchewan, 3 July 1994.

44 Telephone interview with Jayson Arnold, 2 January 1995.

EPILOGUE

1 Lori Baker, *Saint John Dictionary, Fifth Concise Edition* (Fredericton: Non-Entity Press, 1992).

2 Interview with Eric Teed in Saint John, 26 January 1995.

3 Interview with Ann Condon in Saint John, 27 January 1995.

Index